The Courtship Novel
1740-1820

The Courtship Novel
1740-1820
A FEMINIZED GENRE

Katherine Sobba Green

THE UNIVERSITY PRESS OF KENTUCKY

Copyright © 1991 by The University Press of Kentucky
Scholarly publisher for the Commonwealth,
serving Bellarmine College, Berea College, Centre
College of Kentucky, Eastern Kentucky University,
The Filson Club, Georgetown College, Kentucky
Historical Society, Kentucky State University,
Morehead State University, Murray State University,
Northern Kentucky University, Transylvania University,
University of Kentucky, University of Louisville,
and Western Kentucky University.

Editorial and Sales Offices: Lexington, Kentucky 40508-4008

Library of Congress Cataloging-in-Publication Data

Green, Katherine Sobba, 1949-
 The courtship novel, 1740-1820 : a feminized genre / Katherine
Sobba, Green.
 p. cm.
 Includes bibliographical references.
 ISBN 0-8131-1736-4
 1. English fiction—18th century—History and criticism.
2. Courtship in literature. 3. Feminism and literature—Great
Britain—History—18th century. 4. Feminism and literature—Great
Britain—History—19th century. 5. Women and literature—Great
Britain—History—18th century. 6. Women and literature—Great
Britain—History—19th century. 7. English ficiton—Women authors
—History and criticism. 8. English fiction—19th century—History
and criticism. I. Title.
PR858.C69G74 1991
823'.0850906—dc20   90-41569

CONTENTS

ACKNOWLEDGMENTS

LIKE ALL scholarly projects, this one represents stages of growth and indebtedness no longer fully recoverable even by the author. I would especially like to thank the following for their assistance and support.

For his initial suggestion that I look at Joyce Hemlow's article on courtesy novels, and for his attention to my work in its early stages, I am indebted to Carl Kropf.

For their questions and interest, I remember the fellows of the Folger Institute seminar "Love in the Western World" (1985). I am especially grateful to Jean Hagstrum, whose reflections on his own work during the seminar inspired me to read more closely and whose enthusiasm and suggestions for my study improved later drafts.

For a rigorous immersion in feminist criticism, I thank Naomi Schor, whose NEH seminar "Women and Representation in Nineteenth-Century Fiction" (1986) provided the theoretical bases on which my study is grounded. I am particularly indebted to the other fellows (Dale Bauer, Sarah Gallagher, Diana George, Sue Huseman, Pat Johnson, Mary Pinard, Brenda Powell, Pat Sharpe, Janice Sokoloff, Sharon Udall, and Carol Wenzel-Rideout) for their camaraderie and for their careful readings of my work in progress.

I thank Joyce Rothschild for her insightful readings of large portions of the current work and for her unfailing support over many lunch discussions. Among my debts to Kathy Graney, I number her partisanship, commiseration, and encouragement during multiple stages of revision.

Finally, to the men in my life—Sean, Robert, Aaron, Nathan, and especially Bill—I am grateful for their tolerance of closed doors, their patience with my travels, and their respect and support for my work.

INTRODUCTION

MARRIAGE MEDIATES the patterns according to which heterosexual women and men—real and fictional—live. It harmonizes the natural, the familial, the social, and the transcendental. That is, marriage accommodates the diverse reagents of life: nature's coupling and breeding, existing interfamilial patterns, society's contracts, and the church's ministerial function. Tony Tanner conjectures that the wife's role, for instance, "ideally contains the biological *female* , the obedient *daughter* (and perhaps sister), the faithful *mate*, the responsible *mother*, and the believing *Christian*."[1] Marital failure is inevitably attended by role conflict, and, Tanner reasons, this dynamic potential makes adultery the main topic for the bourgeois novel—especially within the nineteenth-century context of growing emphasis on the individual.

This is not to say, however, that individualism simply sprang into being, fully developed, in the nineteenth century—in time to cast the bourgeois novel and to power the Industrial Revolution. What historians term "possessive" or "affective individualism" began coalescing much earlier, from a mixture of ideas associated with Puritanism and capitalism.[2] By the eighteenth century a person had come to be viewed primarily as owner of her- or himself. Historians Lawrence Stone, Randolph Trumbach, and John R. Gillis have argued that coincident with this new understanding of individual rights in the eighteenth century was a new conception of the spousal relationship, a shift from marriage based on parental arrangement and familial convenience to marriage based on an affective relationship between husband and wife.[3]

For heterosexual women in this period, especially, the ideology of companionate marriage involved such thoroughgoing revisions in self-perception that a new literary form was required to represent their altered roles. To appreciate the extent to which this must have been true, one need only return to Tanner's observation that marriage mediates all potential roles—the natural, the familial, the social, and the transcendental. First, if marriage was a matter for family determination, then it was woman's place to forgo individual autonomy in favor of familial and social interests. But once woman was encouraged to choose her partner on the basis of affect, then the process of coupling was immeasurably complicated by all the indeterminacies of personality.[4] Second, whereas earlier matches were made by familial agents for familial interests, under the new system interests were much more likely to vary among family members, particularly between generations, between daughters and parents. Third, social interests, previously served by the class-, status-, and economic-based negotiations inherent in the arranged marriage, were jeopardized because the companionate marriage could cross class, status, or economic lines.[5] Fourth, in accordance with the heightened importance of the individual, especially as promoted by the Puritans, it was believed that in finding a spouse with whom one could share the moral constancy of domestic love, one also gained a helpmate to heaven.[6] In sum, the ideological shift was not only broad enough to modify most of woman's subject positions and roles, but dynamic enough to engender its own literary expression.

That the choice among suitors for the individual woman ideally depended on love and should not be decided on any other grounds— this was the common theme among a group of heroine-centered novels of courtship. Between 1740 and 1820, the subgenre developed and flourished as some two dozen writers, most of them women, treated the time between a young woman's coming out and her marriage as the most important period in her life. Courtship novels, which were written by women and for women—and thus may in some measure be said to have feminized the English novel—are the subject of this book.[7]

What distinguished courtship novels from other contemporary narratives was that thematically they offered a revisionist view: women, no longer merely unwilling victims, became heroines with significant, though modest, prerogatives of choice and action. Naturally, over its eighty-year history the courtship novel varied its formal expression with literary fashion and its politics according to the class and circumstances of its author, so that it is neither desirable nor possible to specify a normative plot outline. More often than not, however, a courtship novel began with the heroine's coming out and ended with her wedding. It detailed a young woman's entrance into society, the problems arising from that situation, her courtship, and finally her choice (almost always fortunate) among suitors. Thematically, it probed, from a woman's point of view, the emotional difficulties of moving toward affective individuation and companionate marriage despite the regressive effects of female role definition. In this sense, the novel of courtship appropriated domestic fiction to feminist purposes. By creating a feminized space—that is, by centering its story in the brief period of autonomy between a young woman's coming out and her marriage—this subgenre fostered heightened awareness of sexual politics within the gendered arena of language, especially with regard to defining male and female spheres of action.

Because the ideological shift from arranged to companionate marriage had as its central question the disposal of the female body (to whom did the right of exchange belong?), it seems fitting to approach the novel of courtship with the theoretical implications of the body in mind.[8] Woman's body has provided and continues to provide a site of ideological conflict. Ever since Simone de Beauvoir, Betty Friedan, and Kate Millett raised the issue, feminist critics have been scrutinizing the implications of women's sexual/textual suppression within male-dominated society.

Historically, woman's sex defined her as chattel in her father's or husband's house, and her body stood in the way of her becoming an autonomous, speaking subject. Until the mid-eighteenth century in England, paternal authority over daughters regularly included their settlement in arranged marriage. And after marriage, Sandra Gilbert and Susan Gubar remind us, common law "coverture" defined a wife's status as an individual suspended by the fact of her marriage.[9] Ideally a woman inhabited a dependent space within a male territory, so that she never appeared as a litigant or head of household. Even the less public form of expression, writing, was considered to be at odds with women's duty. When they did violate the taboo, female authors found themselves unfairly gauged by a biological essentialism. Such praise as they received linked female writers' physical beauty and purity—or, conversely, physical deformity and depravity—with analogous qualities in their texts. Modest Katherine Philips, the "Matchless Orinda," became a paradigm for the proper woman writer, while Aphra Behn, the "Astraea" who wrote bawdy stories and lived an unchaste life, became a model for the immoral female hack. Thus Jane Spencer notes that by the late seventeenth century the physical analogy was also being employed to undervalue women's writing, as critics argued that inevitably their texts, like their bodies, were weak.[10]

The congruities between the essentialist interpretations of eighteenth- and nineteenth-century readers and twentieth-century theorists of language acquisition are suggestive, to say the least. The Freudian/Lacanian explanation of the entry into the Symbolic relies on a polarized view of the sexes that similarly underestimates and devalues female experience and expression. According to this theory, because woman is removed from the psychic disturbance of the Oedipal drama, she lacks the impetus for full investiture in symbolic language.[11] As Gilbert and Gubar extrapolate it in *Madwoman in the Attic*, the question is "if the pen is a metaphorical penis, with what organ can females generate texts?"[12] Among such French feminists as Hélène Cixous and Luce Irigaray the problem of *l'écriture féminine* has been a particularly vexed one.[13] On this side of the Atlantic, Margaret Homans has deployed an alternative version of language acquisition as proposed by Nancy Chodorow,[14] theorizing that because a mother experiences her daughter as an extension of herself rather than a sexual other, the daughter, intuiting that identification, requires no copula, no phallus. Correspondingly, because the father experiences no sexual challenge from the mother-daughter relationship, he issues no threats of castration. Homans hypothesizes that the daughter's entry into the Symbolic, if easier, is never as wholehearted as the son's, that she is never as completely invested in language because she never recognizes a lack of the phallus. Finally, Homans answers Gilbert and Gubar (at least implicitly) when she suggests in *Bearing the Word* that a woman's text emanates from her womb: the child/word that woman bears becomes a trope for literal language.[15] Yet, in considering Homans's theory, one may object that to identify the literal as the woman's mother tongue is to return to a form of essentialism, to render once more the equation text = body.

No less reductive have been Marxist approaches to the history of the novel, which in general have tended to lose women's issues in the apparently infinite regress in pursuit of the means through which goods and ideology are produced.[16] In this vein, Nancy Armstrong's *Desire and Domestic Fiction*—though brilliant in its theorization of the sociopolitical causes and effects of the domestic novel and insightful in its attention to women's sudden appearance on the novelistic scene—consistently subsumes the feminized tradition of the novel and the gender politics within the novel under what for Armstrong are the more pressing questions of class and status. A pertinent instance, to which I will return in the last chapter, is Armstrong's discussion of *Pride and Prejudice*, which renders the relationship between Darcy and Elizabeth to suit the critic's theoretical focus. She maintains that although the heroine "wins Darcy's heart on the basis of what amounts to a direct violation of the female ideal, Elizabeth renounces all her pertness the instant she agrees to marry him."[17] In her effort to demonstrate that Austen redistributes authority and translates "political conflict into psychological terms" (51), however, Armstrong neglects to mentions Austen's concluding explanation that Georgiana Darcy, initially disturbed by the way her brother changes after his marriage, begins "to comprehend that a woman may take liberties with her husband, which a brother will not always allow in a sister more than ten years younger than himself."[18] Elizabeth's "pertness" is still intact, still a model for the younger woman's behavior, because Austen no doubt had in mind the benefit other young women could derive from having male authority challenged. The salient point here is that insofar as Armstrong views the domestic novel primarily as an agent for bourgeois purposes, she devalues what must have been the experience of its female readers.

It is not my purpose to try to resolve the contradictions evident in even so cursory a summary of contemporary criticism but rather to acknowledge that, for a study of heroine-centered courtship novels, such inconsistencies raise important questions. Is it possible for women, acculturated by a social system that privileges male and bourgeois interests, to express themselves counterideologically, or are all such divergent voices fated (as Nancy Armstrong and Mary Poovey seem to argue) to be assimilated by the hegemony? Moreover, if gender construction makes essential differences between male and female, is it also true that these differences are invested in discrete modes of expression (e.g., symbolic and literal, masculine and feminine)? If so, how can one account for a writer like Richardson, whose literary involvement in the feminist concerns of his day I will argue in the following chapters? Analogously, how do female authors represent masculinist rhetoric?

An obvious beginning for theorizing intratextual coincidence of the masculine and the feminine is provided by M.M. Bakhtin's theory of dialogism within which one finds ample warrant for asserting that texts contain different voices and that authors do not and cannot restrict ideologic content to one cohesive view. Texts—and this is particularly true of novels—are characterized by their heteroglossia, their multiple voices. Also pertinent is Bakhtin's explanation, in an obscure yet suggestive passage of *The Dialogic Imagination*, of the psychological process of individuation. According to his progressive scenario, individuation results from a person's internal experience of conflict between two language categories. On the one hand there is the language of authority—a prior discourse, which Bakhtin characterizes as fixed, unyielding, and not to be questioned: "religious, political, moral; the word of a father, of adults and of teachers." On the other there is the language of internal persuasion, which impels an individual toward autonomy, "denied all privilege, backed up by no authority at all, and . . . frequently not even acknowledged in society . . . not even in the legal code."[19]

Bakhtin's pattern for individuation, however, in common with Marxism and with the broad range of poststructuralist theory, holds two questionable premises: the idea that there exists such a thing as a unitary subject or individual and the idea that within that subject may be found a privileged, nonideological space. As Paul Smith argues insightfully in *Discerning the Subject*, poststructuralism, despite its stance against unitary notions of the individual, fails to dismantle the basic subject/object dyad. The subject, Smith explains, is always "cerned," always implicated in the circle of its own theory. Attempts to avoid this critical debacle have failed: "Current conceptions of the 'subject' have tended to produce a purely *theoretical* 'subject,' removed almost entirely from the political and ethical realities in which human agents actually live."[20] Specifically, Smith complains of the neo-Marxists that they do not adequately theorize the possibility of resistance to hegemonic ideology.[21]

Smith's critique may easily be extended to include Bakhtin's *Dialogic Imagination*, for behind Bakhtin's explanation of individuation one finds a similarly unidimensional concept of the subject. Like some of the theorists Smith challenges, Bakhtin seems to assume that at the individual's core is a privileged, nonideological space. Moreover, his notion of conflicting voices, one external and authoritative, the other internal and persuasive, negates or obscures what for Smith is an integral relationship among the subject, language, and the conditions for resistance. First, because the subject's self-awareness depends on language, and language is inherently ideological, there can be no possibility of a subject outside of language, independent of ideology, or generating its own internal voice. Second, according to Smith's theory, resistance, rather than being autogeneic, presupposes a subjection to ideology: "Oppositional or conservative activity on the part of any person is primarily a mark of a certain engagement with meanings as they exist, circulate, and become fixed within the practices of any given social formation."[22]

Such a theory holds several implications for a reading of heroine-centered courtship fiction. It argues that resistance arises from a conflict among subject positions, from an individual's experience of tension among interpolated ideologies. In the case of feminism, then, because "patriarchy has defined and placed woman as the other . . . if women begin to speak and act from the same ground of cerned subjectivity and identity as men have traditionally enjoyed, a resistance is automatically effected."[23] It follows that whenever a speaking/writing female subject is excluded from a universalist stance (from telling mankind's story, for instance) and nevertheless voices her resistant, progressive, or radical position, the text is necessarily marked by a gendered conflict. Moreover, courtship novelists demonstrate what is now a commonplace, that language has too frequently been appropriated by the male hegemony or that women often find themselves, in one way or another, at a loss for words. Yet the novelists prove that even the hegemonic—in Bakhtin's terms the authoritative—word can be subverted. Commodification can be exposed, for instance, and the insufficiencies of masculinist representations of women can be uncovered.[24] Finally, novelists discover in this genre an opportunity to forward such feminist or resistant ideals as marriage for love, egalitarian domestic relationships between men and women, and improved education for women.

I am concerned in the following chapters not only to describe the historical parameters of the courtship novel but also to give substantial attention to individual novelists. Thus my consistent practice in each of the five parts is to follow broader discussion of narrative techniques and themes with chapters devoted to selected authors. Adopting a loosely chronological order, I give more thorough readings to novels by Eliza Haywood, Mary Collyer, Charlotte Lennox, Samuel Richardson, Frances Brooke, Fanny Burney, Mary Wollstonecraft, Jane West, Mary Brunton, Maria Edgeworth, and Jane Austen. Part I of this study entertains the idea that Eliza Haywood, Mary Collyer, Samuel Richardson, and their successors feminized the novel. Part II, "Feminist Reception Theory," considers the theory and practice of appealing to women readers. Part III, "The Commodification of Heroines," treats the ways courtship novelists appropriated masculinist rhetoric to feminist purposes. Part IV examines progressive ideas about education as being integrally related to the new roles required of women in companionate marriage. Part V considers women's new affective expectations for courtship and marriage.

PART I

A Feminized Genre

ONE

The Courtship Novel

TEXTUAL LIBERATION
FOR WOMEN

HOWEVER ENLIGHTENED our understanding of patriarchy, when
we thumb back through eighteenth-century conduct books we expect
to find a language of containment and circumscription that preempts
female hopes and desires—the monitory gesture, uplifted forefinger,
and glowering brow, usually belonging to male conduct writers. A
line from the Reverend John Bennet's *Letters to a Young Lady* (1792)
conveys the stereotypic patriarchal attitude: "If I was called upon to
write the history of a woman's trials and sorrows, I would date it from
the moment when nature pronounces her *marriageable*."[1] Addressing
boarding-school students, Bennet outlines a bleak prospectus for a
woman's life—coextensive with her body, woman's history begins
with puberty. Ominously, a woman becomes eligible for heroinization
in the male-authored text only when she is objectified, when nature
"pronounces her" an object of choice ("marriageable"). Writing as
late as 1792, Bennet can still obscure the happier prospects of choice
and love by adopting traditional cautionary tones. The future he predicts for his young female audience is dismal, and his advice for them
is nothing more than passive acceptance. Against the essentializing
"when nature pronounces her marriageable" there can be no re-
course.

Bennet's easy assumption of the writerly pose stands in contrast
to the authorial difficulties contemporary women faced. His "history
of a woman's trials and sorrows" will begin at an emblematic moment
of sexual differentiation, a biological rite of passage associated with
woman's quietism. Ironically, a woman scripting such a story could
never leave her body behind, never speak or write without admitting
her gender, and yet to admit her womanhood would be to raise the
question of her culpability. This gender-specific association between
textual and sexual availability began, Ann Rosalind Jones conjectures,
in the Renaissance: "The link between loose language and loose living

arises from a basic association of women's bodies with their speech: a woman's accessibility to the social world beyond the household through speech was seen as intimately connected to the scandalous openness of her body."[2]

In fact, both somatic/semantic oppression and its ancillary trope recede into history as they are pursued, leaving modern readers to wonder whether the female writer has ever escaped the collocation text = body.[3] As far back as the autobiography of Chaucer's contemporary Margery Kempe, for instance, one may find a well articulated oral example. Seized for public preaching, Margery Kempe was taken before the archbishop, whose first question pressed to the patriarchal heart of the matter: "Why goest thou in white? Art thou a maiden?"[4] To whom does her body belong? The somatic test, which seeks to place her within the age-old masculinist tale of pursuit and conquest, would not have been applied to a male evangelist. Required to give her oath not to "teach or challenge the people" in the archbishop's diocese, Margery Kempe evasively defines a less public, less professional semantic position that resembles the subterfuges of the Renaissance poets Jones discusses. "I preach not, sir, I come in no pulpit. I use but communication and good words, and that will I do while I live."[5] Doughty Margery Kempe would speak, even if she could not usurp patrilogial space ("no pulpit") or the universal authority which that space defined. Her accommodations of cultural norms were nothing short of exemplary: wearing white garments that signed her body unavailable, she would not pretend to male prerogatives of speech ("preach") but instead use those available to her as a woman ("communication and good words"). When it actually came to writing her book, Kempe had another problem. She was illiterate. But, daughter to a mayor and wife to a tax collector, she could afford to employ scribes. Her father's and husband's status were essential determinants of her limited access to written expression.

For the increasing numbers of women producing public texts in the early 1700s, the somatic/semantic trope that had forced circumspection on Kempe and her Renaissance successors still held as one of the material conditions within and against which they wrote. This much one can guess from their anomalous and usually defensive prefaces. Aphra Behn, Delariviere Manley, Eliza Haywood, and others told risqué stories even while their prefaces persistently claimed moral purposes. Eliza Haywood's dedication of The Rash Resolve (1724) rehearses a common demur: "The Misfortunes of her who is the subject of it . . . cannot fail of exciting compassion in a generous Mind: and how blameable soever her Conduct may appear . . . the Train of Woes it drew on her, prevail to soften the severity of Censure."[6] Haywood's prose is conflicted, shifting unsteadily between two requirements:

making the expected denunciation of the fallen woman's conduct and attempting to enlist reader sympathy or identification with her heroine.

Finally, such circumspection did not protect Haywood from Alexander Pope's censure in the *Dunciad*. Representing her as whore/writer, Pope insisted on the physical proximity of her biological and literary products. "See in the circle next, Eliza plac'd, / Two babes of love close clinging to her waist; / Fair as before her works she stands confessed."[7] "Babes of love" and "works," he implied, were interchangeable effects of sexual/textual depravity. It is not clear from what we know of her personal history whether Haywood was merely daunted or altogether converted by her public humiliation; the demonstrable fact is that she retreated to writing anonymously, eventually turning to genteel courtship plots. Beyond standing as an example of how the somatic/semantic trope affected women, Eliza Haywood's mid-career conversion, her definitive shift from masculine plots of pursuit, seduction, and betrayal to feminine ones of courtship and marriage, illustrates how early women novelists feminized their genre, avoiding or ameliorating the deleterious association between their bodies and their works.[8]

Because its domestic setting and linear plot easily accommodated not only conventional wisdom about women's roles but also incipient resistant ideologies, the courtship novel was an ideal medium for expressing middle-class women's values and issues. If they did not always adopt what we would recognize as feminist strategies or feminist causes, courtship novelists nonetheless feminized the genre in several important ways. First, they valorized the experience of the middle-class "proper lady" by making her the central figure in the plot while reducing male characters to minor roles.[9] Second, they brought the reader into the ordinary sphere of women, typically using domestic settings—country houses, with their dining rooms, closets, sitting rooms, groves, carriages, grounds, tenants' houses, and neighboring estates; or London houses, with their similar interiors and nearby parks, shops, and theaters. Third, by the nature of their heroines, settings, and issues, courtship novelists rendered their works gender-specific, appealing selectively to a community of identificatory readers, women of the middle and upper classes. Fourth, unlike many contemporary writers, these novelists did not usually include in their works prolonged scenes of sexual pursuit, machinations that, in any case, were never successful with their prudent heroines. Finally, courtship novels were didactic; they theorized overtly on women's conduct—at times replicating the repressive views of male-authored conduct books, and at other times expressing the incipient feminism that had begun to question received roles for women. They exposed threats to women's peace: authoritarian parents, rakish suitors, and even fashionable London. On the two issues of education and marriage, especially, courtship novelists sought to raise women's expectations.

It is important to recognize that the feminization of the novel was not an isolated phenomenon but part of a general shift in consciousness in eighteenth-century England. Among the circumstances that shaped receptivity to the new novelistic form, two were particularly important. The first was that, as a result of the currents of sensibility running through England, the courtship novel was part of a broader social imperative to legitimize women's self-actualization as affective individuals. The second, related circumstance that prepared the way was that courtship novels were aligned in their redefinition of feminine roles with two other textual forms that similarly expressed the tensions of ideological change—conduct books and periodicals. Each of these developments in the history of ideas, given adequate scope, would provide matter for a book-length study. The following is necessarily an abbreviated and partial summary of the climate that fostered the growth of women's courtship novels.

Any discussion of sensibility and affective individualism must begin with Lawrence Stone's *Marriage, Sex and Family in England, 1500-1800* and give some account of the heated debate that followed Stone's assertion that human affections underwent a major course correction in the 1700s. According to Stone, *affective individualism* originated in a complex of social change toward greater freedom for children and more equal partnerships between spouses, toward increased separation of the nuclear family from the community, toward more affectionate relations between parents and children and husband and wife.[10] Notwithstanding the large amount of textual evidence Stone amassed, certain vexing questions about the verifiability of changes in marriage patterns continue to stimulate debate among historians: precisely whose lives were actually affected? how can the alteration in marriage patterns be documented? But while such questions are germane to historical study, I suggest that they do not shape the most fertile ground for literary inquiry. On the contrary, it is precisely the change in conceptualization and representation, the field of ideology, that must interest the literary scholar, and in this regard the evidence is both extensive and persuasive. Whether or not the British population actually changed its nuptial practices, historians have demonstrated that, at least within the realm of ideas—that is, within period texts—companionate marriage made a substantial impact on eighteenth-century England.[11]

Among the studies that have followed and clearly been influenced by Stone's, three merit special attention here for their elucidation of the relationship between affective individualism and literature: Jean Hagstrum's *Sex and Sensibility: Ideal and Erotic Love from Milton to Mozart* (1980), Edmund Leites's *The Puritan Conscience and Modern Sexuality* (1986), and Nancy Armstrong's *Desire and Domestic Fiction: A Political History of the Novel* (1987). Writing from somewhat different perspectives, Hagstrum and Leites are in general agreement in tracing a causal relationship between seventeenth-century Puritan beliefs and the subsequent upwelling into eighteenth-century literature of a new interest in affective individualism. Nancy Armstrong, on the other hand, observes that the Puritans had tried to replace a monarchy with a meritocracy in the seventeenth century, and that their theories continued to be useful in contesting the dominant political order, which, in this case, "depended . . . on representing women as economic and political objects."[12] In Armstrong's view, the new interest in affective individualism was merely a new way of achieving the old goal of domesticity. Within the domestic scene, merit and affect displaced the old system of status considerations as a means of determining relationships.

In *Sex and Sensibility*, Jean Hagstrum observes that, while the relationship between social change and the arts is never simple enough to permit us to chart cause and effect, it seems likely that some literary event conditioned Restoration and eighteenth-century receptiveness to changes in familial relations. Seventeenth-century Puritanism, then, was an important root of affective individualism. According to Hagstrum, it was the prelapsarian love between Milton's Adam and Eve that served as the literary model for new domestic relationships. Such writers as Steele, Addison, Thomson, and Fielding were disciples of the Puritan Milton, "who regarded marriage as satisfying the demands of body, mind, and spirit in a union more total than any that had been hitherto conceived of as realistically possible."[13] Thus, after Milton, love came to mean a fusion between sex and sensibility— more specifically, of three essential terms, *body, mind,* and *spirit.*

Hagstrum neglects to mention, however, that it was not until the mid-eighteenth century advent of the courtship novel that women finally mythologized the new reality for themselves. Moreover, when it came to literary expression, the textual interpretation of women's experience of love—the fusion of sex and sensibility, or body, mind, and spirit—was substantially different from men's. Sensibility largely devalued or displaced libidinal sexual passion, supplying instead the term "esteem," and in women's courtship novels the suppression of physical passion was still more rigorous, with *body* (Hagstrum's first term) finding only the most covert expression or being relegated to minor characters. To an even greater extent than in male-authored or male-centered fiction, blushings, faintings, tremblings, and other signs of the sensible body largely replaced "youthful dalliance," the passion and conjugal union Milton specifies. No doubt this absence of overt sexuality in courtship heroines marked the beginning of what Hagstrum, Sandra Gilbert and Susan Gubar, Mary Poovey, Edmund Leites, and Nancy Armstrong have variously referred to as a spiritualization of the domestic scene, or *angelisme*.[14]

Another reason why sexuality was displaced in women's texts may have been the novelists' desire to distinguish their texts from contemporary romances. In this light, one can read the omission of *body* as an attempt to differentiate woman's history from masculinist representations, which depended heavily on the conventions of male libido—pursuit/prey/objectification. Avoiding these patterns (which were later revived in the Gothics), women centered their novels on the limited space provided for female autonomy within courtship. If overt references to *body*, to sexual passion, are absent in female-authored courtship novels, this was not the case for Hagstrum's second and third terms, *mind* and *spirit*. The ideology of affective individualism included the notion that men and women were to be intellectual companions, an ideal that naturally raised questions about women's mental preparation for marriage. At the same time, some period writers, no longer believing in accomplishments and domestic arts, exhorted daughters and parents to view education more as a method of self-actualization than as a narrow means to an end.

The third term in Hagstrum's taxonomy, *spirit*—which may have provided the strongest impetus behind the move toward affective individualism and companionate marriage—appears only sporadically in courtship novels. After Milton, who represented Adam and Eve's prelapsarian love as a spiritual experience that enforced their relationship with God, seventeenth- and eighteenth-century writers encouraged marriage for love and inveighed against arranged marriages as spiritually corruptive. Thus Hagstrum emphasizes, as does Leites, that the new literary topos of spousal love was indebted to Puritan ideals.

One of the more common criticisms of Stone's work has been the charge that he obscures the complicitous relationship between liberal humanism and patriarchy.[15] On the whole, the vogue for interrogating so-called liberal tendencies (in this case, the move toward more egalitarian relationships within the family) has been a valuable strategy in the postmodern quest to dismantle ideological monoliths. But such strategies also produce their own systemic oversimplifications.

Just as we now recognize that the concept *patriarchy* must be read complexly, with historical specificity, so we must also acknowledge the same principle for the range of human experience (marriage, conjugal love, divorce, and so forth) associated with the term *affective individualism*.

Writing in this vein, Edmund Leites warns, in *The Puritan Conscience*, that in attempting to correct earlier historical naiveté, revisionist historians may go too far. Arguing against the practice of simplistically labeling liberal humanist ideals as cooptive strategies, he points out that conjugal love, in particular, has its own complex history—a genealogy that bears significantly on its implementation. Leites suggests that the new appreciation for married love in the eighteenth century was a natural development from the earlier Puritan desire to avoid an oscillating temperament. He locates as a motive force behind individualism John Locke's view that, while children must give ultimate allegiance to their parents, adults owe that ultimate allegiance "to no other person; they must not find other 'mothers' and 'fathers.' Their knowledge of law alone should command their obedience to civil authorities."[16]

Leites's theory is that the two complementary ideas—the Puritan interest in moral constancy and Locke's view of marriage as a contract between two autonomous beings—cohered as part of the concept of affective individualism that subsequently became so important for eighteenth-century England. Leites suggests further that the valorization of moral constancy led inevitably to a reciprocal hierarchy between the sexes—"a new set of complementary potencies": "The purity of women made them dependent upon men, for men, unlike women, could be commanding and animal without violating their place in the hierarchy. Inasmuch as women needed animality and a forceful, dominating power in their own lives, they had to get it exclusively from men. And men, in their animality and amoral will to power, needed the civilizing presence of women." Thus, while he acknowledges that seventeenth- and eighteenth-century English culture was formed largely by men, Leites emphasizes that gains made through gender role definition were reciprocal and denies that "the idea of female purity answered only masculine interests."[17]

Leites's theoretical perspective is especially relevant to a study of women's literature in this period because it problematizes the male/female dichotomy in relation to affective individualism. While finding inherent disadvantages for both sexes in their socialization according to a reciprocal hierarchy pattern, Leites also acknowledges that this pattern to some degree empowered each sex. Thus, while he avoids the tendency of altogether reducing affective individualism to masculinist propaganda, he provides a groundwork for understanding why in this period women suddenly began writing courtship stories. In effect, one can argue on the basis of Leites's reciprocal hierarchy theory that women's new charge of maintaining domestic calm and civility gave them an empowering space from which to speak and to write.

Like Hagstrum and Leites, Nancy Armstrong acknowledges that there were significant changes in gender role definition during the eighteenth century, but for her purposes the more interesting question is how domestic fiction served the rising middle class in its power struggle with the aristocracy. She theorizes in *Desire and Domestic Fiction* that popular novels, by presenting a decontextualized, depoliticized surface, and by valorizing affective individualism, forwarded a middle-class power quest. Armstrong's point is that desire was reconstituted so that "language, which once represented the history of the individual as well as the history of the state in terms of kinship relations, was dismantled to form the masculine and feminine spheres that characterize modern culture." The gendered conflict that provides so much of the material for the domestic novel Armstrong consistently reads as a displacement of class conflict. She argues convincingly, for example, that in the domestic novel, the male party to an exchange usually approximates Richardson's Mr. B. "He is likely to bear certain features of the ruling class that inhibit the operations of genuine love." Then, in the course of the novel, he will be remade in the image of a new ruling class, one that, like the gentry, is permeable—a class one could enter through marriage.[18]

Such a reading of the domestic novel has its drawbacks, however. One of these, inherent in any systematization, is the difficulty of accommodating widely divergent texts written over a considerable period of time. In fact, the weakest aspect of Armstrong's study is that, while she offers a complexly developed theory, she includes relatively few discussions of literary texts. There is something basically suspect, moreover, in the way such a Marxist reading first recognizes the artificiality of dividing human culture along gendered lines (e.g., domestic vs. political) and then implicitly assumes the traditionally masculinist, politically-invested, class-conscious view of history as a basis from which to describe domestic fiction. In effect, Armstrong reenacts the marginalization of the female, reducing once more precisely those voices and texts that historically have been labelled "minor," not representative of hegemonic views. Thus, while she constructs an interesting hypothesis for the largely unconscious process by which affective individualism and class struggle integrate within eighteenth- and nineteenth-century texts, Armstrong does not sufficiently credit and explain the more or less conscious resistances so many women authors expressed through their domestic novels. It is with this question that I will be primarily concerned. In other words, this study of the courtship novel largely confines itself to a purview of the community of women writers and readers whom affective individualism brought together in the domestic sphere.

A second circumstance that conditioned the reception of courtship novels was the presence of similar themes in women's conduct books and periodicals. If women were to be responsible for choosing in a new matrimonial game of chance with higher stakes, it followed that they had to be educated about how to weigh the odds, how to play their hands, and how to read the faces opposite theirs. Roles as well as rules had to be redefined. Jean Hagstrum observes that such a milieu of changing social patterns, where those patterns are inadequately expressed in literature, normally evokes new literary "filiations": "It would be surprising if . . . alternations of the magnitude that [Lawrence] Stone investigates—a truly profound reorientation of human desires and habits—were not also accompanied by linguistic enrichment and a body of internally related literature and art—by works, that is, that possess the power to mythologize reality."[19] Granted, the relationship between actual experience and ideology is more complex than Hagstrum's words would suggest, for, as Paul Smith's *Discerning the Subject* reminds us, the question whether lived experience or ideological representation comes first nearly always remains unanswered.[20] Nonetheless it is important to observe about the contemporary eighteenth-century milieu that among the texts a young woman would have had available to her from mid-century on were two "nonliterary" forms calculated to be especially accessible to female readers and specifically meant to inspire their imitation: conduct books and periodicals written for women.[21]

Valued for their didacticism, conduct books like John Burton's were so similar in content and purpose to novels written for women that one could well argue, as Joyce Hemlow does in a 1960 article, for using the term *courtesy novel* to describe some period fiction. Hemlow remarks that Fanny Burney was one among several writers who "attempted to justify and dignify their new art by including the reputable and useful matter of the courtesy books."[22] To read Burney's novel and others of its kind, then, is to discover "the books of laws and customs *a-la-mode*" that the embarrassed Evelina wished for when caught in her first social faux pas. But the question of where Evelina gets her advice raises a gender issue that both Joyce Hemlow and Mary Poovey neglect—an issue that bears complexly on the history of women's novels. For any discussion of the tandem development of women's novels and conduct books, it is crucial to recall that it was only late in the history of conduct literature that the conduct books ostensibly written for women really began serving as a means of *self-definition* for them.[23] By and large, it was men rather than women themselves who advised and, by extension, defined women, and no doubt male-authored conduct books for women were as suspiciously self-serving as many of those written for servants by their masters, for the simple reason that the group being addressed was not given the prerogative of self-definition. Nonetheless, Mary Poovey is largely correct in linking the general run of conduct books with ideologies one might broadly term bourgeois and patriarchal; it was literally the case that Evelina and other women had few alternatives to the law of the Father until the last quarter of the eighteenth century.

I mean, however, neither to argue that male-authored conduct literature was universally exploitative and repressive nor that there was a coherent and invariable patriarchal line. We know, for example, that Burney's contemporaries were reading both François de Salignac de la Mothe Fénelon's *Traité de l'éducation des Filles* (reprinted in translation five times during the 1700s) and the Marquis de Halifax's *New-Year's Gift: Advice to a Daughter* (which achieved sixteen editions by 1765). In fact, these two very popular books express quite different male attitudes toward women. But whether Fénelon encourages women intellectually or Halifax reminds them they are inferior in nature and in station, the salient fact is that as a group women were still being defined by men—a situation that was not to improve significantly until quite late in the century.

Granted, among the more benevolent male advisers was Samuel Richardson, whose involvement with conduct literature had begun with his printing of Fénelon's *Traité* (1721) and Defoe's *Religious Courtship* (1729). Richardson had written his own conduct book for apprentices, *The Apprentice's Vade Mecum* (1733). Interestingly, one of his last authorial efforts records in its title the kinship he took for granted between conduct literature and the novel: *A Collection of the Moral and Instructive Sentiments, Maxims, Cautions, and Reflexions Contained in the Histories of Pamela, Clarissa, and Sir Charles Grandison* (1755). Richardson, however, sympathetic though he proved himself, was merely another man who chose to advise women.[24] More remarkable than any advice he himself gave women was the fact that his large and shifting female coterie included early women writers both of conduct books and of novels. His friends Hester Mulso Chapone and Jane Collier wrote conduct books; Charlotte Lennox, several courtship novels.

Beyond Samuel Richardson's works and coterie, the most important collective sources of texts written for women in this period were two distinct literary communities, each of which contributed both female-authored conduct books and courtship novels to what one might broadly call the feminist cause. First, there was the select group of men and women who met for informal conversation and who quickly became known as the Bluestockings. Among early members were prominent society figures: Elizabeth Vesey, wife of a member of the Irish parliament; Elizabeth Montagu, wife of the wealthy Edward Montagu (whose grandfather was the first Earl of Sandwiche). Also attending were men of artistic and literary renown—David Garrick, Edmund Burke, Sir Josuah Reynolds, and Samuel Johnson—and literary women, several of whom became famous for their achievements—Elizabeth Carter, Fanny Burney, Hannah More, Anna Laetitia Barbauld, Fanny Boscawen, and Hester Chapone.

This elite company could be termed radical only insofar as they imported a new social custom from France: they exchanged the two-parlor system of entertaining company—which relegated women to gossip, cards, and tea while it favored men with more rational conversation, cigars, and sherry—for the salon, which brought together intellects of both sexes. For this real and symbolic divergence from somatic/semantic strictures, the English *bas bleu* were deservedly famous. In addition, a number of female Bluestockings devoted themselves to advising other women, producing works that were relatively progressive and feminist for the times.[25] Hester Chapone's *Letters on the Improvement of the Mind* (1797) and Hannah More's *Strictures on Female Education* (1799) were popular conduct books promoting better education for women. Anna Laetitia Barbauld, capitalizing on her teaching experiences, also flourished as a writer of children's books. More's *Coelebs in Search of a Wife* (1808), though undeserving of comparison with even the least of Fanny Burney's novels, belongs with *Evelina* (1778), *Cecilia* (1782), and *Camilla* (1796) among novels of courtship advice. No doubt it was this textual legacy of the first English salon, along with the later radicalization of women's issues during the French Revolution, that subsequently converted the term *bluestocking*, originally applied to both sexes, into a gender-specific label of approbrium for the female pedant.

The "Feminist Controversy," the second feminist movement to yield an important body of conduct books and courtship novels, evolved during the heady period of the Revolution, when even equality between the sexes seemed possible. Preceded by the socially acceptable blues but perceived as being much more dangerous, Mary Wollstonecraft was the central figure of this movement.[26] After everything revolutionary began appearing suspect, the women in the "Feminist Controversy" were attacked for their association with the excesses of Revolutionary France. Meeting at the house of publisher Joseph Johnson, Wollstonecraft's circle was, in fact, comprised of radicals—sympathizers with the Revolution, brilliant but erratic people such as Swiss painter Henry Fuseli and poet and artist William Blake. Neither her early conduct book, *Thoughts on the Education of Daughters* (1786), nor the novel that followed two years later, *Mary, a Fiction* (1788), was particularly inflammatory. But in 1792, fired by Talleyrand's report on public education, which ignored questions of equality between the sexes, Wollstonecraft published her most provocative feminist statement, *A Vindication of the Rights of Women*. Whether her contemporaries agreed with her works, were inspired by the *Zeitgeist*, or wrote in outraged response to the brutal frankness of William Godwin's biography of her life, the decade of the nineties saw prolific publication of conduct books and courtship novels, many of which evoked Wollstonecraft's name in their prefaces.[27]

As I have briefly outlined it, then, the relationship among women's conduct books and their novels is much more complex than either Mary Poovey or Nancy Armstrong would allow. It is true that proper women novelists accepted and incorporated without question most traditional ideals of female decorum included in male-authored conduct books—in regard, for example, to choosing friends wisely, refusing clandestine correspondence, and treating servants kindly while maintaining the proper distance from them. In all probability male and female writers alike unconsciously served hegemonic interests by the kinds of advice they gave young women. But to read conduct literature as doing no more than this is to oversimplify its complex and often contradictory messages. On some matters—improving women's education and marrying for love, for instance—female novelists and female conduct writers alike took unusually liberal and feminist positions.

Not surprisingly, at the same time that conduct books were being feminized, parallel changes were taking place in some periodicals. A few instances will suffice to illustrate the accommodations magazines began making for their growing female readership. Too well known to need recapitulating, Addison's and Steele's early efforts at domestic reform were succeeded by such women's journals as the *Female Tatler*, which echoed their incipient feminism, blaming parents who forced their daughters into marriage.[28] By mid-century, women's issues and interests, especially advice on choosing husbands, were spilling into Eliza Haywood's *Female Spectator* (1744-46) and Frances Brooke's *Old*

Maid (1755)—whose editors, coincidentally, also wrote courtship novels. Beyond providing marriage guidance, Haywood was an especially enthusiastic advocate of improved education, claiming that she hoped "to bring learning into fashion among women" by promoting studies in philosophy, geography, history, and mathematics.[29]

Meanwhile, the *Ladies Magazine* (1749-53), one of the more entertaining publications for women, included not only a course of history by question and answer and a detailed account of contemporary crimes but also "verse, riddles and puzzles, a diary of events at home and abroad, play reviews, and short discourses on topics of general interest."[30] "Jasper Goodwill" is known to have borrowed most of his material from other periodicals, yet in one section of the magazine he made a signal change, to all appearances a calculated appeal to his female readers. His marriage announcements were not the customary baldly financial accounts, particularly of the young women's fortunes, which had long been the mainstay of such columns in the *London Magazine* and the *Chronicle*. Instead of quantifying the bride's fortune or listing the pound valuation of both spouses, Goodwill merely mentioned the respective families of bride and groom (as in the first two examples below). On the rare occasions on which he made reference to fortune at all (as in the last announcement), Goodwill did so only in the context of providing other "reasons" for the young woman's desirability in marriage:

MARRIAGES, Sir William Baird, Bart. at Edinburgh to Miss Gardener, one of the Daughters of the brave Col. Gardener, killed at the Battle of Preston-l'ans.----Peter Neville, Esq. to Miss Wilson, Daughter of the late John Wilson, of Chichester, Esq.;----Mr. William Halstead, a Gentleman of Estate, and Merchant of London, in Merton Chapel, Oxford, by the Rev. Dr. Leybourne, Principal of Alban-Hall, to his Niece, Miss Caswall, a young Lady of 6000£. Fortune. Particularly admired for her skill in Musick, and the Sweetness of her Voice; her Good Humour, good Sense, and every Accomplishment requisite to make a Husband most happy.[31]

Although, the phrases "a Gentleman of Estate" and "a young Lady of 6000£. Fortune" convey the idea that in simple pecuniary terms both families would have been content with the Halstead-Caswall marriage, there remains some inequity in the specificity with which Miss Caswall's fortune is listed. One may, however, read trends of broader social significance in Goodwill's treatment of Miss Caswall's personal qualities ("particularly admired for her . . ."): the growing claims of affective individualism and an increasing consciousness of a female audience. In making an effort to edit out or at least to diminish the language of the marketplace, Goodwill is accommodating the designated audience for his *Ladies Magazine*.

Another indication that journal editors were becoming increasingly conscious of female readers is that by 1751 even such decidedly male-oriented journals as the *London Magazine* (1732-83) were attempting to appeal to them. In the July 1751 issue, for instance—along with transcripts of Parliamentary debates, abstracts of books, accounts of trials, descriptions and maps of various cities, and mathematical questions—subscribers were offered an essay entitled "Cautions concerning Marriage, with a remarkable Story." Two summers later, in July 1753, the magazine was largely taken up by the Parliamentary news and contemporary debate surrounding Lord Hardwicke's "Act for the better preventing of Clandestine Marriage," a contretemps, as I will demonstrate later, that bears on the representation of heroines, and consequently on the understanding of female role definition in this period.

TWO

Eliza Haywood

A MID-CAREER
CONVERSION

WHETHER Eliza Haywood was convinced by her own appraisal of the market or forced into caution or repentance by Pope's *Dunciad*, she demonstrated a marked shift toward the morality of Jane Barker, Penelope Aubin, and Mary Davys in her works (largely anonymous) published after the 1728 *Dunciad*. At fifty-one, caught by shifting literary fashions, Haywood returned to topics she had already attempted in the *Female Spectator*, restyling her novels to suit new audience demands for moral heroine-centered tales. One might assume from the dates of *The Fortunate Foundlings* (1744) and *The History of Jemmy and Jenny Jessamy* (1753) that Haywood took the hint for her new direction from Samuel Richardson's enormous success with *Pamela* in 1740. But given the scope of literary activity during the period, it is injudicious to assign cause and effect labels, and certainly too simplistic to assume that the history of the novel can be compassed by beginning with the major author. The question of influence, moreover, is as appropriately posed in relation to Haywood's on Richardson as to Richardson's on Haywood. After all, Haywood had been publishing novels for two decades before Richardson's servant girl made such a splash on the literary scene, and her heroines were already taking feminist positions, if only by virtue of their resistance to being made sexual playthings.[1] As early as *Adventures of Eovaii, Princess of Ijaveo* (1736), one finds Haywood relinquishing her salacious stories for more sedate ones, and at the same time, by having Eovaii educated to rule her people, taking what could be termed a feminist stance.

Of the two novelists, it was Haywood who first initiated separate plots and spheres of action for the sexes, a practice Richardson subsequently adopted in *Grandison*. The fact that she went to great lengths to separate female and male plots in both *The Fortunate Foundlings* and *The History of Jemmy and Jenny Jessamy* is unmistakable evidence that she conceived these late novels in terms of sexual politics. But if Haywood tried to maintain an equilibrium between male and female plots and ideologies in both novels, the implicit balance falters, with the female plot alone manifesting a radical energy, an "internally persuasive" voice, that compels the reader's attention.[2]

Published four years after *Pamela*, *The Fortunate Foundlings* recounts the story of twins, raised and educated by Dorilaus, the gentleman in whose garden they were abandoned as infants. To all appearances its title aligns the novel with contemporary benevolent projects such as the establishment of foundling hospitals[3] and against Thomas Malthus's principle of noninterference with poverty. Yet Haywood does not shape the story as a polemic in favor of the lower classes. These foundlings, it turns out, are not members of a lower class elevated by Dorilaus's benevolence and their own virtue but rather his own illegitimate children. The divided plot permits each twin to mature through separate gender-determined adventures. First, the male twin, Horatio, with their guardian's reluctant approval, joins Marlborough's forces, hoping to make a name as a soldier so that he may "become the head of a family." Later, when Dorilaus falls in love with her and turns suitor, the female twin, Louisa, flees their guardian's home. On the whole, Horatio's difficulties are less sympathetic than his sister's, perhaps because his choices—between the young woman he loves and the military, between obeying Dorilaus and fulfilling his duty to the king of Sweden—merely repeat an age-old love/duty debate.

In Louisa's case, though, the conflict between love and duty—between holding out for a love match and marrying their guardian out of gratitude—presents a psychological crux so new, for the heroine and presumably for her audience as well, that she can scarcely find words to refuse her Dorilaus: "She blushed;—she trembled;—she was ready to die between surprize, grief and shame:—fain she would have spoke, but feared, lest what she should say would either lose his friendship or encourage his passion.—Each seemed equally dreadful to her:—no words presented themselves to her distracted mind that she could think proper to utter."[4] Louisa dutifully tries and fails to return her guardian's love, her reason at odds with her emotional response: "What unaccountable prejudice is this then that strikes me with such horror at his love!—what maid of birth and fortune equal to his own but would be proud of his addresses; and shall I, a poor foundling, the creature of his charity, not receive the honour he does me with the utmost gratitude!" (20). Dorilaus's family and fortune make him a good match, and Louisa believes herself as much his "creature," his to dispose of, as if she were his biological daughter (which in fact she is). She acknowledges feeling "duty, reverence, and gratitude," but "as for any other sort of love I know not what it is; were it a voluntary emotion, believe me, sir, I gladly would give it entrance into my soul, but I well see it is of a far different nature" (19).

If the dynamics of the earlier scene mark its ideological content as emergent, then it should be no surprise that subsequently the "different nature" of marital love becomes a recurrent theme for the female plot, this early scene initiating a persistent conflict between a male rhetoric that coopts and objectifies and a female affective individualism that remains almost speechless (aphonic). Louisa realizes that the love she can neither clearly describe nor control is so vital to her self-definition that, although she has no friends or means of support, she prefers to leave Dorilaus's house rather than risking his "seizing" his happiness as he has threatened. Later, from her vantage point as a seamstress, she begins to understand that her choice isolates her as well from the fashionable people who patronize the milliner's shop where she works. They would think her senseless "did they know I chose rather to work for my bread in mean obscurity, than yield to marry where I could not love.—Tenderness, mutual affection, and constancy, I find, are things not thought requisite to the happiness of a wedded state; and interest and convenience alone consulted" (30). In claiming her right to marry for love, her affective individualism, Louisa in effect claims a natural virtue and positions herself as a rebel, against Dorilaus's power as her guardian, against the authoritative word ("duty") she has internalized, and against the worldly ideology and status system represented by the fashionable crowd. By the care with which all this is argued, one may read Haywood's invitation to her readers to identify with the relatively new position her heroine takes and to enjoy a corresponding liberation from outdated notions about woman's submissive role in courtship.

Haywood is cautious not to oversimplify the matter of choosing for love. Employed as a traveling companion to a fashionable woman, Louisa witnesses at close hand the treachery of affective language and tries ineffectually to persuade her mistress, Melanthe, not to be duped:

What is there in this love . . . that so infatuates the understanding, that we doat on our dishonour, and think ruin pleasing?—Can any personal perfections in a man atone for the contempt he treats us with in courting us to infamy!—the mean opinion he testifies to have of us sure ought rather to excite hate than love; our very pride . . . should be a sufficient guard, and turn whatever favourable thoughts we might have of such a one, unknowing his design, into aversion, when once convinced he presumed upon our weakness. [167]

Haywood's choice of the plural pronoun ("we doat on our dishonour") at once attests to Louisa's cautious diplomacy in advising the fallen Melanthe and promotes the reader's understanding of gender politics, in which language is man's tool ("his design") in the contest with woman ("courting us to infamy").

Altogether unmoved by Louisa's warning, Melanthe persists in a flirtation that finally becomes an affair with Count de Bellflour, whose glibness doubly falsifies, not only veiling his lack of feeling for her but also disguising his designs on Louisa. Frustrated by Louisa's denials, de Bellflour eventually manipulates Melantha into discharging her, and while she is en route to England, gains access to her hotel room by posing as her husband. Again Haywood's heroine is virtually speechless, for, lacking de Bellflour's fluency in Italian, she is unable to convince the innkeeper that she is not his wife: "As she spoke very bad Italian, and the man understood no French, the count being very fluent in that language, had much the advantage, the innkeeper was fully satisfied, and they were again left alone" (199). Just as the rake is about to force himself on her, though, Louisa springs from his arms and seizes his sword. In this posture, she manages to keep him "from closing with, or disarming her" (200) until she reaches the lower floor, where she is relieved by the arrival of her true love, de Plessis. By drawing the sword, Louisa challenges the count's fatuous assertion that she should be grateful for his attentions, and reveals the attempted rape for what it is, a violence to her person. Yet it is obvious that even the physical protest would have been futile had not de Plessis appeared, just as Louisa ran downstairs, to reassert the truth, which in her voice has so far been ineffectual—to deny the count's assertion that she is his wife. Thus Haywood consistently records as a gender difference the fact that language is almost completely at the service of male characters and male machinations.

A final instance of the power of false male rhetoric to bind women in disadvantageous positions occurs in the scene that reunites Louisa with her estranged guardian. Haywood has Dorilaus, whose passionate declaration of his love originally drove Louisa from her home, claim her as his "natural" daughter:

Yes, my Louisa . . . and [I] flatter myself, by what I have observed of your disposition, you have done nothing, since our parting, that might prevent my glorying in being the parent of such a child.

The hurry of spirits she was in, prevented her from taking notice of these last words, or at least from making any answer to them, and she still continued crying out,—Dorilaus, my father!—Good heaven! may I believe I am so blessed!—Who then is my mother! Wherefore have I been so long ignorant of what I was! [317-18]

But even Dorilaus's paternal and, in this scene, recuperative role is rendered problematically, for in view of his earlier behavior such an assertion of paternal and judgmental rights is awkward at best. Louisa fails to answer what, under the circumstances, seems a presumptuous question ("you have done nothing . . . "), yet what she does say—"Dorilaus, my father! . . . Who then is my mother"—recalls his guilt for fathering the illegitimate foundlings and for attempting (however innocently) an incestuous relationship. Further, what is not said—Haywood's suppressed condemnation of the double standard, of the flawed male authority figure—charges the conclusion. By implication, Haywood legitimizes Louisa's original "prejudice" against marrying Dorilaus as a natural instinct, and establishes her right to act as an affective individual. In this way, though she affords her heroine little more than physical resistance (running away and drawing a sword are examples), Haywood uncovers and protests the affectively repressed and muted position woman holds in society.

By the time she wrote *The History of Jemmy and Jenny Jessamy* nine years later, Eliza Haywood's feminist strategy was more verbal and hence more explicit than the largely physical resistance she had employed in *The Fortunate Foundlings*. Furthermore, by 1753, tales of heroines holding out for companionate marriages were no longer uncommon. Jemmy and Jenny Jessamy, distantly related, have been raised knowing that their fathers intend them for each other, and when both are orphaned within a few months, it seems to everyone that their marriage must follow shortly. But during the interim period of mourning, Jenny, watching other lovers, comes to believe that she and Jemmy "ought to know a little more of the world and of ourselves before we enter into serious matrimony."[5] Her plan determines the plot of the three-volume novel and proposes a similar program for her readers: "Every one before they engage in marriage should be well vers'd in all those things . . . which constitute the happiness of it;—this town is an ample school, and both of us have acquaintance enough in it to learn, from the mistakes of others, how to regulate our own conduct and passions, so as not to be laugh'd at ourselves for what we laugh at in them" (1:56). From its initial pages, Haywood's novel takes an overtly sceptical approach to marriage, its plot rendered even more radical by the fact that Jenny, a woman, suggests that the marriage be postponed.

More conventional is the divide between male and female, which coincides with the separation between experience and theory, between participant and spectator. While Jemmy is personally exposed to the temptations city life affords young men—the seductive Liberia, who trades her honor for gambling debts, and the amorous Lady Hardy, whom he rejects when he discovers she is a friend's relation—his fiancée's lessons commonly place her in a spectator role. Haywood implies for her female readers positions at once identificatory and adjudicative, inasmuch as they must not only sympathize with the educational aspect of Jenny's (and, to some extent, Jemmy's) experiences but also participate in judgments of those they encounter. From the number of negative exempla she includes, it would seem that Haywood is especially concerned to insure her female readers against the disillusionment that too often follows marriage. Haywood's feminist perspective is even more explicit when she reveals her male character's mistakes and then invites her female readers' judgments of him (a technique she does not reverse). Her frame-breaking comments appeal specifically to the female reader: "I am very much afraid that poor Jemmy has lain for a great while under the displeasure of my fair readers" (2:196).

Overall, Haywood's persistent scepticism about marital happiness lends the work a kind of thematic unity despite its episodic structure and disruptive alternations between male and female plots. More distinctly than in *The Fortunate Foundlings*, the author outlines woman's disadvantaged position in the verbal arena. When, for example, Jenny censures the difference between a couple's behavior before and after marriage, she specifically faults the husband for his disingenuous use of language:

Who that sees a man a husband would ever think he had been a lover?—till she was a wife he would not have presumed to argue with her on any point she took upon her to assert;—he would not then have opposed his reason to any folly she committed; . . . if she is proud,—imperious and vain, it is on his own too obsequiousness he ought to lay the blame. Oh, why will men endeavour to persuade us we are goddesses, only to create themselves the pains of convincing us afterwards that we are but mortals! [1:75-76]

Power, which to all appearances belongs to the woman during courtship, is shown by the reversals of marriage to have lain all the while with the husband, whose manipulative use of language made it appear otherwise. The role of goddess, as Haywood sees all too plainly, exists solely for deception; it functions as a mere stratagem of male representation.

In fact, so unilaterally is male rhetoric invested with power in Haywood's novel that even when Jenny confronts Jemmy with proof of his intended infidelity (a love note he has written to Lady Hardy but misdirected to her), the author permits her heroine only the mild stipulation that "when we marry you will either have no amours, or be more cautious in concealing them;—and in return, I promise never to examine into your conduct" (3:58). Haywood, as she is careful to point out, does not idealize her hero; hence, her exposé of contemporary manners implies that Jemmy's concupiscence is natural, that even the best of men may be unfaithful. To phrase it differently, one might note that while in some respects courtship—and the ideal of moral constancy that Edmund Leites outlines—comes into its own in Haywood's divided plot structure, it is also true that the novelist, having not yet taken full measure of the new domestic territory that legitimizes her voice, has her heroine speak somewhat tentatively what will later be voiced with more authority.

In keeping with her sometimes grim pragmatism, Eliza Haywood's constant concern is to disabuse her readers, particularly her female ones, of their romantic notions about marriage. Women, the author seems to suggest, should approach marriage with as much cautious circumspection as Lady Speck, who shudders a little at venturing a second time because of "the remembrance of some disagreeable passages in her former marriage" (3:264). Such a scene as Lady Speck's hesitation before marrying Mr. Lovegrove both raises seriously the threat of a mismatch and advances the possibility of a new ideal for domesticity. The author's urgent message here as elsewhere in the novel is that in far too many cases, *love* turns out to be mere courtship rhetoric. Yet even while she reveals that love is a currency debased by glib practicers against women, Eliza Haywood is insisting that *true love* is an indispensable prerequisite for happy marriage.

In a very practical manner, Eliza Haywood's late novels conveyed the adjustments required in social dynamics if women were to express themselves as affective individuals. Parental authority and social custom alike threatened to unravel all the progress made toward the ideal future of domestic love.

THREE

Mary Collyer

GENRE EXPERIMENT

ALL THAT is known about Mary Mitchell Collyer is that she married Joseph Collyer, a compiler and translator, and had one child; beyond this, her personal life is a blank, unrelieved by contemporary diarists or reviewers. Yet she is important to a discussion of the courtship novel not only because her works raise intriguing possibilities of mutual influence when aligned with Samuel Richardson's novels, but also because her sole novel, *Felicia to Charlotte* (1744, 1749) is in its own right one of the better minor novels of the eighteenth century.[1]

While there is no biographical evidence that Mary Collyer ever met Samuel Richardson, nor that he was acquainted with any of her anonymous publications, it seems probable that it was her translation of Marivaux that provided the idea for *Pamela*. Traditionally scholars have looked to *Vie de Marianne* (1731-42) as Richardson's model, but in the original, Marivaux breaks off before completion, leaving the heroine ruined and deserted by Valville. To trace Marivaux's novel as a direct inspiration for *Pamela*, then, one must imagine Richardson experiencing it with revisionist insight, transforming the self-consciously alluring Marianne into a virtuous maidservant who is no less an object of pursuit, though an unwilling one. This argument can begin from John Lockman's more or less faithful translation, which Richardson could have read while employed by Charles Davis, the publisher who issued it in installments from 1736 to 1740. But Richardson may also have read Mary Collyer's *The Virtuous Orphan*, which, according to Ronald Paulson's editorial notes, dates not from 1743, as has been believed, but from 1735.[2] The earlier year is significant, reversing the usual assumption that Collyer was influenced by Richardson.

Very possibly it was the substantial liberties Collyer took with the text that made her Marivaux translation a favorite English version into the 1780s. Addressing women readers in her preface, Collyer hoped that her "English dress" would make *The Virtuous Orphan* more palatable to them. Collyer actually translated only about a third of the original text and appended to Marivaux's story a conclusion in which a repentant Valville legitimizes Marianne by marrying her. Most significantly, Collyer added sensibility to Marivaux's text; the novel's tender scenes, its sentimentalized and recuperated Marianne elevated by marriage after a series of persecutions by her upper-class lover, substantially anticipate Richardson's practice in *Pamela*.

When the first volume of Collyer's sole novel was published anonymously in 1744, her husband's name appeared in the credits—"printed for J. Payne and J. Collyer, London, 1744." There were few contemporary notices. But when a second volume appeared in 1749, the *Monthly Review* (January 1750) reviewed it positively: "The first volume of these letters was published about four years ago, and met with so favourable a reception from the public, as not only to occasion a new edition in a short time, but to encourage the ingenious author to publish a second volume; which, in our opinion, is not inferior to the first."[3] The only evidence that Richardson may have been aware of the novel is the fact that among its admirers were "a select group of bluestockings, including Mary Wortley Montagu and Richardson's friends Miss Catherine Talbot and Miss Elizabeth Carter."[4] But when one considers that the first volume of Collyer's novel *Felicia to Charlotte* was published four years after the initial *Pamela*, four years before *Clarissa*, it appears quite likely that Richardson and Collyer were mutually influential.

Felicia to Charlotte opens as so many later feminized novels (including Richardson's *Sir Charles Grandison*) were to do, with a "remove"—with the heroine's first substantial journey from home. Quitting fashionable London to visit her aunt, Felicia promises faithful correspondence with her friend Charlotte: "I intend to discover all the secret folds of my heart, and to unbosom myself to you without the least reserve."[5] Felicia has scarcely arrived in the country when she overhears a young man's voice and discovers Lucius delivering an enthusiastic reverie in the middle of a wood. From this point, her letters to Charlotte record contending allegiances—her love for Lucius, worthy though poor son of a profligate father—and for her own father, who will not (she assumes) approve the unequal marriage. Meanwhile, an aging "prude" who also loves Lucius sends Felicia's father an anonymous letter alleging that his daughter is ruined. The charge is disproved, but the tensions persist between father and daughter until Charlotte provides Felicia's letters, evidence of her friend's unvarying filial duty. The first volume ends with Felicia and Lucius planning to marry, their union finally blessed by her father.

What resources did Collyer draw from Richardson, and which might he have found in her novel? Like Pamela, Felicia is heroine of an epistolary story, a one-sided correspondence. Much as Pamela's letters to her parents record for Mr. B.'s later reading and reformation her unfailingly correct attitude toward his attempted seduction, so Felicia's letters record her virtue, to be appreciated later by her father and aunt. Like Pamela (and Richardson's subsequent heroines), Felicia—coextensive with her own text—self-reflexively experiences its reading. When Charlotte sends the letters proving Felicia's innocence, Felicia follows her father and aunt into a closet, where she describes them, "both seated with their backs towards me, with the escrutore, before which they were sitting, cover'd with papers. The good lady was listening to my father, who continued reading with a low voice, while she look'd over him; but I had not stood a minute in this situation, when turning their heads so that I discovered half their faces, on which were imprinted some lively traces of satisfaction, they gave each other a glance, my father crying out at the same time, in a transport, O the dear girl!" (1:279).

When she makes a noise at the door, Felicia receives the ironic rebuke, "We were reading your soul, it was talking to us; and here you, like a little impertinent, must come and interrupt the entertainment you yourself were giving us" (1:279). At this complaint, Felicia supplements their text with the letters Charlotte sent to her, thereby completing an epistolary story of which we have only half. It seems likely that Collyer remembered Pamela's writings being prized from her a few at a time until the desirous Mr. B. had read the whole. Subsequently, Richardson was to find use for similar bracketing strategies, stories within stories, in *Clarissa* and *Sir Charles Grandison*.

Aware, no doubt, of the awkwardness charged to Pamela of living pen in hand, Collyer has Felicia comment self-consciously on her own habit of writing down even trivial matters. And, perhaps originating the device Richardson uses frequently in *Grandison*, Collyer avoids the implausibility of Felicia's recalling lengthy discussions by having the speakers act as their own scribes, recording their ideas in writing (Lucius, for example, obliges Felicia by writing down his speech on benevolence). Further, to a remarkable extent, one finds in this first English novel based on female epistolary friendship the relationships and themes later played out in the more sophisticated exchanges of Richardson's Clarissa and Anna Howe, Harriet Byron, and Charlotte Grandison.

Unlike Haywood's novels, Collyer's *Felicia to Charlotte* is not subdivided into male and female plots, and, perhaps for this reason, her gender politics seem less simplistic than Haywood's. To some degree the new vogue for sensibility and the feminist issue of affective individualism are overlaid by a pastoral ethic that works to their apparent advantage. Opposed to the pastoral setting Felicia visits, the spheres of city and court, which she has left behind, are characterized by their vicious stratagems, their artificial and emotionally bankrupt language. Felicia discovers that in moving from city to country she has arrived at a place where ideal domesticity, natural benevolence, and integrity of language and feeling—something like the Puritan ideal of moral constancy—if not guaranteed, are at least possible.[6]

Initially, accustomed to artificial town language, Felicia is impressed by Lucius's fluency, but when he falls in love the obverse is true. Then, she values his lack of rhetorical sophistication as a sign of his sincerity: "the person who a minute before entertained us with such elegance of thought and expression, instantly become speechless. . . . His eyes which had a remarkable languor, and a pleasing softness, were still fixed upon me; but I no sooner met his glances, than with a disordered look he cast them to the floor" (1:20). In effect, the scene may be read as a primer instructing young women how to recognize and value verbal sincerity. Thus, Collyer appropriates for feminist purposes the contemporary thread of sensibility that she had first employed in *The Virtuous Orphan*.

In a later analysis, Felicia enlarges on her appreciation of Lucius's sincerity by parodying the artificial strains she would have expected of a city suitor:

You are now ready to imagine that I shall describe him throwing himself at my feet, while with a flow of rapture, he admires my superlative goodness, blending his praises with two or three hundred adorables, transcendent excellencies, infinite perfections, incomparable creatures, and abundance of other fine things of the same strain; and that to conclude his panegyric, he tells me how astonished he is, that a goddess so heavenly fair, can have the condescention to cast the lustre of her brilliant eyes, and raise to life a wretch so contemptible, so absolutely beneath her least regard. [1:69]

The corrective Felicia supplies for her friend Charlotte is also, one may suppose, intended by Collyer for her readers: extravagant male rhetoric—deification and panegyric—is not to be trusted. Lucius's occasional difficulty in speaking, his simple style register his true esteem: "In short, in spight of his humility his love was incapable of blinding him so far as to make him forget that I was a very woman still, a being of the same species with himself, and therefore he neither debased himself, nor attempted to please me with flattering praises" (1:69-70).

As Lucius himself explains, the male practicer of artificial rhetoric enjoys an unfair advantage: "We ought not to wonder if an artful villain can sometimes triumph over a mind, who knowing itself incapable of deceit, can hardly be brought to suspect another, especially the man she loves, of a guilt the most black and shocking to nature" (1:112). The hyperbole is underscored by an interpolated story in which the minor character Lucy grants the "last favor" only to have her well-intentioned fiancé die and leave her to bear their illegitimate child. Thus, Collyer's caution extends even to sincere male rhetoric as having unfortunate consequences for the woman who steps beyond social bounds of female decorum.

This is not the only occasion when Collyer exposes male rhetoric as running counter to woman's best interest. In one of the novel's wittiest scenes, Felicia meets Mellisont, a minor character whose verbal extravagance affords a strong contrast with Lucius's sincerity. Following her from the stream where she has been weaving garlands, the quixotic young man immediately rattles off a catalogue of praise: "Thus he run on for a quarter of an hour together, without giving either my aunt or me an opportunity of speaking a single syllable; he was all life and gaiety, and attempted to divert me at the same time that he strove to find a way to my heart. He thought it possible that I should be insensible to the force of flattery, and therefore attack'd my vanity with incessant praises" (1:128-29). When Felicia challenges this fanciful suitor for being an "unworthy knight," he dresses himself accordingly—pleased, in helmet and pike, to extend his game on a sartorial level. His disguise admits visually what Felicia has understood all along, that his language misrepresents and trivializes what should only be spoken from the heart.

In another scene near the beginning of her second volume, Collyer raises for critique a different form of male rhetoric, the misogynist language and attitude of men who are witty at the expense of new brides: "Horses were the subject we found them upon, when we enter'd the room. . . . so strictly did they adhere to it, that their very jests had a smack of the groom, mingled with an indecency the most shocking and distasteful, and too coarse and indelicate, even to deserve the name of a double entendre" (2:31). Felicia and Charlotte suffer this treatment only until Lucius, once more demonstrating his sensibility, decides to decline future wedding visits rather than subject his wife to the customary risqué jests.

In either case, whether it under- or overvalues, the implicit agenda of masculinist language is power over women. On the one hand there is Mellisont's fetishistically appropriative language; for his own pleasure, he would fix Felicia as he first saw her: "He even offered to go himself and fetch the flowry wreath that so much became me . . . and asserted that if I would consent to be his, he should ever after our marriage, oblige me to perpetuate the remembrance of that happy day, by wearing upon it a like blooming crown" (1:128). On the other, the "rabble of baronets and squires" who visit presume upon the power of their "considerable estates" when they insult a new bride. Lucius specifies the power inequity behind the situation: "Is there any merit in putting a lady to the blush?—It is cowardly, mean, and scandalous; below the dignity of a gentleman" (2:33). The corrective implied for Collyer's readers is obvious: they must resist, must not allow themselves to be falsely delimited, by male language.

Beyond these analyses of the language that undergirds sexual politics, the novel is precocious for its metatextual commentary and its appeal to women readers. When Collyer resumed her story after a five-year hiatus, she included what amounts to a metatextual commentary on the form she had chosen. Acknowledging at the beginning of the second volume that the true story that she has been recording occasionally approaches romance, Felicia admits that in telling it she has made herself a heroine and Lucius a hero. Yet she has restricted herself to truth and nature, and her hero's obstacles are not the fiery dragons and enchanted castles one expects in romance: "And indeed whatever name is given to my story, whether of rural adventures, novel, or romance, I should be very well satisfied, though all the world thought it fictitious, might I at last . . . have it concluded, like the most celebrated pieces of imaginary scenes of love and gallantry, in a happy catastrophe" (1:123). Read as generic commentary, this passage confirms Mary Collyer's self-conscious adherence to a new form that invites the female reader's identification with a heroine whose story ends in an ideal marriage. But while the author has Felicia anticipate such a "happy catastrophe," one reads in the apology for an ending "all the world" may think "fictitious" Collyer's reluctance to imply that companionate marriage is a normative or inevitable part of female experience.

But this is not the only means Collyer takes to orient her story toward a female audience; she foregrounds a complex of issues related to women's changing social roles: arranged versus companionate marriage, equal versus love matches, and old female decorums versus new. On these issues the lines of debate are already drawn between the voices of authority and those of an emergent feminism. Thus, for example, from the beginning of her relationship with Lucius, Felicia anticipates her father's objections to him. Indeed, when her aunt describes the young man in affective language, Felicia's father responds in authoritarian terms, regretting Lucius's virtue because "it will be so much the harder for my daughter to comply with what I have to propose to her. I have engaged my word to sollicit her consent to marry the son of one of my most intimate friends; and have assured him, that she pays so strict an obedience to my will, that he need not doubt of my success" (1:250-51). More than paternal authority, the difficulty is conventional, societally enjoined wisdom against unequal matches. (In this case, the inequality is entirely financial.) A young woman's friends, Felicia explains, are "almost always blind to merit when unattended with riches: for as they sincerely wish us every blessing, they cannot bear to think of our wanting so essential a one" (1:49).

Yet against that authoritative word, Felicia takes a fairly radical stand, reassuring Lucius's sister that his addresses are not misplaced: "Why not? . . . it would be a great misfortune, if we were never to be honoured with any company but such as were upon a level with us, with respect to fortune. . . . The charms of a virtuous and upright mind are internal; they constitute a real merit, and reflect a glory upon the possessor. A glory in comparison of which all other advantages are superficial and trifling" (1:61). The newer, affective ethic that Felicia adopts privileges not only the individual woman's prerogative of choice over her family's right of determination but also the merits of a "virtuous and upright mind" over the more tangible advantages of fortune. Sensibility has become the standard by which marriages are made.

In a similar vein, as she falls in love with Lucius, Felicia complains about old-fashioned proscriptions against women expressing their affection: "Why should we disguise our hearts, and teach our looks a reserve that we are far from feeling? These little arts should never be used to a man of sense, and merit; as for the rest, we ought to have no care about them. Nor indeed need I blush to own that this silent intercourse of souls gave me more pleasure than I ever received from any of my conquests" (1:48). The expression of sentiment is legitimized by the ethical code of sensibility, which links feeling with virtue, overturning older feminine decorums. In comparable language, Richardson's Harriet Byron admits her feelings for Sir Charles Grandison long before he makes a declaration of his own.

As Mary Collyer was writing her second volume, perhaps about the same time she was expecting her first child, she must have recalled the original and sequel volumes of *Pamela*, a novel Richardson "concluded" with his heroine's marriage and then took up again. It is no doubt with intentional irony that Collyer has Felicia write to Charlotte in the first pages of the new volume, "My story, Madam, is now finish'd; I have been married these three weeks; and, from the serene tranquil state, I am in at present, you have no reason to expect any more romantic adventures" (2:4). Indeed, for most writers in this period, marriage was the preferred conclusion to a heroine's adventures, and Collyer's second, thinner volume was one of the few period novels that took its heroine into married life.

When the novel does conclude, it is with the birth of Felicia's child—an opportunity for once more aligning sensibility with the feminist cause. The child in her lap, Felicia writes movingly in the last pages: "May these lips, that now draw thy sustenance from me, be ever the fountains of truths ever pure in their expressions, and strangers to the wanton's kiss: may the joys of innocence, and as much peace as mortals can know, always dwell within this little heart: and when this heart shall melt with softness for some lovely maid, may she return, with purity, thy flame, and render all thy happiness compleat!" (2:276). Felicia's wish for her son is that he, like his father, may avoid the corruption of male rhetoric. The utopian vision Felicia offers originates in the somatic relationship between mother and child; she hopes that her son's future relationships with women will be as orally innocent. Significantly, the blessing incorporates all the elements of sensibility—body, mind, and spirit, and looks forward to another domestic relationship characterized by moral constancy.

We fail to appreciate the full scope of Mary Collyer's originality if we do not remember that in the years 1744 to 1749, the individual woman's affective entitlement to companionate marriage had not yet been widely adopted as a literary *topos*. The developing issues of affective individualism had appeared in the *Spectator* and were being handled contemporaneously in such periodicals as the *Ladies Magazine* and Eliza Haywood's *Female Spectator*. And, among novelists, Eliza Haywood and Samuel Richardson had made a beginning. But, against the context of contemporary fiction, *Felicia to Charlotte* reads like a radical innovation: in effect, Mary Collyer's story is an experimental foray into a new genre—the courtship novel.

PART II

Feminist Reception Theory

FOUR

Early Feminist Reception Theory

CLARISSA AND
THE FEMALE QUIXOTE

INSOFAR AS WE are accustomed to gauging Daniel Defoe's feminism by the attention he devotes to those ample heroines Moll Flanders and Roxana, we may miss the fact that, beyond supposing his readers to be "virtuous" or "honest," he does not particularize his audience. Against this context, the detail that his contemporaries Jane Barker, Penelope Aubin, and Mary Davys addressed their female rogue fiction specifically to women makes theirs an innovation worthy of consideration. Jane Barker, for instance, selectively addressed herself to "the only Part of Mankind that must act a Scene on this World's Theatre, without being permitted to con their Part beforehand."[1] By appealing categorically to "proper" women readers—an audience that by association legitimized the authors' textual exposure—these writers effectually made the body/text association work to their own advantage instead of against them.[2] Thus, long before Mary Collyer, Eliza Haywood, Samuel Richardson, and Charlotte Lennox began writing feminocentric courtship novels, the initial move had been taken toward a new dynamic of feminist reception. The basic assumption for Barker, Aubin, and Davys, and perhaps for their female readers as well, was that they operated within a closed system shaped by their commonalities: their sex, their concern for propriety, and their new empowerment over issues relating to love and marriage.

Recognizing the lack of literary role models for women, Jane Barker recommends *Exilius* (1715) as a "pleasant Story" that might interest the reader "who flies a serious Lecture." Aside from lessons about love, her audience could "reap many Handfulls of good Morality, and likewise gather some Gleanings of History, and Acquaintance with the Ancient Poets" (Preface). Seven years later, in *A Patch-Work Screen for the Ladies* (1723), Barker claims "Patch-Work" as a suitable pattern "for Discourse and for 'Needle-Work,' " especially as the "Uncommonness of any Fashion, renders it acceptable to the Ladies."[3] Comparable gender-specific overtures punctuate Penelope Aubin's *The Life and Adventures of the Lady Lucy* (1726) and Mary Davys's *The Reform'd Coquet* (1724). Aubin is apologetic about the "one ill Woman" she includes in her novel, expressing the partisan hope "that my own Nation, can furnish a great many Women of all degrees, whose Characters and Virtues are unquestionable."[4] In a similarly feminist and nationalistic tone, Mary Davys dedicates her novel to "The Ladies of Great Britain," challenging everyone to "join with my Opinion, that the *English* Ladies are the most accomplish'd Women in the World."[5] Among these early writers of women's fiction, Davys's desire—to "make some impression upon the young unthinking Minds of some of my own Sex" (ix-x)—was a common motive. The fact that each of them consistently appealed to "proper" female readers in their prefaces, and that they published successfully (Barker producing four novels, Aubin six, and Davys three) suggests that they succeeded in part because of their authorial marketing strategies.

Some twenty years later, addressing his intended audience in *Clarissa* (1749), Samuel Richardson made similar overtures to a female audience: "What will be found to be more particularly aimed at in the following work is—to warn the inconsiderate and thoughtless of one sex against the base arts and designs of specious contrivers of the other . . . to warn children against preferring a man of pleasure to a man of probity, upon that dangerous but too commonly received notion that a reformed rake makes the best husband."[6] Here Richardson underlines what is often diplomatically obscured in texts written by women writers for women readers—that one of their major concerns is to forewarn women against various forms of male persuasion that threaten their physical and moral integrity. Curiously, it is precisely this dynamic of early feminist reception theory that modern critics have so often ignored or oversimplified.

For the Marxist critic, especially, the heroine-centered plot of the courtship story seems bound inextricably to interests at once bourgeois and male, and for this reason its feminist dimensions go largely unremarked. Thus, Terry Eagleton's *The Rape of Clarissa* finds a perspective for one of the most provocative readings of Richardson in the material, socioeconomic facts determining the novelist's production of *Clarissa*, his representation of the heroine, and her reception by the English public. Eagleton sees all of Richardson's novels, *Clarissa* included, as agents rather than mere accounts "of the English bourgeoisie's attempt to wrest a degree of ideological hegemony from the aristocracy in the decades which follow the political settlement of

1688." Viewed in this light, fiction becomes one means of artificially constructing "a powerless, ghettoized 'feminine' culture" and making ideological advances against the aristocracy in the name of benevolence and humanitarianism. Inevitably, in Eagleton's schema, eighteenth-century feminism becomes a byblow of the more powerful ideological movement: "the 'exaltation' of women, while undoubtedly a partial advance in itself, also serves to shore up the very system which oppresses them." Eagleton offers Richardson's relationship with members of his coterie as collateral evidence for the novelist's participation in English class struggle. He suggests that for the rising bourgeoisie, professing humanitarianism was a way to insure women's acquiescence, even as for Richardson, exercising the bourgeois values of humanitarianism and benevolence was a way to promote his solidarity with a family of readers in which he preserved a patriarchal role.[7]

To be sure, Richardson's novel is something of a special case. While *Clarissa* bears an ideological affinity with the feminocentric stories with which I am concerned, the rape effectually displaces Clarissa from the middle-class respectability required of courtship heroines. Yet there is enough similarity between Richardson's fiction and novels by such writers as Charlotte Lennox, Fanny Burney, Maria Edgeworth, and Jane Austen, to prompt the question whether, given the considerations Eagleton raises, courtship novels could be written to forward feminist ends. No doubt Richardson's novels did serve middle-class purposes, but Eagleton's overarching theory, by subsuming all ideology under the label "bourgeoisie," neglects even to acknowledge adequately whatever is not capitalist, masculine, and dominant. To phrase this objection another way, do we not lose by failing to acknowledge ideologic diversity, intertextuality, and dialogism? Or, as Barbara Johnson poses the question, can literature "somehow escape or transform power structures by simultaneously espousing and subverting them?"[8] Clearly, given woman's problematic position in a class system defined by male labor, to focus solely on ideologic hegemony as Eagleton does is to oversimplify. It is to lose sight of changes in the material conditions of life for the minority, and to lose sight of counterideologies of the oppressed, among whom a great number will be women, regardless of class. Finally, it is to lose sight of the audience to whom Richardson avowedly addresses his story.

While Eagleton probes for sources of power, carefully profiling some of the social factors that come together in the Clarissa-Lovelace correspondence, he consistently neglects gender for class, though to do so undervalues Clarissa's role as the heroine. He observes, for instance, that it is Clarissa's narcissism (her writing and reading of

self) that permits her to escape various forms of circumscription that
patriarchal and class society have prepared for her—an arranged marriage, the reductive labels of her family and of Lovelace: "By virtue
of her profound narcissism, not by dint of being fetishized to the
phallus . . . Clarissa is finally able to slip through the net of male
desire and leave the hands of Lovelace and her family empty. Her
elaborate dying is a ritual of deliberate disengagement from patriarchal
and class society, a calculated 'decathecting' of that world whereby
libidinal energy is gradually withdrawn from its fruitless social in-
vestments into her own self."[9] Typically, Eagleton's physical metaphor
for Clarissa's separation does not register the complexity of her situation. In the first place, if it is by narcissism, by redoubling her subject
position as woman (through writing and reading her own story) that
Clarissa escapes the social forms of bourgeois society, does she not
invite identification and/or imitation by female readers? Eagleton
slights the compelling invitation that Clarissa, heroine and novel, issues: the invitation to read as a woman. Clarissa's sex, after all, is a
material fact that at once conditions her own role and choices and the
readers' reception of the novel.

No less important is a fact that Eagleton records but, in his choice
of the neo-Freudian term *decathecting*, loses sight of—Clarissa's individuation, her separation from or resistance to ideologic systems
that threaten to overwhelm her as sign. As a model of greater complexity, Paul Smith's explanation of resistance comes closer to describing the psychological separation Clarissa experiences. Resistance,
according to Smith, is a dialectic process that results from conflicting
subject positions.[10] In Clarissa's case, this means resistance to the
hegemonic symbolic order, both of Lovelace's rakish encomiums and
of her family's monitory patriarchalism. Her only means of escape,
both from Lovelace's assertion of proprietorship over the body he has
used and from her family's attempts to recoup their power of exchange
over her, is death. In death, Clarissa writes herself as sign, as individuated woman, against phallocentric persuasion, against patriarchal
law. In death, Clarissa bespeaks a feminist subject position against
the objectifications of male desire and patriarchal exchange.

As Nancy Miller has reminded us, the experience of reading
changes substantially when we "imagine while reading the place of
a woman's body."[11] Precisely to the extent that it neglects to do so,
Eagleton's otherwise astute reading fails to do justice to Richardson's
novel. A gender-conscious reading of *Clarissa* and other period heroine-centered fiction entails recognizing certain constant assumptions
of early feminist reception theory. Women were generally presumed
to be naive, identificatory readers requiring instruction in their re-

ception both of actual male rhetoric and of fictional texts. Because their respectability proscribed the ritual experiences afforded by the Continental tour, women sought vicarious experience—coaching in discriminating or resisting reading of the world, of people, and of texts—as an essential step toward maturity or individuation. In a very real sense, then, if a woman wished to avoid conscription into the texts of male desire or marriage for convenience, she had to script her own story.[12] Especially interesting from this perspective is *The Female Quixote* (1752), a novel by one of Richardson's contemporaries, Charlotte Lennox.

On several accounts, Charlotte Lennox's feminization of the quixote myth occupies a signal intersection between gender and genre, one crucial for the modern reader's understanding of eighteenth-century fiction. First, as an antiromance published within the same decade as Samuel Richardson's *Pamela* and *Clarissa* and Henry Fielding's *Tom Jones*, *The Female Quixote* implicitly reinforces the new paradigm for fiction. Here one can argue Lennox's discipleship, her intimate participation as a protégée of Samuel Richardson and Samuel Johnson (she consulted both while writing the book) in the politics of the paradigm shift from romance to novel.[13] Second, Lennox's novel inspired analogous female quixotes or pedants in novels written over the next several decades (in Fanny Burney's *Camilla*, Mary Wollstonecraft's *Mary*, Maria Edgeworth's *Belinda*, Eaton Stannard Barrett's *The Heroine*, and Jane Austen's *Northanger Abbey*, to mention only a few). Finally—and this transecting line of argument will be the focus here—the metatextual strategies of the novel and the reduplicative transactions of its author and heroine reflect a significant development in the relationship between gender and genre for eighteenth-century readers and writers.

From the purview of reader-response theory, what is quixotism but an identificatory model taken too far? In the case of Lennox's heroine, Arabella, identificatory reading in bad translations of Scudéry and Calprenède enrolls her under the masculinist illogic of romance: "Supposing Romances were real Pictures of Life, from them she drew all her Notions and Expectations. By them she was taught to believe that Love was the ruling Principle of the World . . . she was alarmed by every trifling Incident, and kept in a continual Anxiety by a Vicissitude of Hopes, Fears, Wishes, and Disappointments."[14] As the author's title implies, the radical nature of her quixote is her gender. The female quixote's perception of herself through the distorted mirror image of romance entangles her in an ominously fragile imaginary construct, for to be heroinized in romantic ideology is to value oneself only as reflected by the male gaze, as an object of pursuit.[15]

The situation for Arabella (and by extension for Lennox's readers) is that by choosing to identify with romantic heroines, she voluntarily gives herself over to a system of objectification. Moreover, the female quixote colludes in her own immasculation (Fetterley's term for reading as a male): "Her Glass, which she often consulted, always shewed her a Form so extremely lovely, that, not finding herself engaged in such Adventures as were common to the Heroines in the Romances she read, she often complained of the Insensibility of Mankind, upon whom her Charms seemed to have so little Influence."[16] Arabella's narcissism is not, as Eagleton suggests for Clarissa, a complete separation from the male hegemony, but simultaneously yet paradoxically an identification with it and a self-objectification. She is both objectifier and object, reader and text.

Naturally, in the romance plot she scripts for herself, Arabella's agency is circumscribed—a romance heroine is one to whom things *happen*—so that her evasions of male desire (real or imagined) define a hunter-prey relationship with the men who pursue her. Misprising the real world according to her identificatory romantic reading, the female quixote expects that every eligible man will declare himself her lover, that every letter she receives must be a *billet doux*, and that frequent plots will be laid for her abduction. In response to her neighbor's bold stare in church, for instance, she takes refuge behind her veil, as ineffectual and unstylish a visor as Don Quixote's pasteboard one. A fish-poaching gardener is presumed to be a disguised nobleman whose despairing love brings him to river's edge, and approaching horsemen are taken for abductors who can only be escaped by plunging, like the "renowned Clelia," into the Thames. The imaginary plot of male desire prompts Arabella's false accusation of her neighbor as "an impious Ravisher, who, contrary to all Laws both human and divine, endeavour to possess yourself by Force of a Person whom you are not worthy to serve" (20). This kind of heroinization, as Rachel Brownstein, Sandra Gilbert and Susan Gubar, and Mary Poovey have maintained, reinscribes woman in the repressive system she tries to escape.[17]

The identificatory model is not only a theory of reception but, at least implicitly, one of production as well; if to read a heroine is to become one, then it follows that becoming a heroine is much like writing one. When, in the best romance tradition, Arabella confides all her secrets to her maid, she, like Clarissa before her, anticipates her own history as construct. Furthermore, she discloses the untenable relationship between the lived life and the romance as genre:

You ask me to tell you what you must say; as if it was not necessary you should know as well as myself, and be able, not only to recount all my Words and Actions, even the smallest and most inconsiderable, but also all my Thoughts, however instantaneous; relate exactly every Change of my Countenance; number all my Smiles, Half-smiles, Blushes, Turnings pale, Glances, Pauses, Full-stops, Interruptions; the Rise and Falling of my Voice; every Motion of my Eyes; and every Gesture which I have used for these Ten Years past; nor omit the smallest Circumstance that relates to me. [121-22]

The fetishistic proliferation of detail in Arabella's projected "history" makes ironic, or, in Margaret Homans's terms, "literalizes," the romance heroine's role.[18] It emphasizes the paralysis and emotional dependence of the woman who waits for adventures to happen to her. When Arabella describes the truly heroic life she imagines for Miss Glanville (her suitor's sister), her language similarly punctures the notion of a romance heroine's activity: "You have questionless . . . gained many Victories over Hearts; have occasioned many Quarrels between your Servants, by favouring some one, more than the others: Probably, you have caused some Bloodshed; and have not escaped being carried away once or twice: You have also, I suppose, undergone some Persecution, from those who have the Disposal of you, in Favour of a Lover whom you have an Aversion to; and lastly, there is haply some one among your admirers, who is happy enough not to be hated by you" (110-11). Because the ideology of romance is demonstrably at odds with proper female subjecthood, the young woman is understandably affronted by the history attributed to her. As Arabella's description implies, the heroine of romance is more object of exchange, to be quarreled over or stolen, than an autonomous, self-constructing subject.

Standing in the wings during the lengthy period of Arabella's quixotism is a perfectly ordinary suitor whose arms she loads with romances and whom she tries unsuccessfully to convert to heroic language and plot. It is this commonplace suitor and the conventional courtship plot he implies that eventually reclaim Arabella from the romantic imaginary by which she is enthralled. In this way, the courtship plot becomes counterideology. Significantly, this emergent feminism achieves its fullest expression through a socially responsible countess who undertakes Arabella's cure by questioning her fascination with "adventure":

Pardon me, Madam, reply'd the Countess, recovering herself, if the uncommonness of your Request made a Moment's reflection necessary to convince me that a young Lady of your Sense and Delicacy could mean no Offence to

Decorum by making it. The Word Adventures carries in it so free and licentious a Sound in the Apprehensions of People at this Period of Time, that it can hardly with Propriety be apply'd to those few and natural Incidents which compose the History of a Woman of Honour. And when I tell you . . . that I was born and christen'd, had a useful and proper Education, receiv'd the Addresses of my Lord ———— through the Recommendation of my Parents, and marry'd him with their Consents and my own Inclination, and that since we have liv'd in great Harmony together, I have told you all the material Passages of my Life, which upon Enquiry you will find differ very little from those of other Women of the same Rank, who have a moderate Share of Sense, Prudence and Virtue. [327]

Thus, the countess opposes to Arabella's still determined identification with the masculinist romance plot a definition of the "history of a woman of honour," a story of feminine resonance that combines the desirable qualities of sense, prudence, and virtue. From this point in the novel, Arabella's self-heroinization oscillates toward a climax in which, following a lengthy illness, she converts (via a talking cure) with the cautious assistance of the local minister.

In one sense, the countess speaks not merely for the heroine but for the reader and the author as well; that is, the passage may be read as Charlotte Lennox's own response, as writer and reader, to the course of Enlightenment fiction. For the eighteenth-century British reader, and particularly if that reader was female, romances were dangerously removed from the code of respectability. And it was also true of an authorial "woman of honor" that she would do well to avoid "adventurous" literature. The countess's definition of a woman's history may be read not only as initiating Arabella's readerly and self-scripting reclamation but also as expressing Charlotte Lennox's metatextual disavowal of masculinist plot, her avoidance of the text/body association that rendered stories of "adventure" dangerous for modest women. Arabella's cure legitimizes Lennox's abandonment of episodic romance for the comforts of a courtship plot and a concluding marriage. Interestingly, this programmatic change was borne out subsequently in Lennox's career, for her later courtship novels are barely levened with romance.

I am not suggesting that within Lennox's *Female Quixote*, feminism successfully routs patriarchy or that one should not be suspicious of the class implications of Lennox's having chosen an exemplary countess to enroll her middle-class ingenue in the courtship plot. One could argue, along Eagleton's and Poovey's lines, that codes of respectability being another form of repression, the courtship plot merely reinscribes Arabella in a system that preempts any real subjecthood for her—in the process joining relatives' estates and serving rising middle-class interests. Yet this is to give a totalizing view, to conceive of the male hegemony or what has been termed "patriarchy" as effectually occluding or superseding all divergent ideological expression.

Moreover, in examining the feminist issues that inform the novel, it is important to notice that in the conclusion Lennox herself distinguishes between two types of marriages that are celebrated:. "We chuse, Reader, to express this Circumstance, though the same, in different Words, as well to avoid Repetition, as to intimate that the first mentioned Pair [Miss Glanville and Sir George] were indeed only married in the common Acceptation of the Word: that is, they were privileged to join Fortunes, Equipages, Titles, and Expence; while Mr. *Glanville* and *Arabella* were united, as well in these, as in every Virtue and laudable Affection of the Mind" (383). The author's frame-breaking reference to her readers explains the difference between the common "marriage," which joins goods and titles, and the uncommon "union" of virtue and affection. Thus, even while she is apparently following the prescribed pattern for conclusions, Lennox insists that hers is not a utopian closure masking a material agenda. She seeks rather to demystify marriage, to distinguish between the "common acceptation" of the word and its uncommon or true meaning in reference to the "union" of Mr. Glanville and Arabella.

Nonetheless, one should not, while probing the feminist strategies of Lennox's text, go so far astray as to underestimate the cooptive power of the predominantly male hegemony. Indeed, a detail from one reader's actual reception of the novel illustrates how problematic the intersections of reader/writer, gender/genre could be. If one adopts the perspective of Erasmus Darwin, writing at the turn of the century, some four decades after the novel was originally published, *The Female Quixote* becomes part of the syllabus for a girls' boarding school. In his *Plan for the Conduct of Female Education* (1797), Darwin first divides novels into "the serious, the humorous, and the amorous" and entirely omits the last category. He explains that to such serious novels as *Sandford and Merton, The Children's Friend, Tales of the Castle, Robinson Crusoe*, and *Edward*, "may be added some other modern novels, the productions of ingenious ladies, which are I believe less objectionable than many others; as the Evelina, Cecilia, and Camilla of Miss Burney. The Emmeline and Ethelinda of Charlotte Smith, Inchbald's simple story; Mrs. Brook's Emely Montague; and the female Quixote; all which I have here introduced from the character given to me of them by a very ingenious lady, not having myself read them with sufficient attention."[19]

Darwin's recommendation of these novels prompts several observations. First, we should note that, perhaps because of the residual fear of quixotism, sentimentalism, or worse associated with reading romances, novels rarely found a place in such educational tracts. Second, Darwin recognizes in these books he has not himself read with "sufficient attention" a separate category of novel written by women for women. And third, he expects that the young boarders will be identificatory readers for whom, if "amorous" (male plotted) novels are dangerous, "serious" (female plotted) novels are instructive. A few sentences later he outlines these supposed benefits more specifically, recalling a "lady of fortune" who read them too late:

It is true indeed, that almost all novels, as well as plays, and epic poems, have some exceptional passages to be found in them; which might therefore be expunged, before they are allow'd to be read by young ladies. But are young women therefore to be kept in intire ignorance of mankind, with whom they must shortly associate, and from whom they are frequently to chuse a partner for life? This would be making them the slaves rather than the companions of men, like the Sultanas of a Turkish Seraglio. And how can young women, who are secluded from the other sex from their infancy, form any judgment of men, if they are not to be assisted by such books, as delineate manners?—A lady of fortune, who was persuaded by her guardian to marry a disagreeable and selfish man, speaking to her friend of the ill humour of her husband, lamented, that she had been prohibited from reading novels. "If I had read such books, said she, before I was married, I should have chosen better; I was told, that all men were alike except in respect to fortune." [34]

Serious novels, particularly those written by certain women writers, would be especially helpful to young women who must choose partners for life. In the novels that follow *The Female Quixote*, what I have called the female plot—the courtship story—takes precedence, and the female quixote, when she appears at all, is a minor character. Thus, it is possible to consider the development of the courtship plot and heroine as functioning not only as a literary but also as an affective enfranchisement for women and to read Darwin as a well intentioned if patronizing tract writer for women's education.

It is well to remember, though, that identificatory reading may be coopted all too easily by the male hegemony. As a case in point, one should consider the conditions under which Darwin produced his *Plan*. The book was written to aid the Misses Parker, who were establishing a boarding school in Lichfield. The young women were the physician Darwin's illegitimate daughters, whom to his credit he had openly acknowledged and carefully educated so that they would be able to provide for themselves. When Darwin, a widower, remarried later in life, the daughters of his second marriage were sent to school to the Misses Parker.[20] The ironies compound when one considers that an essential purpose served by the school, one given careful consideration in Darwin's *Plan*, was the preparation of young women for marriage. At this point, the economies of exchange become too complex to pursue further.

But even if we must recognize in this cultural sample I have drawn from Charlotte Lennox and Erasmus Darwin the glutinous texture of male hegemony, of patriarchal exchange, which always rises to the top, there is also suspended in the crucible a stubborn admixture of feminism. Placing Lennox's *Female Quixote* against the cultural context of a change in nuptialization patterns, one may read the novel as an important confluence of gender and genre; its valorization of the courtship plot was an empowering strategy both for the identificatory readers who had new prerogatives of choice in marriage and for the "women of honor" who were to write women's histories in the future.

Indeed, if one is tempted to read courtship novels solely as propaganda that duped women into unwary acceptance of a domestic ideal, one should remember that although these novels generally concluded with the obligatory wedding and a foreshadowing of conjugal bliss, their minor characters alone—women won with promises, ruined, and abandoned, wives turned shrews—would have sufficed as a warning about how uncommon the ideal domestic relationship was in real life. For every love match depicted in novels, periodicals, and conduct books, there were several exposés of failed marriage.[21]

Perhaps the most persuasive evidence against reading courtship novels as works of naive optimism lies in the personal experiences of the writers themselves—experiences that were an integral part of the material conditions within which they produced their novels. Though most of these women preserved their middle-class respectability despite failed marriages, their lives largely corroborated the fictionalized details of marriage à la mode that filled contemporary magazines. A cursory reading of available biographical sketches reveals that about half of the two dozen women courtship novelists who did marry eventually separated from their husbands. Charlotte Ramsay Lennox (1729-1804) married "an indigent and shiftless Scott" when she was nineteen and suffered for forty years before separating from her husband; Charlotte Turner Smith (1749-1806), who married at fifteen to avoid living with her new stepmother, left the father of her twelve children after twenty years; and Sarah Robinson Scott (1723-1795), wiser or braver than her contemporaries, parted from her husband after only one year.[22]

For some, the perils of marriage must have seemed too formidable.

Fanny Burney did not become Madame d'Arblay until the advanced age of forty-one, and Maria Edgeworth and Jane Austen never did marry. It cannot be coincidental that women writing novels of courtship advice—many of whom were reluctant brides or unhappy wives—inventoried women's options from a woman's point of view. Ironically, in a period when ideology far outstripped reality, when the companionate matches poets and novelists endorsed were rare, writing courtship stories was one of the few means a woman had of earning a living and hence of preserving her independence from a less than ideal liaison. For the women who made up a large portion of the novel-reading public, as well as for the women who wrote novels, the progression from girlhood to womanhood was a natural plotline because the courtship situation had autobiographical resonances that were by no means always positive.[23]

FIVE

Charlotte Lennox

HENRIETTA, RUNAWAY INGENUE

IN *Henrietta* (1758), published six years after *The Female Quixote* (1752), Charlotte Lennox once again examined the problems a young woman faced as she came to terms with the world—this time not through the deflation of a romance-reading heroine but through the more realistic disappointments and surprises of an ingenue run away from her guardian. As she had done in the earlier novel, Lennox shaped her heroine's story to convey a broader lesson to women readers by weighing the advantages and disadvantages of social rebellion.

Perhaps because she herself was orphaned just as she entered adult life, one of Lennox's special talents as a novelist was her physical evocation of the subject position of an unchaperoned woman in a man's world. She quickly establishes reader identification with her heroine by describing Henrietta's difficulties as she boards a crowded London stage. While the coachman receives the "slender young body" simply as an additional fare, benevolence motivates one passenger, a grave man who wishes "it possible to make room for the young gentlewoman." Among the women passengers, "making room" has unfortunate class implications, however; protesting herself unaccustomed to riding in common stages, one woman flatly refuses to be crowded until she is shoved, cooperatively forced against a window, by a plump lady and a young woman in riding dress. Meanwhile, motivated by quite different feelings, a young man resigns his seat, "extremely glad he had an opportunity of obliging such a handsome lady. He then jumped out of the coach, and taking the stranger's hand to help her in, stared confidently under her hat, which put her into a little confusion."[1]

Once Henrietta has found a seat, the other passengers continue to focus their attention on her: "A Profound silence now prevailed among the company in the coach; the eyes of all were fastened upon the fair stranger, who appeared wholly insensible of the scrutinizing looks of her fellow-travellers" (1:6). The women passengers, facile readers of the class/status testimony of clothing, are less impressed by Henrietta's person than by "the elegance of her morning-dress" (1:7). The haughty woman takes satisfaction in the idea that "this stranger was probably more unhappy than herself" (1:7), and the lusty matron imagines she has obliged someone of a superior rank. The other young woman passenger, whose vanity is flattered by the "acquisition of so genteel a fellow-traveller" (1:8), addresses "civil speeches" to Henrietta. Through this scene, Lennox both rouses her reader's identification with the heroine and at the same time shapes that reader's opinions through the assessments of others in the coach.

Thus far in the novel, the reader understands that Henrietta is a young attractive woman apparently of superior status to the other passengers, and that her presence in the coach is suspect. As an unchaperoned gentlewoman wearing a morning dress, she raises questions, the most obvious of which involves her physical and social "place"—her body and her role. To whom does she belong? A young gentlewoman who steals herself away as Henrietta does defies the patriarchal system of power and authority; until she is old enough to be considered a spinster, a woman of the middle or upper classes is legitimized by obedience to her parents, to a male family member, or to a designated guardian. Thus, as Henrietta's experience will illustrate, a woman who absconds is liable to be suspected by those who should respect her, affronted by men who misunderstand her character, and befriended by those whom informed prudence would reject.

In effect, *Henrietta* rephrases the story of failed utopia that Lennox had written in *The Female Quixote*: an idealistic young woman rebels against a pragmatic and repressive older generation. Eventually, as in the earlier novel, Lennox's heroine will be reconciled with the ruling social order by a concluding marriage, but it is her earlier resistance that compels reader interest. We empathize with the all too familiar confusion of youthful idealism out on a limb as the coach to London gradually empties: " 'Lord bless me!' said miss Courteney, lifting up her fine eyes swimming in tears, 'What shall I do? what will become of me?' " (1:8). The young woman in riding dress, now the only other passenger in the coach, receives Henrietta's appeal with enthusiasm:

You have obliged me excessively by this unreserved confidence . . . and you shall find me not unworthy of it. From this moment I swear to you an inviolable attachment. . . . I have formed a hundred violent friendships, but one accident or other always dissolved them in a short time. . . . I am charmed, I am ravished with this meeting. Who would have imagined that

by chance, and in a stage coach, I should have found what I have so earnestly
sought for these three months, a person with whom I could contract a violent
friendship, such as minds like our's are only capable of feeling. [1:10-11]

If Lennox thus far has seemed to overemphasize the opposition
between the lone woman and the unpleasant microcosmic society of
the London coach, here she provides a corrective. Miss Woodby's
romantic language parodies youthful idealism. In effect, the ludicrous
pledge of "inviolable attachment" is a conservative nod to strictures
against unchaperoned travel. Henrietta's new acquaintance goes further, proposing that they adopt romantic names to give "a spirit to
the correspondence between such friends as you and I are" (1:11).
The pseudonym Clelia, doubly appropriative, reflects the fact that in
leaving home, Henrietta voluntarily heroinizes herself at the same
time she quite literally forfeits her identity, her real name and her
social role.

Moreover, from Miss Woodby's insistent recurrence to the romantic and from her professed inability to advise the heroine, the
reader can infer the impracticality of a young woman's leaving home:
"Lord! my dear . . . one young creature is not qualified to give another advice upon such occasions" (1:16). Henrietta's misgivings
about being decontextualized, her understanding that she has removed herself from safety to an alienating place of adventure, are
only heightened by Miss Woodby's sympathy: "I Protest . . . your
fears are very natural upon this occasion. I should in your situation
be almost distracted. Even our parents' watchful cares are hardly sufficient to guard us against the attempts of insolent men: how much
more then are those attempts to be dreaded, when we are left de-
fenceless and exposed" (1:14).

While Miss Woodby imagines an ideal relationship between parents and daughter, the more common story in this novel is of unre-
lenting and capricious guardians who not only deny the possibility
of affective individualism to their wards but seek, physically and socially, to repress them. It is significant that Henrietta is not left solely
to her own initiative in deciding to resist her guardians' coercion, for
she has the legitimizing precedent of her parents, who lived poor but
happy rather than relinquish each other. Further, the power of this
precedent is intensified and reinforced by her "scribbling" mother's
written account and by her own unfortunate encounters with her
father's family.

Indeed, the reader learns through the story Henrietta gradually
unfolds for Miss Woodby that she has already borne her share of

oppression. As a young woman of no fortune, she has suffered the insults of dependence on those whose generosity was really self-gratification. One of these false benefactors, Lady Manning (a soap-boiler's daughter), schemed to marry Henrietta to a man whom her family raised from a parish school to become their steward. Conscious of her own place as "an earl's niece" and "Mr. Courteney's daughter," though, Henrietta rejected the proposal. In Lennox's terms the match is objectionable on more than one ground—it would mean a gross inequity in status as well as an alliance without love.

Later, as Lady Manning repeats the story of the match she tried to arrange, another benefactor fortuitously hears it and comes to Henrietta's rescue. But Lady Meadows, the heroine's estranged aunt, turns out to be no less motivated by selfishness, and in her house Henrietta suffers the double oppression of her aunt and a chaplain, both of whom try to convert her so that she may marry a Roman Catholic baronet. As Lady Meadows lays the case before Henrietta, her refusal of the proposed match is directly at odds with her familial position: "What, is it not possible for you to make a good wife to an honest gentleman, without bringing with you all that romantick passion which forces girls to jump out of windows to get to their fellows; and, for the sake of a man who possibly a few weeks before was an absolute stranger to them, break through every tie of natural affection, and to be a wife, be contented to be neither daughter, sister, or niece" (1:145). Henrietta's reply is peremptorily stopped by her aunt's hand on her mouth: "I have hitherto treated you as my own child; if you comply you shall find me a mother, if not I am only your aunt; and you know how some who stand in that degree of relation to you behave" (1:145). Henrietta's choice lies between mute submission to an arranged marriage, which would insure her a familial position (wife, daughter, sister, niece) and her assertion of individual affective rights, which may mean exclusion from familial protection and role definition.

When Henrietta finally meets her uncle, the earl whose title clearly figures in her self-esteem, she finds him no less interested in exchanging her and no more concerned for her feelings than were her other protectors. In fact, when she tries to explain why she left her aunt's house, he signals his unwillingness to listen to anything besides concessions. "I am afraid you are going to say some silly thing or other" (2:143). His sole concern, Henrietta soon realizes, is to exonerate himself from any blame for having neglected her. Later, in relating his version of their meeting, Henrietta's uncle forgets to mention, that he tried to force Henrietta to change her religion or that her reward was to be her aunt's fortune and marriage to an earl's son. The omission of these circumstances "gave such a colour to Henrietta's behaviour, that she was considered by all, who heard her uncle's account of it, as an unhappy young creature, who would ruin herself, and be the blot of a noble family" (2:147).

What her heroine understands and what Lennox is interested in conveying to her female readers is the fact that young women who venture to assert their resistance to the patriarchal order are not likely to receive a fair hearing. When Henrietta thinks of leaving her aunt's house, for instance, she realizes that, partly because of social restrictions on young women, she has no alternative but to hazard taking a room in London: "Mr. Bale, whose protection I might have requested with honour, was not in town; my brother was abroad; none of my father's relations would receive me; I had no acquaintances but such as were my aunt's, to whom my application would have been very improper, as I should have found very strong prejudices to combat with; it being a received maxim among persons of a certain age, that young people are always in the wrong" (1:156). Such prudential wisdom, she observes, prevents "many a kind interposition; so that we seem to live only for ourselves" (1:157). Young people, and particularly young women, who ran away—even with good cause—generally found themselves excluded from polite society.

The tension between her oppressive guardians and Henrietta's individual resistance lingers unresolved until well into the second volume, when she unexpectedly meets her brother, whom she has not seen for years. By this point, Henrietta has fled her aunt's house and found a position as companion to a lady who travels to France to avoid the importunities of a married man. En route, Henrietta and her mistress become acquainted with two Englishmen traveling incognito, one of whom (a marquis who introduces himself as Melvil) falls in love with Henrietta and she with him. Misunderstanding her character, the tutor tries to arrange a sexual liaison between his charge and Henrietta but discovers to his horror that the woman he has propositioned is his sister: "What a wretch have I been! . . . Indeed, my dear sister, I never shall forgive myself for having ignorantly practised on your virtue!" Her brother is caught, as Henrietta cleverly points out to him, in the logical extreme of the double standard: " 'Oh! that my brother,' replied Henrietta, 'would be taught by this accident never more to form designs against innocence; and, in cases like mine, to consider every virtuous young woman as a sister' " (2:226). Insofar as it would eliminate the sexual oppression of women, the reform Henrietta proposes is idealistic: if men considered all women as sisters instead of objects for their use, there could be no rakes and no female victims.

By this time, only too glad to return to some form of protection, Henrietta repents of her former rebellion. Much as in *The Female Quixote* Arabella's sudden conversion propels the novel toward conclusion, so Henrietta's submission to her brother's authority prepares for a denouement in this novel. Naturally there is some dissatisfaction on the modern reader's part that Henrietta, who has managed quite well by herself since the beginning of the novel, must now resign herself to her brother's keeping. As an agent of the marquis's father, her brother cannot even promote her marriage to his charge, and Henrietta herself asserts that "if the marquis was a thousand times more amiable than he is, and were I ever so much prejudiced in his favour, I have too just a sense of what I owe to my birth, to your honour, and my own, to admit of a clandestine address" (2:239). Read against her earlier alternatives, Henrietta's submission is the choice of a resistant character who, within certain bounds, reconciles herself to the social forms required of her, but who at the same time hopes to find in her brother what she has lacked in other guardian figures—someone whose affection makes him concerned for her feelings, someone who will settle her in the marriage of her choice.

In terms of class/status parity within marriage, and in terms of the submission of women to authority, the novel takes a fairly conservative position. Henrietta is, after all, infected with enough aristocratic pride to reject the idea that she, an earl's niece and Mr. Courteney's daughter, should marry a steward. But lest readers misunderstand the author's motives, we must remember that her heroine also rejects the idea of marrying a Catholic baron merely for his position and estate, and that her father, disinherited for marrying beneath his family, was nonetheless happy in his domestic situation. The implied class ethic is further problematized when the heroine meets and falls in love with Mr. Melvil, who is a marquis in disguise, for this event at once allows Henrietta to make what even advocates of arranged marriage would consider a good match, while at the same time permitting her reconciliation with the repressive older generation of her father's family.

Moreover, if initially the novel breaks neatly along a faultline that separates an older class-conscious generation from a young generation of lovers—Henrietta's parents from her father's family, Henrietta from her uncle and aunt, the marquis from his father—eventually all these rifts are healed by the concluding nuptial celebration. Thus, even while Lennox goes to some length to exercise feminist issues in relation to marriage, and while her heroine outlines a model for rebellion against female socialization, her denouement neatly restores the social fabric to a seamless whole. For a representative image, one may return to the initial scene of the novel. Even if society may be brought to make room for an individual woman, her situation, like Henrietta's in the London coach, will most likely be cramped and uncomfortable.

SIX

Frances Moore Brooke

EMILY MONTAGUE'S
SANCTUM SANCTORUM

FRANCES MOORE's first literary venture was *The Old Maid*, a periodical that ran from November 1755 through July 1756. "Mary Singleton, Spinster" invited correspondence from old maids, addressed such current issues as the war with France and the establishment of foundling hospitals, and advised her readers on the behavior of theater audiences, the management of a young woman's courtship, and friendship. Although her magazine halted publication abruptly when Frances Moore (age 32) married the Reverend Dr. John Brooke, she continued writing, having two plays staged as well as publishing several translations and three novels.[1]

Her husband's stint as First Chaplain of Forces in Quebec provided Brooke with materials for an innovative novel combining elements of courtship and travel stories. Although it was supported by subscription, *The History of Emily Montague* (1769) did not sell well initially, and Brooke regretted that she had felt obliged to stretch it out to four volumes. But during her lifetime the novel eventually ran into a sixth edition despite its flaws, becoming especially popular in Canada and France.

By transplanting the British novel of courtship to the New World, Brooke gained not only travel-book matter but also a new multicultural perspective from which to view the institution of marriage and the role of women in British society. The travel aspect of the novel blends naturally into its epistolary format, as when Rivers, the young man who is Brooke's principal tourist, describes the approach to Quebec: "It stands on the summit of a boldly-rising hill, at the confluence of two very beautiful rivers, the St. Lawrence and the St. Charles, and, as the convents and other public buildings first meet the eye, appears to great advantage from the port. The island of Orleans, the distant view of the cascade of Montmorenci, and the opposite village of Beauport, scattered with a pleasing irregularity along the banks of the river St. Charles, add greatly to the charms of the prospect."[2]

As one might expect, Brooke's novel also reflects the nature of her husband's assignment in Canada. Several letters compare religious practices in the New World, and William Fermor's scrutiny of the North American Indians forms the basis of an extended critique of Jean-Jacques Rousseau's exaltation of primitive man. On the whole, the travel-book material shapes a realistic exchange of letters, which in itself would have been compelling reading for Brooke's contemporaries.

Unlike most novels of courtship, though, Brooke's epistolary novel begins from a male point of view—that of Ed. Rivers, who is preparing to settle on the Canadian property to which he has a right as a lieutenant on half-pay. The complex interrelationships among friends and siblings would have reminded Brooke's readers of Richardson's *Grandison*, published fifteen years earlier. Aside from Rivers and his friend, John Temple, and another pair of male correspondents who exchange a few philosophizing letters, all the correspondents are female—Emily Montague with her guardians and with Arabella Fermor; Arabella with Lucy Rivers. Eventually the letters converge around the developing courtship of Ed. Rivers and Emily Montague, with secondary relationships developing between Fitz Williams and Arabella, and John Temple and Lucy Rivers.

When Rivers acknowledges, in an early letter to his friend Temple, that he prefers "mature" women, he initiates a plot movement that will conclude in his marriage with Emily Montague. At the same time, by raising the issue of female character, the author prepares for a series of comparative studies of women, whose combined effect is an argument for social reform. From the male character's viewpoint, the salient question is which among the various ethnic groups of women is the most eligible for his attentions. Writing to Temple, Rivers describes Indian women as being fairly accessible before marriage, but afterward "chastity itself." As married women "they become coarse and masculine, and lose in a year or two the power as well as the desire of pleasing" (1:22). Writing a similar letter to his sister, Rivers accommodates the change in audience by focusing on the political advantages enjoyed by Indian women: "The sex we have so unjustly excluded from power in Europe have a great share in the Huron government; the chief is chosen by the matrons from amongst the nearest male relations, by the female line, of him he is to succeed" (67-68). Rivers extends the contrast, drawing his sister's attention to the inequity English women suffer: "In the true sense of the word, *we* are the savages, who so impolitely deprive you of the common rights of citizenship, and leave you no power but that of which we cannot deprive you, the resistless power of your charms. By the way, I don't think you are obliged in conscience to obey laws you have had no share in making; your plea would certainly be at least as good as that of the Americans, about which we every day hear so much" (1:69). While Brooke does not go so far as to have her character propose that women become revolutionaries or candidates for office, Rivers's implication that women should be enfranchised depends on an unusually egalitarian acknowledgment of female subject positions. The analogical terms in which he presses his argument are forceful: like the Americans, women have been denied their citizenship, their prerogative of self-determination.

Similarly, Rivers's account of the middle rank among Canadian women, though not so politically charged, also initiates a comparative study, this time of the general character of women of different ethnic backgrounds. The Canadians have every other charm, according to Rivers: "They are gay, coquet, and sprightly; more gallant than sensible; more flatter'd by the vanity of inspiring passion, than capable of feeling it themselves" (1:23). Those Canadian women who confine themselves in convents Rivers believes to be misguided: Are they "rational beings, who think they are serving the God of mercy by inflicting on themselves voluntary tortures, and cutting themselves off from that state of society in which he has plac'd them, and for which they were form'd? by renouncing the best affections of the human heart, the tender names of friend, of wife, of mother?" (1:30). Brooke has Rivers describe the women who inhabit Catholic convents as amiable, even while his disavowal of Catholic practice leads him into what we would term an essentialist formulation—"friend . . . wife . . . mother." Similarly, while Rivers's depiction of the native peasants is harsh in general, he finds the conversation of their women "lively and amusing" (1:35).

On the whole, the effect of Rivers's comparative study is to multiply the focus on woman's social role, and to this constantly reiterated question Brooke's heroine is clearly meant as an answer. Rivers finds her beauty more than physical: "I adore beauty, but it is not meer features or complexion to which I give that name; 'tis life, 'tis spirit, 'tis imagination" (1:40). He especially values her understanding and "the natural softness of her soul, which gives her the strongest desire of pleasing" (1:41-42). There can be no doubt that Brooke intends Emily Montague to be a role model for the woman of sensibility.

Yet, to permit oneself sensibility is a choice more individualist than conformist. In deciding against the man her guardians have chosen for her, Emily Montague overturns their plans and thwarts, in a general way, the expectations of society: "This sweet girl has been two years wretched under the bondage her uncle's avarice (for he foresaw Sir George's acquisition [of fortune], though she did not) prepared for her. Parents should chuse our company, but never even pretend to direct our choice . . . a conformity of taste and sentiment alone can make marriage happy, and of that none but the parties concerned can judge" (2:34-35). Brooke outlines the principles behind her heroine's resistance. Emily Montague's friend protests that choice begins with individual taste and sentiment, and for this reason parents and guardians should confine themselves to choosing a young woman's company—a pool from which she may select a suitable partner. Emily's change of heart is an issue, moreover, that divides the generations, beginning with Arabella's father and extending to the large community. "The prudent mamas abuse her for losing a good match, and suppose it to proceed from her partiality to your brother, to the imprudence of which they give no quarter; whilst the misses admire her generosity and spirit, in sacrificing all for love; so impossible it is to please every body. However, she has, in my opinion, done the wisest thing in the world; that is, she has pleased herself" (2:48-89). Arabella's commentary points out the anomaly in her friend's situation: the issue of her marriage, which preoccupies so many of her acquaintances, instead should be altogether her individual decision.

Later, in writing to Lucy, Arabella presses home the point about affective individualism by noting a parallel between convents and unhappy marriages: "The cruelty . . . of some parents here, who sacrifice their children to avarice, in forcing or seducing them into convents, would appear more striking, if we did not see too many in England guilty of the same inhumanity, though in a different manner, by marrying them against their inclination" (3:29). Even if parents are initially to blame for marriages of convenience, though, the young woman herself bears the ultimate responsibility. As Arabella explains, "I think marrying, in that expectation, on sober prudent principles, a man one dislikes, the most deliberate and shameful degree of vice of which the human mind is capable" (3:32). Arabella's words emphasize that giving in to an arranged marriage is a vicious passivity into which no woman should allow herself to be persuaded.

Significantly, it is one of Brooke's male characters who describes the preferred affectionate marriage. Quoting advice from Madame de Maintenon, Ed. Rivers hopes Lucy will see the conduct writer's limitations. Thus, he challenges the commonly received idea "that women are only born to suffer and to obey":

That we are generally tyrannical, I am obliged to own; but such of us as know how to be happy, willingly give up the harsh title of master, for the more tender and endearing one of friend; men of sense abhor those customs which treat your sex as if created meerly for the happiness of the other; a supposition injurious to the Deity, though flattering to our tyranny and self-love; and wish only to bind you in the soft chains of affection.

Equality is the soul of friendship: marriage, to give delight, must join two minds, not devote a slave to the will of an imperious lord; whatever conveys the idea of subjection necessarily destroys that of love, of which I am so convinced, that I have always wished the word *obey* expunged from the marriage ceremony. [2:194-95]

The fact that Brooke gives this speech to Rivers makes the proposal seem less radical than in fact it is. By displacing the notion of equality, by having a male character explain it, Brooke effectually takes this feminist issue farther than she might otherwise have gone.

Significantly, much as Rivers's description of marriage—without subjection, with "the word *obey* expunged"—makes psychological space for the individuated woman, so, analogously, he provides a physical space for Emily when he marries her. She is to have a room of her own, he writes to Fitz Gerald, "a dressing room and closet of books, into which I shall never intrude: there is a pleasure in having some place which we can say is peculiarly our own, some *sanctum sanctorum*, whither we can retire from those most dear to us" (4:42). In effect, Brooke's anticipation of Virginia Woolf's "room of one's own" epitomizes the demonstrably feminist agenda that informs her novel.

By 1769, when Frances Brooke's novel was published, the ideal of sensibility, firmly lodged in the British psyche, could be used to justify a young woman's differences with her guardians and society. Moreover, *The History of Emily Montague* presses the logical consequences of female subjecthood beyond courtship into the relationship of wife and husband within marriage. Brooke holds out for her readers the kind of relationship she appears to have had herself—a friendship in which there was mutual respect, in which the dread command "to obey" was replaced by affective consideration.

PART III

The Commodification of Heroines

SEVEN

The Blazon and the Marriage Act

BEGINNING FOR THE COMMODITY MARKET

INTRODUCED in Parliament in 1753, Lord Hardwicke's "Act for the better preventing of Clandestine Marriages" stipulated that marriages were to be performed by ordained Anglican clergymen in the premises of the Church of England, the banns to be called three times or a special license purchased from a bishop. Most crucially, parental consent for those under twenty-one was to be strictly enforced. The Hardwicke Act outlawed ecclesiastical suits brought on the basis of contracts *de praesenti* or *de futuro*; the ceremony, not the agreement, would be the test of English marriage. The centuries' old conflict over who properly held power over the marriage contract persisted, however.[1] Critics variously faulted the act for increasing parental power over daughters, for insuring aristocratic privilege and wealth, for preventing younger sons from marrying middle-class heiresses, for obstructing marriage among the poor, and for creating hardship for women who had been seduced.[2] Indeed, when Hardwicke himself referred to the law some nine years later in the case of the Earl of Buckinghamshire versus Drury (1762), he seemed to assume that the law had decided the power struggle in favor of parents, yet the list of motivations he attributed to them was no more than a summation of the previous debate: "There are many considerations, which may induce them, besides strict equality in settlements—inclination of the parties—rank and quality of the person—convenience and propriety in families—bringing together and uniting different parts of the same estate; all these are proper reasons."[3] Making a rhetorical flourish for the purposes of the settlement case on which he was giving his opinion, Hardwicke's language starts in the direction of liberalism—"besides strict equality in settlements"—but returns immediately to the service of class endogamy: "rank and quality of the person—convenience and propriety in families—bringing together and uniting different parts of the same estate."

So complex and varied was rhetoric on either side of the bill that disentangling it yields few meaningful generalizations. But arguments from upper-class proponents did tend to invoke the terms of patriarchy while those of middle-class opponents called on the terms of commercialism. A similar divergence of views persists among latter-day historians. Lawrence Stone, Randolph Trumbach, Alan Macfarlane, and others have offered widely divergent interpretations of motives of proponents and opponents, of what was gained and what was lost, but they have tended to agree in viewing the new taste for companionate marriage as a primary motive for the passage of Hardwicke's Act in 1753. More recently, Erica Harth has objected that while romantic love was at issue, "it was neither the pivot on which the vote in the House of Commons turned nor the main concern. . . . For those in power . . . considerations of love and marriage were embedded in those of money and property." Both sides claimed to be concerned for female virtue, but the virtue claimed by the bill's proponents was class determined, "directed at the propertied alone." Bringing such diverse ideas as the free circulation of love and money and the protection of female virtue into cooperation, the Hardwicke Act, as Harth reads it, "was a victory for patriarchy and capitalism."[4]

Protest against marriages of convenience, which continued after the "Act for the better preventing of Clandestine Marriages," had of course begun much earlier, in, among other places, pamphlets addressed to the general public. Whether they collected advertisements for the lovelorn or advocated institutional reform, pamphleteers used catchphrases ("matchmaking," "maneuvering," and "marriage market" are examples) that carried overtones of class conflict central to the issue of how marriage should be regulated. In 1750 one such pamphlet, *A Serious Proposal for Promoting Lawful and Honourable Marriage*, began stylishly, its anonymous author prefacing the work with details of an aunt's courtship misfortunes. The young woman's guardian and matchmaker was "one of those wise People, who consider a Woman only as a Skin of Parchment, whereon to engross the Conveyance of so much Land to one's own Use; or as a stained Canvass, whereon to continue the Family Pictures; or as the most legal Method of strengthening and securing so much Interest in a Borough-Election."[5] The object of these denunciations was the aristocratic family, with its royal charter, country estate, and gallery of family portraits.

In place of matchmaking guardians, the pamphleteer outlines for "the Unmarried, of both sexes" a remarkably liberal scheme anticipating today's computerized dating service. Public offices at opposite ends of town will house files of eligible singles, "the Ladies' Office" near Temple-Bar and the Gentlemen's" near Charing-Cross. Labeled "Batchelor or Widower," a sample file catalogues "vital statistics" for perusal. The registrant's age, height, complexion, and condition in life are recorded—the file providing the status terms "Esquire," "Gentleman independent," "Profession," "Trade," and "Calling." Fortune may be measured "either in general (as) well to pass: moderate, good—or more particular, as . . . thought proper." On looking over an opposite register, a gentleman or lady who approves "of any Description, and Circumstances, as there entered" may send a letter to arrange an interview. Initial meetings are to be held at guarded houses with no locks on the doors; ladies are to be permitted veils. But, aside from these gender distinctions, the proposal extends to both sexes, in an egalitarian way, the prerogative of choice and the disadvantage of commodification—the advantages of affective individualism and the requirements of a free market.[6]

In brief, the progress from the marked exploitation of the "Skin of Parchment" to the gender egalitarianism of the "registers" parallels in some measure the shift historians have taught us to expect of eighteenth-century nuptial patterns; coincidentally, the move from preface to proposal also adumbrates the shift outlined by Harth from the conservative language of land and privilege to the progressive language of trade. The pamphlet is suggestively bourgeois and feminist in its apparent focus. Behind the surface objectifications of the dating service (which, granted, resemble the calculations of arranged marriage) lie the very real advantages of choice—a prerogative that patriarchal exchange largely denied women of the nobility and gentry but which was generally fostered by capitalism and, more specifically, by the ideology of companionate marriage. Moreover, the eighteenth-century "dating service" codifies what Michel Foucault has termed a period fascination with "representations of representations." Of the three epistemological domains Foucault attributes to the eighteenth century—grammar, taxonomy, and monetary exchange—the latter two are enlisted in the "dating service" registration.[7] Registrants practice an auto-taxonomy, one category of which, "fortune," refers to monetary exchange. In other words, as in today's cryptic personal advertisements, while registration insures choice, it also requires self-commodification, an attempt to measure one's own exchange value.

Setting aside for the moment apparent contradictions between taxonomy, monetary exchange, and eros, I want to look at the integral part commodification played in the representation of women in this period. Often, eighteenth-century England was anything but sympathetic to women's interests—objectifying, commodifying, displaying overt misogyny. But alongside the rakish encomia and early examples of fetishism that punctuated some texts was a form of tropic commodification that revealed women's disadvantaged positions within the male hegemony—a combination of taxonomy and monetary exchange to which I will apply the term *blazon*, borrowed from French heraldric usage. The blazon, as I will explain more fully later, describes a man or woman in terms of a normative taxonomy— beauty, fortune, family, education, and character. Like the *Serious Proposal*, the blazon operates subversively, deploying the languages of male hegemony, of landed interest and incipient capitalism, for feminist purposes. In other words, this trope, like the register houses of Temple-Bar and Charing-Cross, gestures toward a feminist concern with the prerogative of choosing a marriage partner.[8]

In the following discussion, I identify several instances of tropic commodification, selecting for more thorough analysis Samuel Richardson's *Sir Charles Grandison* and touching on the fact (to be developed later with regard to *Pride and Prejudice*) that the blazon became a standard element in Jane Austen's novels.

Richardson published his third and last novel, *Sir Charles Grandison*, in 1753, the year of Hardwicke's Marriage Act. For his heroine, Harriet Byron, whose story will end in a marriage of choice, the psychohistoric context of the 1750s provides a cluster of representations initiating as a feminist theme a woman's right to fall in love, to choose her own love object. The dynamic by which the text proceeds, a gendered dialogism, is well established in the first of its seven volumes. Richardson's presentation of Harriet, whose concerns rival Grandison's for the reader's attention, conveys a marked awareness of what it is to be a woman inscribed within patriarchy, menaced by reductive systems of representation. Consider, for example, Harriet's exchanges with Mr. Greville, one of her most persistent suitors.

From the first letter in this epistolary novel, the reader is enlisted as Harriet's co-conspirator against a form of male consumerism—in this case, against the phallocentric rhetoric and the scopic system associated with the rake.[9] Enclosed with Lucy Selby's letter to Harriet is one borrowed from Mr. Greville—a description of "the celebrated Miss Byron" written for his friend, Lady Frampton. The conflicting requirements of making Harriet the subject (or more significantly, the object) of a letter ostensibly directed to Lady Frampton, yet meant to be read by Harriet, is too complex even for an accomplished rake. The double-voicedness of Greville's encomia marks his protested appreciation of Harriet's mind: "You know I have vanity, Madam: But lovely as Miss Byron's person is, I defy the greatest Sensualist on earth not to admire her mind more than her person. What a triumph would the devil have, as I have often thought, when I have stood contemplating her perfections, especially at church, were he able to raise up a man that could lower this Angel into Woman?"[10] The libertinism he tries to suppress beneath the honorable surface of courtship is as legible as the passages of the letter he ineffectually tries to cover over with lighter ink. Greville's "contemplation," his gaze, he confesses as the devil's work, and with Harriet, Richardson's reader would feel the threat of sexual appropriation.[11]

While Greville claims to admire Harriet's mind, it is after all her person he contemplates. Most interesting for our purposes here is the rakish consumerism of his description: "Let me die, if I know where to begin. She is all over loveliness. . . . Her Stature; shall I begin with her stature? She cannot be said to be tall; but yet is something above the middling. Her Shape—But what care I for her shape? I, who hope to love her still more, tho' possession may make me admire her less, when she has not that to boast of?" (1:11). Through the next two pages, the movement from anatomizing description to anticipated possession fetishizes, morselizes Harriet into "complexion," "forehead," "cheek," "mouth," "nose," "chin," "hair," "neck," "arm," and "hands," replicating the terms of male desire. Unable to see Harriet as whole, self-expressive sexual being, Greville diverts his taxonomic attention to her "parts."[12] In a later scene, when Harriet tells Greville she has never "seen the man to whom I can think of giving my hand," he will rave, "By heaven you have. . . . You shall give it to *me*!—And the strange wretch pressed it so hard to his mouth, that he made prints upon it with his teeth" (1:101). Harriet's presence converts Greville's desire for the fetishized hand into a lack at once gustatory and sexual: " 'And *Oh*!' said he, mimicking (and snatching my other hand, as I would have run from him) and patting it, speaking thro' his closed teeth, 'You may be glad you have an hand left. By my soul, I could eat you' " (1:101).

In his letter, however, Greville is less passionate, more deliberate, eventually trying to recuperate his laudatory excesses within a second semantic system, the language of exchange appropriate to arranged marriage. He hopes to marry Harriet under terms that had obtained largely unquestioned for the middle and upper classes through the first two decades of the eighteenth century. But at the time he prepares his brief in this novel of the 1750s, arranged marriages and the marriage markets that promote them have become targets for parody. This second system of representation, also taxonomic, grows not from a

rakish consumerism but from a consumerism nevertheless—that of
patriarchal exchange; its terms are not psychosexual but socioeconomic.[13]

Reminiscent of the pamphleteer's register entry, Greville's socioeconomic appraisal of Harriet, in the passage I will quote shortly, is
a blazon.[14] The term is borrowed from the Renaissance, recalls Julia
Kristeva in *Desire in Language*. One of several deviations along the
novel's trajectory, the blazon comes "from the fair, marketplace, or
public square. It is the utterance of the merchant vaunting his wares
or of the herald announcing combat. Phonetic speech, oral utterance,
sound itself, become text: less than writing, the novel is thus the
transcription of vocal communication." These "laudatory utterances"
give direct information on war or, more to the purpose here, on the
quality and price of merchandise in the marketplace. Kristeva's discussion of Antoine de La Salle's fifteenth-century prose narrative emphasizes the referentiality of early blazons: "The culture of exchange,
definitively imposed by the European Renaissance, is engendered
through the *voice* and operates according to the structures of the dis-
cursive (verbal, phonetic) circuit, inevitably referring back to a reality
with which it identified by duplicating it (by 'signifying it')." After
the early Renaissance, however, the blazon loses its univocity; it
becomes multireferential—hence, ambiguous. Kristeva applies the
argument to the heroine of de La Salle's *Jehan de Saintré*, whose
"treachery skews the laudatory tone [of the blazon] and shows its
ambiguity." That is, de La Salle's heroine, introduced in glowing terms
at the beginning of the narrative, is later shown not to measure up
to her blazon; she is, in fact, not the faithful lady of her lord. To put
it simply, the advertisement is a scam.[15]

In a similar way, when Richardson raises the crucial issue of marriage in *Sir Charles Grandison*, the blazon, which appears to be as
straightforward a taxonomic representation as the gentlemen's and
ladies' files referred to earlier, actually implies an ambiguity, an inadequacy of the sign. As I use the term here, the eighteenth-century
form of blazon describes a man or woman in terms of a normative
taxonomy—physical beauty, fortune, family, education, and character. The blazon alludes both to a system of patriarchal exchange and
to the bourgeois marketplace, referring to exchanges made by giving
"equal value," by aligning equivalent male and female blazons. It also
gestures toward irreconcilable tensions, rife in contemporary prose—
in the journals and in the preface of the *Serious Proposal*—that only
wanted to be incorporated into the novel. The point is that Richardson
was writing at a time when it was impossible to raise the question of
marriage without also raising the issues of interest versus love and

parental authority versus female autonomy. All of these were implicated in the blazons, which drew at once on what Harth terms the
conservative language of land and privilege" and the "progressive
language of trade."

Thus, Greville's case for marriage with Harriet reveals its inadequacy not only through its fetishism (or "flattery," as Harriet will
term it) but also through its reliance on the blazons associated with
arranged marriages, with the commodification of women within the
system of patriarchal exchange. Greville's outdated ploy is to weigh
his own blazon, his own register entry, as it were, against Harriet's:
"And ought *I* to despair of succeeding with the girl *herself*? I, her
Greville; not contemptible in person; an air—free and easy, *at least*;
having a good estate in possession; fine expectancies besides; dressing
well, singing well, dancing well, and blest with a moderate share of
confidence; which makes *other* women think me a clever fellow: She,
a girl of twenty; her fortune between ten and fifteen thousand pounds
only; for her father's considerable estate, on his demise, for want of
male heirs, went with the name; her grandmother's jointure not more
than 500 £. a year" (1:11).

In market terms, Mr. Greville would be a catch for Miss Byron,
and he knows it. Yet the blazons (his and hers) become ambiguous
or inadequate when read in the context of a fuller understanding of
her character. In his own words, Harriet "can hardly find room in
her heart for a particular Love . . . till she meets with one whose mind
is near as faultless as her own" (1:10). Moreover, Greville has already
alluded to Harriet's privileged autonomy of choice, which must convert his use of the blazon to an empty form. Harriet's grandmother
and aunt will not interfere with her choice, will not exchange her:
"The approbation of their Harriet must first be gained, and then their
consent is ready" (1:11). Significantly, Harriet's female relations speak
the newer language in which autonomy of choice becomes privileged—an epistemology in which Greville's signifiers, "person," "air,"
"fortune," suffer a radical loss of exchange power. Greville is unsuited by a semantic position he can quote but does not comprehend:
love is ineffable, irreducible, to the materiality either of a market
economy or of patriarchal exchange. Moreover, the blazon signals an
irreducible conflict between liberalism, which presupposes individual
access to the marketplace, and feminism, which denies the applica-
bility of market terms to women.

Through Greville's rhetorical facility, Richardson complicates
and marks his representation of Harriet Byron, applying at least two
systems of objectification and commodification—the psychosexual
language of rakish consumerism (fetish), and the socioeconomic lan-

guage of patriarchal and bourgeois consumerism (blazon). The female novelists who followed Richardson adopted the second system of objectification, the blazon, generally shaping it into a formal introduction of their heroines, a programmatic headnote that their texts subsequently revised or erased.

Fanny Burney's *Evelina* (1778), for example, introduces its heroine as having "a virtuous mind" and "a cultivated understanding." An early letter of Mr. Villars's completes the blazon: "This artless young creature, with too much beauty to escape notice, has too much sensibility to be indifferent to it; but she has too little wealth to be sought with propriety by men of the fashionable world."[16] Evelina is the "only child of a wealthy baronet, whose person she has never seen" and who may never "*properly* own her" (18-19). To some degree, Villars's reservations about sending his ward to town signal his pessimistic assessment of her against the London marriage market. Yet, his is a benevolent objectification; beyond desiring to keep her with him, to preserve her from the corruptive influences of the city, he simply wishes to spare her pain. Eventually, the novel will invalidate Villars's doubts about his ward's marriageability. Even before her birth, mystery is publicly resolved and she becomes an heiress, and despite her social awkwardness and rude bourgeois relations, Evelina gains the aristocratic Lord Orville's "disinterested attachment." Thus, the initial measure taken of her, the blazon, is revealed as insufficient by the events that follow in Burney's novel. Villars's objectification, though benevolent, is misguided; tropic commodification cannot assess Evelina's desirability within companionate marriage.

If Burney implies that Villars's social perspective is too limited, then other novelists will go further, vilifying parents or guardians and tracing a generational conflict between adults who adhere to the outdated system of patriarchal exchange and daughters who embrace the newer freedoms of companionate marriage. Maria Edgeworth, Jane Austen's immediate predecessor in the nineteenth century, titles one of her novels *Manoeuvring* as a corrective for matchmaking parents.[17] Her best courtship novel, *Belinda* (1801), all but erects the shop and hangs the shingle "husband wanted" in the first twenty pages. Belinda is the sixth niece of modest fortune her aunt has taken to market: The aunt is a "catch-matchmaker," the phrase implying that Mrs. Stanhope specializes in marrying her nieces above their expectations—in unions where there is an inequity of status or fortune. With such language as "hawked" and "puffing" marking the resemblance between Mrs. Stanhope's matchmaking methods and the crassest mercantile practices, Edgeworth recognizes that the motto *caveat emptor* is as applicable to marriage as to other enterprises.

Belinda is "handsome, graceful, sprightly, and highly accomplished; her aunt had endeavoured to teach her that a young lady's chief business is to please in society, that all her charms and accomplishments should be invariably subservient to one grand object—the establishing herself in the world."[18] The blazon marks Belinda's destiny, according to patriarchal exchange and her manipulative aunt, yet what follows gestures toward Belinda's resistance to being inscribed in a narrative concluding in her establishment: "Mrs. Stanhope did not find Belinda such a docile pupil as her other nieces, for she had been educated chiefly in the country, she had early been inspired with a taste for domestic pleasures, she was fond of reading, and disposed to conduct herself with prudence and integrity" (1). Edgeworth's beginning forecasts a generational conflict, and thereafter Belinda resists her aunt's lessons. In the course of the novel, the marriage-market blazon, if not erased, is at least revised; Belinda successfully resists her aunt's machinations and finds, through her own integrity, love (and a good establishment) with Mr. Hervey.

By the second decade of the nineteenth century, the blazons that introduced heroines were being overhauled because they were recognizably anachronistic or so hackneyed that they could no longer be taken seriously. In *The Heroine* (1813), Eaton Stannard Barrett revives the intertextual tradition of the quixote, drawing on eighteenth-century fiction to travesty the literary conventions associated both with the courtship novel and with the earlier excesses of romance. His Cherry Willoughby ludicrously colludes in her own objectification, assessing her suitability for a heroine's role:

That I am not deficient in the qualities requisite for a heroine, is indisputable. I know nothing of the world, or of human nature; and every one says I am handsome. My form is tall aerial, my face Grecian, my tresses flaxen, my eyes blue and sleepy. Then, not only peaches, roses and Aurora, but snow, lilies, and alabaster, may, with perfect propriety, be applied to a description of my skin. . . .

There is but one serious flaw in my title to Heroine—the mediocrity of my lineage. My father is descended from nothing better than a decent and respectable family. He began life with a thousand pounds, purchased a farm, and by his honest and disgusting industry, has realized fifty thousand. Were even my legitimacy suspected, it would be some comfort; since, in that case, I might hope to start forth, at one time or other, the daughter of some plaintive nobleman, who lives retired, and occasionally slaps his forehead.[19]

By having his heroine catalogue her own qualifications, Barrett complicates the blazon. In fact, Cherry's self-portrait combines fetish and blazon—anatomizing the heroine's physiognomy ("my form is tall and aerial, my face Grecian") as well as detailing her socioeconomic bargaining position (her family is "decent and respectable"; her fortune, fifty thousand pounds). Paradoxically, the portrait also enlists her naiveté—she knows "nothing of the world, or of human nature." Yet this is patently untrue, for in Cherry's self-objectification we can read her understanding of the upper middle-class position her father's "disgusting industry" and her own legitimacy determine for her. In Barrett's representation, Cherry self-reflexively questions her blazon even as she utters it, understanding its program as something to be overturned. Cherry's self-commodification depends on a rather sophisticated rhetorical strategy, a double displacement, for at the same time that the author is glancing at older conventions of romance, he is parodying the more recent blazon, itself an ironic rendition of the "register" entries of patriarchal exchange.

Barrett's *Heroine* was almost certainly in Jane Austen's mind when she revised *Northanger Abbey* (1818) for publication in 1816 or so, for like Barrett, while she makes a parodic reference both to romance and to the courtship novel, she employs the blazon as her beginning. Asserting her inability to list Catherine's qualifications or perfections, the author catalogues her deficiencies, taking for granted her readers' familiarity with at least part of the long tradition of courtship novels, against which her blazon reverberates as a divergent voice: "No one who had ever seen Catherine in her infancy, would have supposed her born to be an heroine." At ten, Catherine has "a thin awkward figure, a sallow skin without colour, dark lank hair, and strong features," and while her looks have "improved" by seventeen, Austen continues to remind her readers that Catherine's beauty falls short of heroic standards. Fortune and family are quite modest commodities for this "heroine" and, by courtship conventions, Catherine's education is deficient. Here is a young woman who is "fond of all boys' plays" and rejects the usual female accomplishments of gardening and music; her writing, French, and accounts are undististinguished. By fifteen, "in training for a heroine," Catherine has no objection to books "provided they were all story and no reflection." Summing up Catherine's character, Austen emphasizes its normalcy and shortcomings: "Her heart was affectionate, her disposition cheerful and open, without conceit or affectation of any kind—her manners just removed from the awkwardness and shyness of a girl; her person pleasing, and, when in good looks, pretty—and her mind about as ignorant and uninformed as the female mind at seventeen usually is."[20]

Catherine is about to enter her courtship period, and though "she had reached the age of seventeen, without having seen one amiable youth who could call forth her sensibility; without having inspired one real passion" (4), her trip to Bath is meant to provide her such experiences. The blazon at the beginning of the novel encourages Austen's readers to judge Catherine's chances on the market, much as Mr. Dashwood, in *Sense and Sensibility* quantifies Marianne and Elinor, predicting by the hundred pounds how well they will marry.[21] Austen insists that Catherine, whatever her allegiance to novels, is not a heroine who can be objectified—commodified—but an individual whose personality and flaws merit our attention.

Through their blazons, Richardson's *Sir Charles Grandison* and subsequent courtship novels gesture toward a semantic field increasingly at odds with marriage practice in England. As places of departure in the novel, blazons exemplify what Edward Said has to say about some "beginnings," that "the truth . . . can only be approached indirectly, by means of a mediation that, paradoxically, because of its falseness makes the truth truer. . . . a truer truth is one arrived at by a process of elimination: alternatives similar to the truth are shed one by one."[22] On the surface, the blazon—the taxonomy of beauty, fortune, family, education, and character—essentializes the heroine's role; within the socioeconomic semantic stratum of patriarchal exchange and the commodity market, the blazon is the heroine's truth. Much as women have internalized a male scopic perspective, so female novelists internalized this form of tropic commodification. As taxonomy, the blazon replicates the reduction of women to cyphers in the manipulations preceding arranged marriage. But as part of the heroine-centered courtship novel, this beginning, this program, necessarily stands under erasure by the remainder of the text. From the feminist semantic field to which the courtship novel belongs, the blazon implicates a partial truth in need of revision, a representation of woman as object, commodity, ready for exchange. The two dozen novelists (most of them women) who wrote courtship novels between Richardson and Austen, between 1740 and 1820, supplied what for them was a truer truth, a representation of woman as a subject whose prerogative it was, within the new nuptial ethic, to choose her own marriage partner—to say with Richardson's Harriet Byron the words that so infuriated Sir Hargrave Pollexfen: "You do not . . . hit my fancy— Pardon me, Sir" (*Grandison*, 1:84).

EIGHT

Fanny Burney

CECILIA, THE
RELUCTANT HEIRESS

BY THE TIME Fanny Burney's second novel was published in 1782, the author was already in place as a favorite among the Thrale circle. Fifteen years later Erasmus Darwin recognized her popularity among women readers by including *Cecilia* (1782), along with the earlier *Evelina* (1778), with the "serious novels" he recommended in his *Plan for the Conduct of Female Education*.[1] When Jane Austen undertook a defense of the genre in *Northanger Abbey* (1818), *Cecilia* was one of the few novels she mentioned. Burney's second novel, as critics have only recently begun to acknowledge, conveys a remarkable understanding of the troubled relationship between society and the female self.

Burney begins by situating Cecilia socially and economically, introducing her heroine through the ideologically-charged shorthand of blazon: "Cecilia, this fair traveller, had lately entered into the one-and-twentieth year of her age. Her ancestors had been rich farmers in the county of Suffolk, though her father, in whom a spirit of elegance had supplanted the rapacity of wealth, had spent his time as a private country gentleman, satisfied, without increasing his store, to live upon what he inherited from the labours of his predecessors." Her parents have left her £10,000, and her uncle's will makes her "heiress to an estate of £3000 per annum; with no other restriction than that of annexing her name, if she married, to the disposal of her hand and her riches." At this point in her introduction, Burney's language veers from socioeconomic concerns to those of sensibility: Cecilia's "form was elegant, her heart was liberal; her countenance announced the intelligence of her mind, her complexion varied with every emotion of her soul, and her eyes, the heralds of her speech, now beamed with understanding and now glistened with sensibility."[2] The divided blazon—family and fortune as against beauty, education, and character—outlines the contested ground on which

Burney's heroine stands, the term "heiress" flying as an ambiguous standard she eventually must desert.

Julia Epstein argues convincingly that Burney's focus is on "money as a medium of exchange for her plot and for her materialist social critique."[3] Cecilia is left to the care of three guardians, two of whom do act in sordidly materialistic ways toward her, each interested in his power over her future. Mr. Harrel, husband of a girlhood friend, games himself into bankruptcy and hopes, by exhibiting his maudlin despair before Cecilia, to coax money from her. The self-made Mr. Briggs, reducing all human motivation to loss and gain, wants to save the entirety of Cecilia's fortune, even from the heiress herself, for its "rightful" recipient, her future husband. The third guardian, Mr. Delvile, is motivated by family pride, and his refusal to permit his son to marry Cecilia is founded on a typically "patriarchal" rationale: if they married, either Cecilia would lose her uncle's fortune or the young Delvile would relinquish his family name for hers; in either case, the resulting exchange, from the elder Delvile's point of view, would be ignominious.

Against this trenchant rendering of virtually everything according to a monetary standard, Burney shapes as the novel's central concern the troubled consciousness of a young heiress facing conflicting duties to society and self.[4] At the beginning of the novel, Cecilia's neighbor Mr. Monckton urges her to accept his maxim that "the opposition of an individual to a community is always dangerous in the operation, and seldom successful in the event;—never, indeed, without a concurrence, strange as desirable, of fortunate circumstances with great abilities" (11). On its face, the advice is innocuous, but Monckton's real purpose is to frighten Cecilia back into the stasis of dependence, to insure that she will not act without his permission and counsel. Although her position as an orphan just a few months short of attaining majority and inheriting a considerable fortune would seem to promote Cecilia's independence, it only guarantees that others will attempt to dominate her. To clear a space for self-determination, then, Burney's heroine must reject male consumerism or commodification, resisting the authoritative infringements of guardians, suitors, and society.

As in *Evelina*, Burney's treatment of certain social scenes forces to the reader's attention the conflict between female autonomy and male consumerism. Framed scenes, unusually heightened spaces within the text, these passages are significant, if merely implicit, counterideological statements by the author.[5] In the first gathering at Monckton's house and in each subsequent framed scene, Cecilia endures a virtual interrogation of her social position. Her mere presence provokes a series of competitions among the men in the party, as Monckton takes a proprietary interest, considering Cecilia and her fortune as reserved for his use when his elderly wife dies.[6] His plans jeopardized by Cecilia's impending departure for London, Monckton hopes, under cover of advising, to predispose her against making new connections in the city. But his plan is thwarted by a forward young lawyer, Morrice, who takes the chair next to Cecilia, forcing Monckton to resort to a feigned proposal to play "move-all" to trick Morrice from his place. When he finally manages to sit beside Cecilia, Monckton details the worldly dangers she will find in London: "sharpers, fortune-hunters, sycophants, wretches of all sorts and denominations, who watch the approach of the rich and unwary, feed upon their inexperience, and prey upon their property" (13). His misanthropic vision disguises his real purpose, which is to insure his own desires by fixing Cecilia at her present stage of development: "Who that knows, who that sees her, would not wish it were possible she might continue in every respect exactly and unalterably what she is at present?" (14). Under the circumstances, the stasis Monckton enjoins is especially sinister, for it denies the possibility of her social maturation, which should be a natural consequence of her visit to London.[7] The position Burney implies for her reader is not unilateral resistance to the kind of social conservatism Monckton advises, though, for behind his cautions one must feel how applicable such words ("sharpers, fortune-hunters, sycophants, wretches") are to the adviser himself. Monckton, as becomes physically manifest in a later masquerade scene, is just such a wolf in sheep's clothing as he warns Cecilia about.

Scarcely has Cecilia entered the Harrels' London house when she is led into a magnificently dressed company (another framing scene), where once more she becomes the unwilling center of attention. With complete disregard for her individuality, the women inventory the visitor's dress while the men debate whether or not she paints. Especially threatening is the attention of Sir Robert Floyer, for whom she becomes "the object of . . . attention, though neither with the look of admiration due to her beauty, nor yet with that of curiosity excited by her novelty, but with the scrutinizing observation of a man on the point of making a bargain, who views with fault-seeking eyes the property he means to cheapen" (31). Only later does Cecilia learn that Sir Robert's consumerism has in a way been legitimized by Mr. Harrel, who has agreed to broker her marriage to Floyer in return for his financial assistance.

By far the most interesting of Burney's framing scenes is the Harrels' masquerade, a set piece, as Terry Castle observes, that functions as a prolepsis for the remainder of the novel. The heroine, herself neither costumed nor masked, attracts by her novelty a group of admirers, each of whom reveals by his dress the role he will play: "Sir Robert Floyer, the lascivious suitor . . . is a Turk; Belfield, the dilettante poet, is a hapless, *raffiné* Don Quixote. Mr. Gosport . . . who becomes Cecilia's instructor in social etiquette, is a schoolteacher." Castle suggests in *Masquerade and Civilization* that Burney's masked ball externalizes the "fantasy of autonomy with which Burney's novel itself begins," a dream that both author and heroine must divest themselves of in the end.[8] Thus Castle argues that Burney's masquerade is a gynesium tragically unfulfilled by the novel's conclusion, in which the author sublimates her reactionary theme, having Cecilia give up the title *heiress* for that of *wife*.[9]

But Castle's interpretation falls short in two important respects. First, because she reads the masquerade as gynesium, a space of female freedom, Castle ignores the claustrophobic and dreamlike disruption, both of self-determination and of expression, that so strongly marks Cecilia's experience at the ball. Second, because she views the contest between individual and society solely through a matrix of patriarchal terms (fortune and name), Castle sees Cecilia's marriage as a tragic and complete capitulation to male power structures.

Granted, both literally and tropically, masquerades are spaces of freedom, but I would point out that these are freedoms Burney's heroine is unable to share. A guest in the Harrels' house, she has followed her friend's counsel that ladies at home need not wear costumes. As a consequence, the social scene is fraught with difficulties for Burney's heroine, who stands exposed, as Kristina Straub has noted—an easy target in a dangerous game whose rules she does not understand: "In one sense, the dress of these masks is an indicator of real identity, but the fact that costume may be directly or inversely related to character underscores the arbitrary logic of the code."[10]

But Cecilia's lack of freedom must be read as something more, I suggest, than mere naiveté or awkwardness. Again and again in the novel, external forces combine to suppress the least sign of individuality in Burney's heroine. Thus, for example, at the same time that she is signalized by the fact that she wears neither mask nor costume, Cecilia is also isolated, and virtually silenced by the first mask to approach her, who "seemed to have nothing less in view than preventing the approach of every other: yet had he little reason to hope for favor for himself, as the person he represented, of all others least alluring to the view, was the devil" (103). From Cecilia's point of view, then, the salient experience of the masquerade is not freedom but frustration, for though the devil's domination is temporarily interrupted by a Don Quixote, he soon returns to growl at her feet until an accident to the colored lanterns precipitates the guests' departure. Ironically, the devil (Monckton in disguise) forwards the very thing he wishes to prevent; his acts of circumscription not only encourage general attention to Cecilia but may be credited with initiating Delvile's courtship.

Far from the carnivalesque freedom of the world upside down that Terry Castle intimates, the masquerade is to Burney's heroine a series of encroachments on her personal liberty, verbal as well as physical. Monckton's mute anguish, brandished wand, and bestial growling interrupt Cecilia's conversations, so that she responds gratefully when a white domino (Delvile) frees her: "I was so tired of confinement, that my mind seemed almost as little at liberty as my person" (108). In another instance, it is Mr. Briggs's approach that prevents Cecilia's speech. Dressed as a sooty chimney sweep, Briggs threatens to pop her into his bag. He warns, "Never set your heart on a fine outside, nothing within" (114). Not only is her conversation with the "white domino" (the younger Delvile) frequently interrupted, but Cecilia finds herself at a loss for words to explain either the fiend's groveling attention or Mr. Briggs's self-appointed role as marriage broker.

Here and elsewhere in the novel, the author draws attention to language as a medium of power; the social initiate Cecilia seems always to owe a debt she cannot pay, to feel a lack she cannot recoup, to suffer an aphonia. Margaret Doody notes that Burney is "one of the first novelists to see that each person is the bearer or representative of what Marxist critics have taught us to call an 'ideology.' "[11] Repeatedly, the reader's attention is drawn to conversations that shape Cecilia's growing understanding of London society. Language may be used to falsify, as in the case of a minor character who salts his speech with French phrases: "I was quite *au despoir* that I could not have the honour of sliding in; I did *mon possible*, but it was quite beyond me" (129). Or conversation may bind one into tedious listening, as when Mr. Arnott persists in talking about their childhood long after Cecilia feels the subject exhausted, or when Miss Larolles impertinently rattles on about her social engagements and wardrobe. Most fashionable among Cecilia's acquaintances is the ennuyé Mr. Meadows, who, Miss Larolles explains for her benefit, can hardly be brought to speak at all: "I assure you sometimes I expect to see him fall fast asleep while I am talking to him, for he is so immensely absent he don't hear one half that one says" (128).

On the whole, Cecilia finds social conversation mundane and trivial. Unable to hear the vocalists at the opera, for instance, she turns to a nearby party of ladies, but gains "nothing but descriptions of trimmings, and complaints of hair-dressers, hints of conquest that teemed with vanity, and histories of engagements which were inflated with exultation" (130). Her next move lodges her behind a party of young men, whose rapt attention holds only for the dancers; after they have left the stage, the young rakes discuss the marriageable women seated about them, in such terms that "their language was ambiguous, and . . . unintelligible: their subjects . . . required some discretion, being nothing less than a ludicrous calculation of the age and duration of jointured widows, and of the chances and expecta-tions of unmarried young ladies" (130). Vain and conniving, language in the novel generally functions as a medium of social corruption, and Burney distinguishes for the reader's notice few characters who speak selflessly, among them Mr. Gosport, Cecilia, the younger Del-vile, and the railleur Mr. Albany.

Cecilia is especially at a disadvantage when negotiating with her guardians and suitors. Thus, when she thinks of taking asylum with Mr. Briggs after her initial disgust with the spendthrift Harrels, she hesitates, "unable to devise any answer," while the lower-class Briggs complains about her "pretty guardian master Harrel" and "old Don Puffabout," Mr. Delvile. When he asks, "Well, my duck, got ever a sweet-heart yet?" he refuses to credit her denial: "all a fib! better speak out: come, fit I should know; an't you my own ward? to be sure almost of age, but not quite, so what's that to me?" (91). Similarly, Mr. Delvile repeatedly demands explanations to which he will not listen. He en-quires about the opera-house dispute between two of her suitors and then refuses to believe her denial that she favors either, though Cecilia "again assured him he had been misinformed; and was again, though discredited, praised for her modesty" (147). Impenetrable, the au-thoritative discourse of her guardians is exposed as self-aggrandizing, patronizing, and, as far as Cecilia is concerned, repressive of any attempt to define herself as an individual.

The effect of male discourse is particularly insidious in Harrel's attempts to broker Cecilia's marriage to Sir Robert. Her guardian's language approaches the active evil of the seducer or rapist as he tries to circumvent Cecilia's denials with persuasion: "With much raillery, he denied the assertion credit, assuring her that he [Sir Robert] was universally admired by the ladies, that she could not possibly receive a more honourable offer, and that he was reckoned by everybody the finest gentleman about town. His fortune, he added, was equally unexceptionable with his figure and his rank in life; all the world, he was certain, would approve the connection, and the settlement made upon her should be dictated by herself" (156). When she persistently refuses Sir Robert, Harrel employs an argument that normal socialization would ill equip a woman to resist; he claims that the marriage is "universally expected." That failing, he resorts to outright duplicity, assuring Sir Robert the match is made while avoiding all conversation with Cecilia.

In recalling Cecilia's paralysis and aphonia, her recurrent inability to act and speak for herself, one should not neglect to mention by way of contrast Burney's matriarch, Mrs. Delvile, whose choric voice is one among few that sanction Cecilia's cautious moves toward self-sufficiency and self-determination. From the first, Mrs. Delvile is Cecilia's friend. During her initial recoil from the Harrels' giddy life, while Cecilia is visiting the Delviles, she confides to Mrs. Delvile that she wishes to be mistress of her own time and society. Sympathetic, the older woman explains the practical difficulties in such a scheme: "I find few who have any power to give me entertainment, and even of those few, the chief part have in their manners, situation, or characters, an unfortunate *something*, that generally renders a near connection with them inconvenient or disagreeable. . . . Yet to live wholly alone is cheerless and depressing" (229-30).

Margaret Doody correctly identifies Mrs. Delvile as an ambivalent character caught, for a time, between patriarchal and feminist motives. With her husband (who is also her cousin) she shares a pride in family name; with Cecilia she finally comes to share a belief that parental authority should not bar young people from seeking partners after their own hearts. In fact, it is possible to read Mrs. Delvile as embodying the kind of conflict among subject positions that Paul Smith, in *Discerning the Subject*, imagines as a source for feminist resistance. Because "patriarchy has defined and placed women as the other," when "women begin to speak and act from the same ground of cerned subjectivity and identity as men have traditionally enjoyed, a resistance is automatically effected." As Smith points out, then, the failure to accord women full subjecthood automatically renders female speech a form of resistance.

In the process of critiquing contemporary Marxist theory, Smith observes that it has not reckoned with the significance of individual experience, from which "purposive intervention into social formations" may be said to originate. Resistance, Smith argues, begins with "the subject/individual's history," a history "not exclusively determined by class or class membership."[12] In the case of Burney's ambivalent character Mrs. Delvile, this model goes a long way toward explaining not only her apparent inconsistencies, but also why the author herself considered the conflict scene involving Cecilia, Mrs. Delvile, and her son so important. Mrs. Delvile's initial strength in the patriarchal cause leads to her bursting a blood vessel and eventually to her becoming an advocate for Delvile and Cecilia against her prideful husband. As Margaret Doody so clearly demonstrates, it is Mrs. Delvile's personal disappointment within her own patriarchally-determined marriage that leads to her own change of heart, and, ultimately, to her separation from her husband.

From Cecilia's position, too, the issue of marriage involves role conflict and resistance to patriarchy. Initially, when the Delviles refuse permission for their son's marriage, Cecilia is coaxed into a clandestine ceremony by Delvile's assertion that "no law, human or divine, can be injured by our union, when one motive of pride is all that can be opposed to a thousand motives of convenience and happiness, why should we *both* be made unhappy, merely lest that pride should lose its gratification?" (560). The law to which Delvile refers is Hardwicke's Act, which presumably they will circumvent by obtaining a special license. Yet almost immediately Cecilia regrets the decision, recalling the requirements of filial obedience and female decorum: "Her consent to a clandestine action she lamented as an eternal blot to her character, and the undoubted publication of that consent as equally injurious to her fame" (607). Significantly and ominously, the scene leading to this first wedding returns to the imagery of the masquerade (to the conflict among the roles), when Cecilia's secret journey into town is discovered by Miss Larolles and a party of friends who suspect a disguised man seen scouting their party to be Delvile. Just as at the masquerade, Cecilia's conversations with Delvile once more suffer interruptions, this time by Morrice, Monckton's agent. Finally, when the clandestine wedding is broken off, Cecilia insists on a new condition, a stipulation that emphasizes the question of female authority lying at the heart of this novel: she will not marry Delvile without his mother's permission.

In an interim period of separation, Cecilia comes into her majority, discharges her guardians, takes up residence in her own house, and begins a program of charities directed by the benevolent railleur, Mr. Albany. As Terry Castle observes, the modern reader cannot help regretting that Cecilia's independence is so short-lived, that just as she has come into her own, Delvile again arrives to propose marriage, this time with his mother's "separate" consent (if Cecilia will give up her name and her uncle's fortune, they may be married).

Even with Mrs. Delvile's approval, however, their clandestine marriage is shown to be problematic when the next heir, hearing that Cecilia has forfeited her uncle's fortune, turns her out of the estate: "Her situation . . . was singularly unhappy, since, by this unforeseen vicissitude of fortune, she was suddenly, from being an object of envy and admiration, sunk into distress, and threatened with disgrace; from being everywhere caressed, and by everyone praised, she blushed to be seen, and expected to be censured; and, from being generally regarded as an example of happiness, and a model of virtue, she was now in one moment to appear to the world, an outcast from her own house, yet received into no other! a bride, unclaimed by a husband! an *HEIRESS*, dispossessed of all wealth!" (848). Burney's description emphasizes the ephemeral nature of the social role Cecilia has held, while at the same time measuring the effects of social and material loss she suffers.

Circumstances continue to combine against Cecilia, when, believing that Delvile has left the country to avoid prosecution (after wounding Monckton in a duel), she seeks advice from their friend Mr. Belfield. Meanwhile, Delvile also visits Mr. Belfield's room, and, misconstruing his wife's presence there, leaves enraged. This last misunderstanding is more trauma than Burney's strong heroine can endure. Turned away from the elder Delvile's door, she spends most of the night searching London for his son, finally giving way to hysteria when a usurious coachman holds her arm, demanding payment: "This moment, for the unhappy Cecilia, teemed with calamity; she was wholly overpowered; terror for Delville, horror for herself, hurry, confusion, heat and fatigue, all assailing her at once, while all means of repelling them were denied her, the attack was too strong for her fears, feelings, and faculties, and her reason suddenly, yet totally failing her, she madly called out, 'He will be gone! he will be gone! and I must follow him to Nice!' " (874-75).

Burney dwells on the emotional and physical claustrophobia of the heroine's situation, as, running through the streets, Cecilia tears herself from those who catch at her riding dress and, eventually exhausted, staggers into an open shop. There, however, she becomes prey to another kind of exchange, when the proprietor—believing her escaped from a private mad house—holds her for a reward. By the time an ad is placed in the paper, Cecilia's desperation has become frenzy: "Whereas a crazy young lady, tall, fair complexioned, with blue eyes and light hair, ran into the Three Blue Balls, in —— street, on Thursday night, the 2d instant, and has been kept there since out of charity. She was dressed in a riding habit. Whoever she belongs to is desired to send after her immediately" (879-80). Posted from the pawn shop, the reductive personal advertisement, an inverted blazon, marks the heroine's fall from individuality into an amnesia, a complete lack of self-knowledge. The experience of self-alienation is common to all of Burney's novels after *Evelina*, remarks Kristina Straub: "A moment comes in the course of the heroine's troubled romance when the familial, sexual, and social pressures of her attempts to gain a just 'reading' culminate in a crisis of self-alienation."[13]

In this trajectory from disease to recovery, and in Cecilia's subsequent talking cure with Dr. Lyster, Burney's novel parallels Charlotte Lennox's *Female Quixote*, discussed earlier. There is, however, a significant difference between the two: although Cecilia, like Arabella, is repatriated into the community following a talking cure, Burney, unlike Lennox, continues to orchestrate the opposition between patriarchy and feminism in her conclusion. There, in crucial ways that Terry Castle does not mention, a feminist counterideology succeeds. Although Cecilia is at first all too willing to assume that filial disobedience was the source of their problems, she is corrected by Dr. Lyster, who traces Delvile and Cecilia's difficulties to patriarchal "PRIDE AND PREJUDICE": "Your uncle . . . began it, by his arbitrary will, as if an ordinance of his own could arrest the course of nature! and as if *he* had power to keep alive, by the loan of a name, a family in the male branch already extinct. Your father, Mr. Mortimer, continued it with the same self-partiality, preferring the wretched gratification of tickling his ear with a favourite sound, to the solid happiness of his son with a rich and deserving wife" (908).

Even their reconciliation with Delvile's parents, Lyster goes on to observe, is owing to pride and prejudice—Mr. Delvile's shame over his daughter-in-law's being lodged at a pawnbroker's. Castigating power, pride, and rhetoric—the terms of marriage exchange—Lyster champions affective individualism as natural for both sexes. One can measure the extraordinary appeal of this passage by the fact that Jane Austen borrowed from it the title and the sentiments for her most famous novel.

Indeed, given Mr. Delvile's position at the end of the novel, it is not possible to read his role as a triumphal one. After all, in marrying his son, Cecilia ignores his prohibition against the match. He also suffers a substantial loss of power when he receives Cecilia into his London house. As Dr. Lyster has predicted, moreover, the elder Delvile's pride turns him against his own former position, so that when the doctor praises Cecilia, Delvile grudgingly acknowledges her worth. Further, with Cecilia sitting primly beside her, Lady Honoria, Delvile's irrepressible niece, sabotages and disrupts her uncle's solemnity with various attacks against male prerogative. Her badinage against gloomy Delvile castle provokes only a feeble defense from him: "The estate which descends to a man from his own ancestors . . . will seldom be apt to injure his health, if he is conscious of committing no misdemeanour which has degraded their memory" (911). To Cecilia she addresses *sotto voce* advice on annulling her marriage

and taking another suitor, and when Cecilia rallies her on her principles, Lady Honoria maintains that a woman's principles do not sig-
nify in the marriage contract: "Not a creature thinks of our principles,
till they find them out by our conduct: and nobody can possibly do
that till we are married, for they give us no power beforehand. The
men know nothing of us in the world while we are single, but how
we can dance a minuet, or play a lesson upon the harpsichord" (912).
When Mr. Delvile, overhearing part of this speech, responds that a
young lady of condition, having a proper sense of her own dignity,
"cannot be seen too rarely, or known too little," she retorts satirically:
"O, but I hate dignity! . . . for it's the dullest thing in the world. I
always thought it was owing to that you were so little amusing" (913).

There is of course some truth in Terry Castle's remark that Burney's conclusion is problematic for modern readers (270), for while
we appreciate the author's gestures of travesty toward Mr. Delvile's
dignified stasis, we regret that he is so little altered by the attacks
made against him. Even though he has had to make some concessions
to nature, to Delvile's and Cecilia's love for each other, the elder Delvile persists unregenerate in his authoritarian and mercantile rhetoric.
His wholly inadequate reading of their relationship is that his son has
lost his chance to marry an heiress while Cecilia has made a good
bargain in choosing his noble family over her fortune. Nonetheless,
even though he is never brought to appreciate the affective grounds
for his son's marriage, Delvile's authority is clearly diminished by the
end of the novel. Perhaps, in eighteenth-century terms, Burney has
gone far enough. In some measure, the implicit promise of masquerade has been fulfilled; patriarchal authority, if not quite overturned, has definitely been unsettled.

PART IV

Educational Reform

NINE

Richardson and Wollstonecraft
THE "LEARNED LADY" AND
THE NEW HEROINE

ALTHOUGH at one point in his *Sermons to Young Women* (1766), James Fordyce assures his readers that there is no such thing as a learned lady—he has never seen one—pages later he applauds the advantages of women's "Mental Improvements": "to adorn and animate the companion, to direct and dignify the mistress, to accomplish the mother and the friend, to spread a charm over the whole matrimonial state, and to relieve those duller hours that are apt to steal on the most delightful condition of humanity."[1] It was at once within and against such apparently contradictory advice as Fordyce's that eighteenth- and early nineteenth-century feminism advanced the call for better education—a broadly based proposal that was not confined to educational tracts but made its way into novels as well.

In this period, women's education was founded on a patchwork of contrasting theories, culled from the wealth of sources available: Classical, Dutch, French, and British.[2] Some conservative educators, perhaps encouraged by Castiglione's courtly woman and her social graces or by Montaigne's idealization of wifely companionship, still emphasized "fashionable education." Boarding schools were often primarily concerned with the externals, "instruction in the social graces and such ladylike pastimes as embroidery and needlework."[3] Even good boarding schools might have superficial curricula, as Phyllis Stock explains. They taught "religion; belles-lettres (some history, geography, biography, natural history, astronomy, poetry, painting, sculpture, architecture, travel stories)" but also "accomplishments" such as "needlework, embroidery, drawing, music, dancing, dress, politeness," and offered "training in manners."[4]

It was in the latter part of the eighteenth century that Rousseau's *Émile* (1762) promoted revolutionary changes in male education; in the future, a student's natural genius was to determine his course of study. But for women, Rousseau proposed nothing really new—his

Émile merely giving fresh impetus to instruction in the social graces. Reasoning that "men's morals, their passions, their tastes, their pleasures, their very happiness" depends on women, Rousseau argued that "the whole education of women ought to relate to men."[5] He defined woman's nature, remarks Susan Moller Okin, "in terms of her function—that is her sexual and procreative purpose in life," and woman as mistress and breeder had little need of books.[6] Rousseau's prescriptions for women were no more progressive than Fordyce's, no less concerned with socializing women to accept subordinate roles within marriage. Over a decade later John Gregory's similarly conservative advice also achieved wide popularity. In *A Father's Legacy* (1774), Gregory cautioned his own daughters against challenging male power preserves, warning them to keep their learning "a profound secret, especially from the men, who generally look with a jealous and malignant eye on a woman of great parts, and a cultivated understanding."[7] His express concern was that education prepare his daughters for marriage, and that undue refinement—reading and conversation that warmed the imagination, softened the heart, and raised the taste above the common level—could make a woman unhappy in her marital lot.

Against such conservatism there arose advocates for educational reform, initially from Richardson's immediate circle and from the Bluestockings, and, by the turn of the century, from Mary Wollstonecraft's group.[8] Interestingly, some forty years before Wollstonecraft's *A Vindication of the Rights of Woman* (1792) polemicized the issue, Richardson himself challenged the notion of relative education in *Sir Charles Grandison* (1753). Engaging her suitors in a drawing-room debate, Harriet Byron expresses her doubts about the validity of using ancient languages as a measure of good education for either sex. Despite her determination to avoid public confrontation—she "would rather . . . be an hearer than a speaker"—there are compelling reasons for reading Richardson's heroine as outlining a progressive position in relation to women's education.[9] First, her theorizing broaches male territorial imperative, and her questioning the utility of "ancient languages" challenges what had long been a distinguishing factor between male and female education. Beyond demonstrating his own feminist sympathies, the rhetorical space Richardson opens for his heroine in this drawing-room debate is symptomatic of what Nancy Armstrong terms a general increase in attention to feminine authority. This was particularly true among novelists, observes Armstrong, because they chose a language of affect associated with moral superiority—thereby rejecting affiliation with Latin, a sexually-specialized language used in male communication.[10] Such authors as Defoe and

Richardson rejected the elitist male position Latin implied, at the same time finding, through courtship and marriage, a means of "talking about conflict and contradiction within the socioeconomic sphere while remaining remote from that world."[11]

A second way in which Richardson's heroine is progressive is that by questioning whether ancient languages are a measure of good education for either sex she suggests a radical egalitarianism, a companionate relationship between equals. From the author's management of the scene, moreover, it seems clear that Richardson endorses his heroine's position. Her Uncle Reeves sanctions Harriet's participation in the debate—initially, by forcing her to argue independently and later by taking her side. When she withdraws from the conflict, Reeves comes to her defense, citing Bishop Burnet's opinion that Latin literature, though noble in thought and sentiment, need not be read in the original if a young man has an adversion to or difficulty with the language. Reeves reminds Harriet's adversary that Locke himself does not enforce a language difference between male and female education: "So far from discouraging the fair sex from learning languages . . . [he] gives us a method in his Treatise of Education, by which a mother may not only learn Latin herself, but be able to teach it to her *son*" (1:59).

Finally, Reeves confronts the unspoken question before Harriet and her suitors—whether a well-educated woman is marriageable— by affirming that in his opinion, "the more a woman knows, as well as a man, the wiser she will generally be; and the more regard she will have for a man of sense and learning." Reeves/Richardson summarizes a nuanced position: women should not be "ashamed either of your talents or acquirements. Only take care, you give not up any knowledge that is more laudable in your sex . . . for learning; and then I am sure, you will, you *must* , be the more agreeable, the more suitable companions to men of sense" (59). In other words, by suggesting a democratization of intellectual discourse, Reeves/Richardson employs a logical and forward-thinking means for enabling companionate relationships between wives and husbands. Thus, muffling his progressive words with cautions and still implying relative positions for women ("companions to men of sense"), Richardson nonetheless anticipates many of the issues that would be raised again by Wollstonecraft at the end of the century.

If, despite the brevity of her career and frequent negligencies of her style, Mary Wollstonecraft has assumed an eminent position in turn-of-the-century literature, it is not solely because her biography and polemics make fascinating reading, but also because, to an even

greater degree than her predecessor Richardson, she unerringly penetrates and exposes male power structures, challenging the "authoritative" or patriarchal word through which women are socialized.
Unlike Richardson, Wollstonecraft recognized that sensibility, often
exalted as woman's psychological birthright, could also be castigated
as her besetting flaw. Signally important in her first novel *Mary* (1788),
the collocation thinking/feeling reappears some five years later in a
novel attributed to Gilbert Imlay, an American with whom Wollstonecraft was having an affair. This coincidence is one of several facts that
argues for including *The Emigrants* (1793) in Wollstonecraft's corpus.[12]
Making occasional references to her other works, this section will
examine the way Wollstonecraft polemicizes the issues of educational
reform and affective liberation in *Mary* and in *The Emigrants*.

Wollstonecraft's first novel makes a significant departure from the
contemporary pattern for heroine-centered fiction because, rather
than an ingenue finding personal happiness and social integration
through courtship, *Mary* outlines the growing awareness, the affective
individualism, of a woman trapped in a loveless marriage. In this
sense *Mary* belongs to the category of texts Nancy Miller describes
as dysphoric.[13] Wollstonecraft's preface acknowledges the novel's difference, challenging the reader to accept a new heroine, "neither a
Clarissa, a Lady G——, nor a Sophie." In her words, "the mind of a
woman who has thinking powers is displayed. The female organs
have been thought too weak for this arduous employment. . . . in a
fiction, such a being may be allowed to exist."[14] Despite the author's
apparently rebellious posture, her novel nonetheless ends with its
heroine still subject to a patriarchally arranged marriage—a fact, Mary
Poovey alleges, that does not argue for a complete overthrow of "the
romantic expectations which eighteenth-century bourgeois society
annexed to female sexuality."[15]

Yet while she never completely breaks from the generic boundaries of her time, Wollstonecraft seems to insinuate that women's only
hope is a revolutionary assertion of their intellectual and affective
rights. To that end, she introduces the main plot with an unusually
long description of the heroine's mother—a negative exemplum of
miseducation from which Mary's own upbringing diverges in ways
as fortunate as they are haphazard. As a girl, the mother was gentle,
fashionable,

with a kind of indolence in her temper, which might be termed negative good-
nature: her virtues, indeed, were all of that stamp. She carefully attended to
the *shews* of things, and her opinions, I should have said prejudices, were

such as the generality approved of. She was educated with the expectation of a large fortune, of course became a mere machine: the homage of her attendants made a great part of her puerile amusements, and she never imagined there were any relative duties for her to fulfil . . . and the years of youth spent in acquiring a few superficial accomplishments, without having any taste for them. When she was first introduced into the polite circle, she danced with an officer, whom she faintly wished to be united to; but her father soon after recommending another in a more distinguished rank of life, she readily submitted to his will, and promised to love, honour, and obey, (a vicious fool), as in duty bound. [1]

Wollstonecraft's language, borrowing from the early days of the Industrial Revolution, objectifies the human being, who is miseducated until she becomes a "mere machine," incapable of feeling or thinking for herself.

In this first novel, as in the later ones, Wollstonecraft shapes her heroine as an individual isolated by unusual ideological affiliations. Thus Mary owes not only her Rousseauistic education, her developed intellect, and her heightened sensibility, but also her natural religion to parental neglect. "Sensibility prompted her to search for an object to love" (5), and not finding it in her parents, she looked to Heaven. It is because she escapes the kind of fashionable training her mother had and is formed instead by haphazard childhood experiences that Mary avoids the conventional female roles, becoming instead an individual who can both think and feel.

Wollstonecraft's first heroine exemplifies the conflicts that will characterize her later ones. Initially, the fact that Mary is a "feeling and thinking" woman contributes to her victimization, but eventually it will cause her to recoil from her societally prescribed role. On the one hand, Mary's father takes advantage of her emotions at her mother's deathbed to force her into a loveless but prudent match with her cousin. Quite literally, Mary is "exchanged," the sole purpose of the marriage being to resolve an estate litigation with another branch of the family. On the other hand, the author measures Mary's strength by contrast with minor female characters whose less fortunate educations have done nothing but prepare them for such a fate. As a victim of fashionable education, Mary's mother, for instance, lacks sufficient mettle either to marry for love, to meet life's difficulties, or to accept with proper gravity the fact of her approaching death.

No better equipped are three women Mary meets at the invalid hotel where she goes to nurse an ailing friend. They have learned languages and music, but all is "words, words, words": "Without having any seeds sown in their understanding, or the affections of the heart set to work, they were brought out of their nursery, or the place they were secluded in, to prevent their faces being common: like blazing stars, to captivate Lords" (24). Bound by propriety and self-objectification, they imitate their kinswoman, a countess, around whom they move as satellites.

Thus, throughout the novel, Wollstonecraft carries a double ideological burden, criticizing fashionable education, which weakens or fails to develop the intellect, while at the same time applauding feminine sensibility.[16] Mary Poovey regards the task Wollstonecraft sets herself—to reconcile intellect and affect, polemics and sentimentalism—as an impossible one. According to Poovey, the difficulty is that Wollstonecraft's "political insights and the sentimental structure" she employs are at odds: "For those 'finer sensations'—and the sentimental genre in which they were characteristically enshrined—were deeply implicated in the very values of bourgeois society which Wollstonecraft wanted to criticize."[17] In other words, the author is implicated in the ideology she tries to escape. Poovey goes on to argue that sentimental fiction serves the needs of the male hegemony even while it seems to offer the woman an escape (via passion) into individuality. Poovey's point is well taken, and her argument accommodates some of the perplexed strategies of Wollstonecraft's novel, but, on the whole, she does not sufficiently acknowledge the resistance of the heroine who, even while she more or less passively suffers its effects, has a full appreciation of her objectified position. It is *as women* that Wollstonecraft's women suffer like martyrs for the cause: Mary in her loveless marriage, Maria in meeting the "dogs of law" and (according to the fragmentary conclusion) deciding to live for her unborn child. This pattern continues, as I will demonstrate, with the effects of Lady B——'s love for P.P. in *The Emigrants*. It is in the Wollstonecraftian woman's resistance to female socialization, in her refusal to accede to feminine decorums, that one finds the author's most feminist statements.

When, for example, Mary blurts out the true state of her affections, she shocks the fashionably educated women at the invalid hotel: " 'I cannot live without her!—I have no other friend; if I lose her what a desart will the world be to me.' 'No other friend,' re-echoed they, 'have you not a husband?' " (26). Mary's *crie de coeur* exposes her societally sanctioned arranged marriage for the sham that it is, and though she understands her own impropriety and shrinks from replying, the force of her outburst is not neutralized by the authoritative word "husband" and she does not retract what she has said.

In a later scene, Wollstonecraft once more urges the importance of affect, this time emblematically, by having Henry (another resident at the invalid hotel) ask for Mary's picture, "with the expression I have seen in your face, when you have been supporting your friend." The tribute—to feeling rather than beauty, to sympathy rather than proprietorship, contrasts painfully with Mary's memories of her earlier portrait. She "recollected that she had once sat for her picture—for whom was it designed? For a boy! Her cheeks flushed with indignation, so strongly did she feel an emotion of contempt at having been thrown away—given in with an estate" (28). Retrospectively, Mary understands that her first portrait merely represented in material form her own objectification within patriarchal exchange.

Significantly, Wollstonecraft permits Mary no facile solutions; she does not back away from the contradictions implied in her feeling/thinking heroine. When Mary falls in love with Henry and begins to regret the lost opportunity of conjugal love, she may bend decorum in nursing Henry during his final illness, but she may not break through the strictures against physical infidelity to her husband. Ultimately—and it is here that Poovey faults Wollstonecraft for wavering in her radical experiment—Mary must defer to social requirements and agree to live with her husband. Poovey's reading overlooks the fact that, while Wollstonecraft refuses to deny the social realities of her age, at the same time she emphasizes Mary's passive and internal resistance: "When her husband would take her hand, or mention anything like love, she would instantly feel a sickness, a faintness at her heart, and wish, involuntarily, that the earth would open and swallow her" (67). Wollstonecraft's concluding sentence allows no real answer but death: "Her delicate state of health did not promise long life. In moments of solitary sadness, a gleam of joy would dart across her mind—she thought she was hastening to a world *where there is neither marrying*, nor giving in marriage" (68).

Like the hero of Sterne's *Sentimental Journey*, Mary experiences a progress in sensibility, but that journey is also a progress in understanding her societally defined role. Beyond the novel's liberal insistence on woman's right to develop her capacity as a thinking, feeling individual, however, the novel is equivocal, implying that, regardless of her inevitable misery, it is preferable that a woman acceed to the conditions under which she lives, even while she fully understands and deplores them. Like Werther, Wollstonecraft's heroine experiences the truth that to live is to suffer. 245645

Given the implicit radicalism of her first novel, it should not surprise us that Wollstonecraft responded as she did five years later to Bishop Talleyrand-Perigord's plan for educational reform. In *A Vindication of the Rights of Woman*, Wollstonecraft demanded that the good bishop reconsider "respecting the rights of woman and national education."[18] Actually, she was simply following the British pastime of sympathizing with and analyzing the Revolution—in her case, protesting Talleyrand's oversight in not proposing equal education for women. She argued that if men were despotic, reserving all the power and responsibility to themselves, they surely could expect no more than that women should act like slaves. Wollstonecraft's proposal, decidedly tame by today's standards, went no further than Locke in suggesting that women be fitted by good education for their important (albeit still relative) roles as companions to their husbands and educators of their children.

The goal Wollstonecraft advanced seems modest, but both her analysis of woman's condition and the language in which she phrased her argument were so inflammatory that the resulting flurry of publications in the nineties has been given the name "Feminist Controversy." Education, she observed, was essential to independence, for without it, men could maintain power over women by degrading their minds; "like the flowers which are planted in too rich a soil, strength and usefulness are sacrificed to beauty." This "barren blooming" begins in "a false system of education, gathered from the books written on this subject by men who, considering females rather as women than human creatures, have been more anxious to make them alluring mistresses than affectionate wives and rational mothers" (73). The author opposes the terms "alluring mistresses" to "affectionate wives" and "rational mothers," gesturing toward a basic incongruence between objectification and her conception of the individuated (thinking/feeling) woman. In important ways, Wollstonecraft's analysis of woman's objectification within phallocentric society anticipates modern feminist theory. To phrase this central idea of Wollstonecraft's *Vindication* in Lacanian terms, one can say that because the dominant discourse is phallocentric, and because within that discourse woman is always signified, never signifier, women's individuation is problematic.[19]

It was almost a year after *A Vindication of the Rights of Woman* was published that Wollstonecraft finally traveled to Paris, arriving in time to see Louis XVI taken to prison. During her residence in France, she had an affair with Gilbert Imlay, an American who sheltered her from arrest and remained with her until their daughter Fanny (half-sister of Mary Wollstonecraft Shelley) was born in 1794. Wollstonecraft's relationship with Imlay becomes particularly interesting when one considers *The Emigrants*, the novel published under his name in 1793. As Robert R. Hare argues in his introduction to the 1964 reprint, there is ample reason to doubt Imlay's authorship; the novel is suspiciously feminist and revolutionary in its principles, principles Imlay is not known to have held. The preface offers a case in point, sympathizing with "the miseries of individuals" and making defensive references to the problems women face: "I have no doubt but the many misfortunes which daily happen in domestic life, and which too often precipitate women of the most virtuous inclinations into the gulf of ruin, proceed from the great difficulty there is in England, of obtaining a divorce. Those who have paid a superficial regard to this subject, will be of a different opinion" (v-vi). Beyond the presence of his name on the title page, there is no other evidence that Imlay, an American soldier and land speculator, had any literary talent or that he would have concerned himself with British women and divorce law. *The Emigrants, &c. or the History of An Expatriated Family, Being a Delineation of English Manners, Drawn from Real Characters, Written in America* is more domestic story than travel tale, more courtship novel than generalized novel of manners, facts that argue for Wollstonecraft's authorship, or at least her extensive collaboration in this epistolary novel.

The strong-willed woman struggling heroically against a male power structure is central to all of Wollstonecraft's novels, and to this pattern *The Emigrants* is no exception. Caroline T——n's mental and physical strength is demonstrated by the fact that she chooses to walk behind the wagons her family rides in as they move from Philadelphia to Pittsburgh. When Captain Arl——ton, joining them on the way, protests the walk is too fatiguing, Caroline first declines his assistance and then sets a brisk pace. She chooses to walk because "here is a continual feast for the mind—every rock, every tree, every moss, from their novelty afford subject for contemplation and amusement" (27). But he suspects that is not the only reason—that she is concerned for the horses which must pull the wagon uphill. In either case, the reader must interpret the incident in her favor, as a sign of her sensibility and her individuality.

In another instance, Caroline explains her interest in natural science, her words adumbrating a broader position statement in favor of improved education for women:

If the education of women have generally been so injudicious, as to prevent their extending their understanding beyond the common limits that custom has prescribed, doubtless it has been the material cause, why illiberal men have estimated our talents at so cheap a rate. For while we have been taught to talk of dress and the things of the day . . . few women have had strength of mind equal to burst the bands of prejudice, and soaring into the regions of science and nature, have shewn that comprehension of mind which gives a lustre and dignity to the human understanding. [91]

Her speech not only challenges the social constraints on women's education but also blames men whose prejudice confines women's speech to "dress and the things of the day." In effect, Wollstonecraft acknowledges the hegemonic confines of language, recognizing that in order to study or talk of science her heroine must "burst the bands of prejudice." What the author describes is Caroline's effort to seize authority, to penetrate what is usually a male verbal space.

This corrective in regard to women's education is not, however, the primary didactic burden of the novel but only a means to an end. Specifically, the burden of *The Emigrants* appears to be Wollstonecraft's (and/or Imlay's) interest in equitable reform of divorce laws. Acting as primary spokesman against the cooption of women's rights in marriage is the heroine's uncle P.P., whose amorous misfortunes are told in a long interpolation. Supposing that change must begin with education, P.P. adopts Rousseau's theory that for individual rights to be recognized, youth must first be taught social responsibility, and he suggests that from the amendment of men that of women will naturally follow. P.P.'s narrative affords some of the novel's most radical passages—a long story of his relationship with a married woman in which he calls for concerted reform of marriage laws. Somewhat laboriously, this radicalism is displaced from the heroine, who, reversing the usual positions of youth and age, judges her uncle's actions and voices society's disapproval of his unconventional behavior. Eventually, however, her uncle's account of the social persecution the couple undergoes brings even Caroline to agree that legal reform is needed.

As a young man waiting for preferment, Caroline's uncle had visited in the household of Lord B——, and while there found the nobleman kind to him but brutally cruel to his wife. In Lady B——'s words, her husband is "one of those extraordinary men, who considered women merely as a domestic machine, necessary only as they are an embellishment to their house, and the only means by which their family can be perpetuated" (111). He uses speech as a means of exerting his power, denying her personhood even at table. He speaks volubly,

upon the excellence of his dogs, the breed of his hunters, and the various pleasures that were to be derived from such manly amusements as coursing and hunting: and while the most interesting being in the world was again reduced to a cypher, if it is possible for love itself to be a cypher, I was forcibly struck with the contrast of ideas, between what was passing, and those of a charming woman, who added to a most lively sensibility, the most brilliant wit and captivating vivacity, which kindled into rapture the admiring senses; for she seemed to breath sentiment, talked like Minerva, and looked like the Queen of Beauty; so that my wonder was for a time suspended by my indignation, excited by the thought, that the prevalence of manners, should not only strike at the root of the colloquial happiness of rational beings, but which substituted the practice of *jejune*, and anomalous conversations, in the place of brilliancy of thought, and elegance of expression, and which imperceptibly, when fine women have their share of it, gives the most lovely polish to manners, and zest to the charms of society. [120]

Wollstonecraft's description idealizes Lady B—— as a woman who both thinks ("talked like Minerva") and feels ("most lively sensibility"). Her prose emphasizes the husband's mental cruelty, his denial of his wife's feelings and personhood, and the fact that society ("the prevalence of manners") sanctions his mistreatment of his wife.

Like the heroine of the novel, Lady B—— challenges the boundaries of her societally defined role. In her first act of resistance against a husband who comes to her "two hours after midnight in a state of intoxication," she decides "never to enter the bed of my Lord B—— again" (113)—thus responding on the physical level because that is the only means of communication her husband will allow her. Eventually, when he is faced with the possibility of leaving no heirs, Lord B—— enlists the law as his accomplice and makes a false accusation of adultery against his wife and P.P. Wollstonecraft's point, both in this interpolated history and in letters related to it is that a corrective is needed for the double standard that permits a man who seeks external comfort from an unfortunate marriage to do so with impunity, while a woman in the same situation invites social ruin.

Whether or not one accepts Wollstonecraft as the sole author of *The Emigrants*, it seems certain, given the strength of its feminist bent, that the novel was at least considerably informed by her interests, or more probably took shape in collaboration with Imlay. That it belongs to the tradition of heroine-centered courtship novels there can be no doubt. In this novel, as in the earlier *Mary*, education is viewed as a means to individuation, but it is too easily coopted by society, with the result that natural sensibility is made to serve patriarchal goals— woman is enslaved to a domestic tyrant. Arguably, in both Henry's and Lady B——'s deaths, one should read Wollstonecraft's capitulation to patriarchal society. But just beyond the grasp of Wollstonecraft's characters one senses a utopia where there would be no capitulation—an ideal space where thinking and feeling women could live happily ever after with the men of their choice.

TEN

Bluestockings, Amazons, Sentimentalists, and Fashionable Women

IF Mary Wollstonecraft stood as a symbol for female education and revolutionary idealism, she also represented in her personal life the worst fears of conservative writers—that education would emancipate women from socially prescribed roles and encourage their radicalism. The autobiographical content of her works heightened her mimetic appeal so that Wollstonecraftian characters populated contemporary novels. Yet, tainted by the social opprobrium surrounding the author's highly controversial life, these figures commonly were presented as negative exempla, patterns of the ills brought on when women rebelled.

The simplest reading of such negative exempla or "little histories" is that they gesture on the mnemonic level toward behavioral patterns to be avoided.[1] Usually, the female characters associated with a heroine are meant to be read, observes Mary Poovey, as "negative counterparts of the heroine's perfect qualities." But these doubles also may provide an opportunity "to play at different roles, to explore, often through the characters of servants or lower-class women, direct actions forbidden to the more proper lady."[2] Such groupings may include figures who act as surrogates for the heroine when the ideological field becomes too highly charged.

In other words, the strategy of the negative exemplum is multi-faceted, a gesture of containment and dispersal, of rejection and acceptance. On the one hand, the minor characters with whom I am concerned in this chapter—bluestockings, Amazons, sentimentalists, and fashionable women—dramatized the extremes to which female education could be taken. If, as Pierre Maranda hypothesizes, "acceptance is an outgrowth of narcissism," then it becomes crucial that a novelist not alienate her identificatory readers by radicalizing her heroine or, if she does (as in Wollstonecraft's case), that she make "poetic justice" reaffirm societal values. According to Pierre Maranda, an author must take into account the duality of interpretation, which accepts "what we recognize, while filtering out what is incompatible with our own semantic charter."[3] Thus, in a way that must have been reassuring to society, such negative exempla hedged against entropy. An author's depiction of an Amazon, then, could be read as part of her defense strategy against instability and disorder, a strategy that at least implicitly reaffirmed the hegemonic world view.

But there is more to these characters than a mere strategy of containment. As Michel Foucault explains in his rule of tactical polyvalence, allowance must be made "for the complex and unstable process whereby discourse can be both an instrument and an effect of power, but also a hindrance, a stumbling-block, a point of resistance and a starting point for an opposing strategy."[4] That is, insofar as Amazons, bluestockings, sentimentalists, and fashionable women could speak and act counterideologically, a novelist could convert the gestures of containment to her own purposes. Under cover of consolidating social rejection of certain subject positions—those of the bluestocking or the Amazon, then—an author could obtain a hearing for subversive or radical discourse that would otherwise be unspeakable to her constituency.

"All that a woman can learn . . . above the useful knowledge proper to her sex, let her learn."[5] Recalling Clarissa's words, Anna Howe praises her friend for having studied Latin before her death. Yet, concerned to hedge against misapprehensions, she also cites her friend's characterization of two negative types of female learning that may be termed the *bluestocking* and the *Amazon*. Thus, at about the same time as the real British *bas bleux* were beginning to meet for intellectual conversations between the sexes, Richardson's heroine was drafting what would turn out to be literary prototypes for the miseducated women who appeared as negative exempla in subsequent novels.

One negative type Clarissa described was the pedant or bluestocking, "fond of giving her opinion, in the company of her husband, and of his learned friends, upon doubtful passages in Virgil or Horace," but not knowing "how to put on her clothes with the necessary grace and propriety which should preserve to her the love of her husband and the respect of every other person" (4:496). Richardson endorses the received wisdom that excessive study promotes social idiosyncrasies—in this case, disruptions of male rhetoric or breaches of decorum in dress. His negative exemplum, by implicitly deflecting charges of pedantry from the heroine herself, at once marginalizes certain kinds of miseducation and justifies Clarissa's efforts toward intellectual improvement.

Often the pedant, like Clarissa's scholar who cannot dress herself, is only foolish and solipsistic, a social bore or naif. One of the most interesting and substantial examples appears in Fanny Burney's turn-of-the-century novel *Camilla* (1796). Influenced, no doubt, by Wollstonecraft's expanded treatment of childhood in *Mary* (1788), Burney begins her novel with several chapters detailing the childhood experiences of Camilla, her siblings, and her cousins. While visiting at her uncle's house, the heroine's sister Eugenia is crippled by a fall and scarred by smallpox, a double impairment that so works on their foolish uncle's conscience that he substitutes Eugenia's name for Camilla's in his will. Just as haphazardly determined is Eugenia's education, which is handed along as though it were an exchangeable commodity of low value. Initially, Sir Hugh employs a tutor for himself, but finding Latin beyond his own capacity, he transfers Dr. Orkeborne to the young people living with him—first to Lionel, who derives a false sense of his own superiority to his uncle; then to Indiana, who will not apply herself; and finally to Eugenia. From these details alone, it is apparent that Burney does not propose education as a general panacea.

Only after this considerable effort to distance herself from a radical encouragement of female learning does the author begin to allow that circumstances have made Eugenia an ideal student: "She had now acquired a decided taste for study, which, however unusual for her age, most fortunately rescued from weariness or sadness the sedentary life, which a weak state of health compelled her to lead. . . . But neither disease nor accident had power over her mind; there, in its purest proportions, moral beauty preserved its first energy. The equanimity of her temper made her seem, though a female, born to be a practical philosopher; her abilities and her sentiments were each of the highest class, uniting the best adorned intellects with the best principled virtues."[6] But while her studies enable Eugenia to bear the isolation of physical deformity in a world that overvalues female beauty, they turn out to be an equivocal blessing, disqualifying her for society.

To understand that Eugenia is doubly marginalized by her pocked face and her reputation as a scholar is not, however, to account altogether for our fascination with her, for the fact that she comes near to supplanting Camilla in our affections. While we may read Burney's pedant as a strategy of containment, a negative exemplum against female pedantry, circumstances in the novel so underscore her position that she challenges Camilla's centrality. Granted, Burney has gathered a cluster of foils about her heroine (Lavinia, Indiana, Mrs. Berlinton, Lady Isabella, and Eugenia herself), but she has made Eugenia a similar nexus among the scholars and readers in the novel. This prismatic effect brings to bear the reader's evaluations of Dr. Orkeborne as a type of plodding pedantry; Mrs. Berlinton and her brother Melmont as indulgers in the literature of sensibility; and Dr. Marchmont as an ideal scholar whose sole flaw is his embittered distrust of women.

If the heroine's mistakes originate in hasty judgment and apparent lack of maturity, Eugenia's derive from a habitual deference, a reliance on the truth of the word as it is presented to her. Although she is textually proficient, Eugenia, as a reader of the world, is no more adept than her sister, so that when Camilla asks for her advice, Eugenia characteristically returns unmediated the word of authority. She naively agrees, for instance, with the plan Miss Margland hopes will bring Edgar Mandelbert around to proposing marriage to her favorite, Indiana—that Camilla should prove her disinterest in Edgar by avoiding him and resisting his advice. Her reading of the love letter Sir Sedley sends to Camilla depends on a similar rhetorical credulity: the terms "*fetters, captive,* and *insensible,* satisfied the heroic Eugenia that Sir Sedley deserved the hand of her sister" (530). In like fashion, Eugenia is persuaded by Bellamy's ardent language, first, to listen to his proposals, and then, when he has taken her by force to Scotland, to agree to the marriage ceremony. By the end of the novel, however, Eugenia's married experience has taught her a painful caution. When their father is arrested for Camilla's debts, Eugenia perceptively advises her sister, despite their mother's written injunction against her return, to ignore the denial, to go home, to seek a reconciliation with her parents.

Our fascination with Eugenia grows in inverse proportion to our disapproval for the compounded foolishness of Burney's heroine, whose sufferings, if pathetic, we cannot but feel are justified. Eugenia's developing resistance to Bellamy's words takes on heroic significance as she steadily refuses to ask her uncle for money despite her husband's abuse. Ultimately, it is this resistance that initiates the denouement of her subplot, when Bellamy, threatening her with a gun, is startled by their coachman and accidentally shoots himself.

It is not until later, when Eugenia, taking advantage of the narrative potential of her life, begins writing a novel, that we recognize what has been latent in her character from the beginning, that as a female pedant she also represents the female author. Appropriately, the preface to her novel measures the disadvantaged position of a physically handicapped woman and records similar disadvantages for the female pedant and author. Contrasting her self-depiction with those of the "young and fair," Eugenia traces her knowledge of her own deformity to the "lords of the creation, mighty men," explaining that "for the value you yourselves set upon external attractions, your own neglect has taught me to know; and the indifferency with which you consider all else, your own duplicity has instructed me to feel" (905). Eugenia makes her indictment from a redoubled position on the verges of society—not only physically handicapped in a world that overvalues female beauty but also intellectually undervalued and even censured for her learning. As a character set apart by her physical deformity and her learning, decentered in negative exemplum, Eugenia may speak of female repression with much greater authority than Burney's heroine.

Burney's pedant is hardly typical, however. More commonly, pedants and bluestockings held quite minor parts in women's novels. Contemporary conduct writers warned that study could be an effectual bar against marriage, but pedantry was considered unpleasant rather than immoral. In Austen's *Pride and Prejudice* (1813), for example, Mary Bennet's fondness for lecturing and for performing tediously on the pianoforte makes her an unlikely candidate for courtship. In *The Memoirs of Mary* (1793), the best of Susannah Minifie Gunning's novels, pedantry is humorously put in its place when the heroine meets Miss Lexington, "the most unbending of all *female* pedants, except to those whose rank and consequence are *much* superior to her own," or when she is "engaged in pursuit of young *unprovided-for* gentlemen, who perhaps have been heard to declare they would rather marry the Witch of Endor than be the husband of a *classical* scholar in petticoats."[7] Miss Lexington is a type character presented in simple contrast to the heroine, whose learning also informs her conversation, though without the same abrasiveness. Thus, even as they supported better education for women, courtship novelists found it prudent to allay societal malaise over the intellectually domineering female.

Less innocuous than the pedant or bluestocking was a second type of woman scholar described by Clarissa, one who affected "to be thought as learned as men" and could "find no better way to assert her pretensions than by despising her own sex, and by dismissing that characteristic delicacy, the loss of which no attainment can supply" (4:496). Sketched in masculine, misogynistic, and sometimes homophobic terms and clearly not meant for any woman's emulation, these characters became known in contemporary patois as Amazons. Felicity Nussbaum observes in *The Brink of All We Hate* that Amazons were popular subjects for misogynistic literature, a fact easily explained if one recalls the attributes of that select female society.[8] In Samuel Johnson's translation of the Abbé de Guyon's *Histoire des Amazones Anciennes et Modernes* (1740), for instance, Amazon virgins were required to kill three men to prove that they were not susceptible to falling in love when they mated. There was no mistaking the direct threat by Amazons to male authority.

But because their radical position insured the displacement of anything they happened to say, regardless of how strident, Amazons were particularly useful to feminist writers. Thus, in Fanny Burney's *Evelina* (1778), Mrs. Selwyn embarrasses the heroine by provoking Lord Merton to say, "Devil take me if ever I had the least passion for an Amazon."[9] Yet Mrs. Selwyn's barbs are well directed, the targets well chosen. Lord Merton and his friends Coverley and Lovel are fashionable fellows whose self-complacency needs disturbing, and what Selwyn implies is true; although they are members of Parliament, they are not her intellectual equals. Burney's "Amazon" may say what her heroine may only think: if no man should be connected with a woman whose understanding is superior to his own, to accommodate all their company "would be utterly impracticable, unless we should chuse subjects from Swift's hospital of idiots" (362). Playing an offensive role that Evelina has no mind to imitate, Mrs. Selwyn nonetheless reminds the heroine (and Burney's readers) that male power is not invincible.

In the post-Revolutionary period, Amazons—borrowing from Mary Wollstonecraft and the Feminist Controversy—spoke a more heightened and abrasive rhetoric. In *Ellinor* (1798), for example, Mary Ann Hanway depicts an irascible Amazon complaining openly against the debilitating influence of women's education: "I commiserate the infirmities of my sex, who, with susceptible hearts, and minds enervated by an education calculated to debilitate both the corporeal and mental system, they look not into themselves for support, but *lean* on man, whose vaunted strength arises from their weakness. Did we make greater exertions, and call into action those powers entrusted to us by the Creator of the universe, we should find that he has distributed his gifts nearly equal between the sexes."[10] Lady John's theme is that women are capable of acquiring arts and sciences with "the same advantages as men" (2:303). The fact that she addresses these remarks to Ellinor, who is personally preoccupied with the problem of finding her own living, translates the invective into a more pragmatic complaint against oppression than was common earlier in the century.

Another work belonging to this ideologically heightened period is Amelia Opie's *Adeline Mowbray* (1804). As a member of Wollstone-craft's group who apparently agreed with most of its sentiments, Opie nonetheless was interested in correcting William Godwin and Mary Wollstonecraft's notions of free love. Not surprisingly, she included in her novel (which is loosely based on Wollstonecraft's life) an Ama-zonian figure who not only challenges masculine verbal dominance but also is the "terror of the ladies in the neighborhood":

She would always insist on making the gentlemen of her acquaintance (as much terrified sometimes as their wives) engage with her in some literary or political conversation. She wanted to convert every drawing-room into an arena for the mind, and all her guests into intellectual gladiators. She was often heard to interrupt two grave matrons in an interesting discussion of an accouchement, by asking them if they had read a new theological tract, or a pamphlet against the minister? If they softly expatiated on the lady-like fatigue of body which they had endured, she discoursed in choice terms on the energies of the mind; and she never received or paid visits without convincing the company that she was the most wise, most learned, and most disagreeable of companions.[11]

Threatening to expropriate intellectual discourse, Adeline's mother makes a power play in the drawing room; clearly, the satire cuts both ways—at the ridiculous figure of the obstreperous Amazon and at the women whose conversation does not rise above the trials of "lying in." As Opie knew, however, the social consequences for such women were severe; like Wollstonecraft, Opie's character is ostracized—Mrs. Mowbray receives no visits—and her daughter, Adeline, imitating her mother's studies, converts to the dangerous theory of "free love." Self-educated and by 1804 a successful novelist, Amelia Opie must have appreciated the parodic value of representing in one scene two extremes of women's education.

If a young woman managed to avoid the two educational aberrations Clarissa described, there were still mistaken ideas she might fall prey to. In particular, women were cautioned against sentimentalism, a softening of the passions usually attributed to reading too many sen-timental novels, or, as in the case of Lennox's Arabella, too many romances.[12] In an age given to sensibility, the quantity of one's tears was often understood as proving the quality of one's heart. Among Richardson's coterie, for example, Lady Bradshaigh complained after reading *Pamela* that she had shed "a pint of Tears."[13] Especially in women's conduct books, novels were viewed as potentially dangerous forms of entertainment for young impressionable women, and, ironically enough, warnings against cultivating excessive sentimentalism were often incorporated by women novelists.

Sentimentalism drew admonitions in such novels as Fanny Burney's *Camilla*, Maria Edgeworth's *Angelina* (1801), Mary Brunton's *Self-Control* (1811), and Charlotte Smith's *Desmond* (1792). Among the characters surrounding Burney's Camilla is Mrs. Berlinton, clearly meant as an example of excessive sensibility: "To all that was thus most fascinating to others, she joined unhappily all that was most dangerous for herself; an heart the most susceptible, sentiments the most romantic, and an imagination the most exalted" (487). Burney traces the defect to its source in inadequate education; aside from faith and her prayers, all that Mrs. Berlinton was exposed to were "some common and ill selected novels and romances, which a young lady in the neighborhood privately lent her to read; till her brother, upon his first vacation from the University, brought her the works of the Poets" (832).

The debilitating effects of Mrs. Berlinton's reading are obvious from Camilla's first acquaintance with this sentimentalist. Walking out on a moonlit evening, Camilla and Miss Dennel surprise Mrs. Berlinton, who is self-indulgently rereading a friend's letter. Just as they approach, she is accosted by a man who pursues her and seizes her garment. Camilla rushes to her assistance, while, oblivious to the physical danger she has just escaped, Mrs. Berlinton snatches up her letter, touches it with her lips, and carefully folding it, puts it into her bosom, tenderly murmuring, "I have preserved thee! . . . O from what danger! what violation" (389). Her speech records an unnatural concern, a transferral of alarm from body to text. Mrs. Berlinton is a dangerous companion for Camilla precisely because, much like Charlotte Lennox's "Female Quixote," her reading is focused on texts to the exclusion of the world.

In imitation of the novels she reads, the sentimentalist may enact a comic role, becoming a self-conscious, self-histrionic heroine—a negative exemplum for identificatory readers. In this vein is Maria Edgeworth's Angelina, who is possessed by the latest novel and runs away to join the "woman of genius" who wrote it.[14] Similarly, a minor character in Mary Brunton's *Self-Control*, becomes victim to her own imagination, altering her facial expression and physical attitude to suit each successive heroine she reads about.[15]

Inveighing against novel-reading and sentimentalism was more than common practice; it was fashionable, as Charlotte Smith implies in *Desmond*. Thus, Smith's heroine explains to her younger sister that their mother has been listening to women who complain against fiction:

> But if every work of fancy is to be prohibited in which a tale is told, or an example brought forward, by which some of these ladies suppose, that the errors of youth may be palliated, or the imagination awakened—I know no book of amusement that can escape their censure; and the whole phalanx of novels, from the two first of our classics, in that line of writing, Richardson and Fielding, to the less exceptionable . . . inventors of the present day, must be condemned with less mercy, than the curate and the barber shewed to the collection of the Knight of the sorrowful Countenance.[16]

Significantly, Geraldine derides the dangers associated with novel reading as a trumped-up charge, borrowed, she alleges, from men of letters interested in preserving their own power. In this way, Charlotte Smith draws a line between the female language of sensibility and the male language of learning, simultaneously inculcating and participating in the intertextual debate over that gendered field of contention, the novel. Sentimentalism could be a serious flaw in a young woman's education, and some courtship novelists joined in cautions against it, but as Smith implies, few were willing to go the length of Don Quixote's friends and burn all novels.

If courtship novelists were cautious about allowing (or seeming to allow) too much latitude to women's education, they were also expecting more of women than "fashionable," "accomplished" learning. "Feminine arts" had lost so much favor by the end of the century, according to Lawrence Stone, that "feminist educational reformers like Hannah More and Maria Edgeworth . . . launched an attack on training in time-consuming aesthetic accomplishments."[17] The arguments earlier educators had advanced for accomplishments, as Maria and Richard Lovell Edgeworth summed them up in their conduct book, *Practical Education* (1798), were that they were "objects of universal admiration," "tickets of admission to fashionable company." According to the Edgeworths' ironic assessment, accomplishments were supposed to "increase a young lady's chance of a prize in the matrimonial lottery," and after marriage, become "resources against ennui."[18] But if excessive study and reading in novels issued dangerous challenges to patriarchal ideology, education in fashionable accomplishments held its own dangers, foremost among them that it pandered to the male scopic economy. As the Edgeworths astutely observed, the trivializing of female education was directly related to the objectification of women within the marriage market.

Novelists had similar criticisms to make. Mary Ann Hanway's most unsympathetic character, the Amazonian Lady John, is empowered to deliver a particularly harsh diatribe against fashionably educated women:

> They are to totter a minuet, rattle the keys of a piano forte, twang the strings of a harp, scream an Italian song, daub a work-basket, or make a fillagree tea-caddie; they are just able to decypher a letter of intrigue, and scrawl an answer; have French enough to enable them to read by the help of a dictionary, *La Nouvelle Heloise, les Liaisons Dangereuses, Les Malheurs de l'Inconstance*, and the *Chevalier Faublas*. Of the authors of their country, of its history, ancient and modern, of its laws or policy, they know as little as a native of Kamtschatka. [2:307]

Accomplishments, she declares, are no longer sufficient education. Through this minor character, the author articulates a contemporary feminist concern: women are caught in a system that virtually insures that they will be educated to consider themselves, first and foremost, as objects for display.

Especially interesting for its treatment of fashionable education is Hannah More's *Coelebs in Search of a Wife* (1808), which inverts the usual courtship schema by featuring a male protagonist "in search of a wife." Rather than a single minor character drawn in for a negative exemplum, Coelebs meets (and dismisses) a string of "accomplished" women. Mindful of his mother's caution that "the education of the present race of females is not very favorable to domestic hapiness," More's hero examines many households before he finds one where there is not patent neglect of intellect for accomplishment, of housewifery for dress, of dress for religion.[19] In one family, he finds the table poorly arranged and the daughters unable to converse about anything but the latest novels in spite of the fact that many masters have been extravagantly paid for teaching them. In another, religion and trivial arts are strangely combined. The mother feels no compunction at her daughters' waste of time; they spend the day moving from one trifling pursuit to the next: from the harp to the piano-forte, to copying drawings, to gilding flowerpots, to netting gloves and veils. This, Coelebs implies, is not suitable employment for "immortal beings." It is what Coelebs's future father-in-law will later characterize as a "Mahometan" education, one that consists "merely in making woman an object of attraction" (335). No easy quest, Coelebs's search for a well-educated woman underscores the fact that much of what passed for women's education was misdirected.

ELEVEN

Jane West

PRUDENTIA HOMESPUN
AND EDUCATIONAL REFORM

JANE WEST's *The Advantages of Education, or, The History of Maria Williams* (1793), obviously calculated for readers following the skirmishes of the Feminist Controversy, appeared the year after Mary Wollstonecraft rushed *A Vindication of the Rights of Woman* (1792) into print. While generally West concurs with Wollstonecraft's complaints against female miseducation, she employs a more restrained rhetoric. Moreover, by using a pseudonymous author, she appeals directly to identificatory readers, yet at the same time she distances herself from the responsibilities and hazards of her authorial position. Much like the Amazons, bluestockings, pedants, and fashionable women discussed in the last chapter, West's spinster novelist, "Prudentia Homespun," defuses a politically-charged situation, affording the author considerable counterideological leverage yet insuring against entropic change in feminine roles. Prudentia herself frames an excuse from the economy of the novel by claiming that she knows what the market will bear and what her readers require.

Discussing possible formats for the novel with a friend, Prudentia rejects (as Wollstonecraft had done) the stock heroine, the young woman whose attributes or blazon determine her remarkably good marriage at the end of the novel:

I do not chuse to hold up matrimony as the great desideratum of our sex; I wish them to look to the general esteem of worthy people, and the approbation of their own hearts, for the recompense of their merit, rather than to the particular addresses of a lover. Men educate their youth upon this principle; they never say, 'do thus,' and the ladies will admire you. Indeed, we ourselves should think such an inducement would only form a coxcomb, or a petit maitre; and can we expect any other, than that our method should produce a romantic prude, or a flirting coquette.[1]

Prudentia's précis closely parallels Wollstonecraft's insistence that female education concern itself with equipping women for life rather than teaching them how to appeal to men. Even Prudentia finds some accommodations to convention necessary, though, for she admits that a friend's immoderate laughter prompted her not only to change her heroine's name from Polly to Maria but also to allow her "beauty and elegance, lest I should not have one reader in her teens" (1:5). Acknowledging and partially revising the norms of women's novels and the subject positions she implies for her female characters, Prudentia heightens her reader's awareness of the problematic terms for heroinization. Thus the self-consciousness of West's spinster author implicitly calls for a similar reflexivity on her reader's part.

Prudentia/West raises specific Wollstonecraftian topics to be treated: boarding-school education, private versus public education, and fashionable education. She tells the story of Maria Williams, whose mother has returned from several years in the West Indies in time to finish (or correct) her daughter's boarding-school education. Much as Prudentia revises our understanding of the heroine, so she adjusts our view, interrupting her introduction to explain that she does not mean to attach a stigma to boarding schools. Against the range of possibilities, the reader is to appreciate Mrs. Williams's method in preparing Maria to enter the world: "Instead of forming genteel connexions for her daughter, enquiring after the most fashionable artists who presided over the different branches of female dress, and performing all the etiquette which is commonly called introducing a young woman into the world," she instructs Maria "to perform her part in it with consistency and comfort" (1:39). In stark contrast is Maria's friend Charlotte Raby, whose accomplished education, fashionable coming out, and considerable fortune do not, as Maria expects, determine her happiness but lead to an unsatisfactory marriage with Major Pierpoint.

The novel follows Maria's developing infatuation with Sir Henry Neville, whose goal is not marriage, as she believes, but seduction. Ultimately, only the heroine's virtue and her mother's caution save her from a fate worse than Charlotte's unhappy union. Maria loves Sir Henry, but not enough to agree to a clandestine marriage or overlook his earlier seduction of Miss Seymour. At the same time, parallel to and impinging on the courtship/seduction plot, there is Maria's maternally-directed "finishing," a central lesson of which is fortitude. Initially, Maria adopts her friend's attitudes, asking her mother, for instance, "if she ever knew any thing so unfortunate and distressing" as Charlotte Raby's disappointment at a masquerade. By way of reply, Mrs. Williams tells of visiting a poor family stricken by smallpox, explaining that by familiarizing her daughter with objects of affliction, "I wish to convince you, that you belong to an order of beings, whose prescribed rule of duty supposes suffering. . . . Do you think that Mr. Raby's affectionate care can always guard his daughter from the pressure of misfortune: or will your friend meet it, when it unavoidably falls on her own head, with more firmness, because she has hitherto been kept ignorant of its effects on others?" (1:76). There is, of course, an authorial prescience in Mrs. Williams's instruction, which foreshadows a time when fortitude will enable Maria to bear the truth about Sir Henry's intentions and later his suicide.

In the context of these plot developments, Prudentia's prefatory denial that she is preparing her heroine for marriage reads differently; the more enlightened perspective of Mrs. Williams allows the reader to understand that education has as its end not marriage but self-respect. By precept and by example, Prudentia Homespun demonstrates that there is life outside matrimony, and that this life is preferable to a misalliance (like those experienced by Charlotte Raby and Mrs. Williams, and that which threatens Maria). It is only after having made this point that West develops in the final pages a better fate for her heroine, a happy marriage with Mr. Herbert, whose literary instructions inspire first friendship and then love.

The most significant thing about West's second novel, *A Gossip's Story* (1797) was that it served as a model for Austen's *Sense and Sensibility* (1811). West enlarged the cast of idiosyncratic characters by including Prudentia Homespun's society of gossips. The stories of "the scandalous club," gathered during weekly meetings, concern the developing courtships of Louisa and Marianne Dudley, young women recognizable as prototypes of Austen's Louisa and Marianne. Beyond these characters, Austen would have discovered in West's Prudentia an ironic narrator not unlike the persona she herself assumed—a savante in accommodations between individual psychology and the often ungenerous and foolish expectations of society.

Louisa, who has been carefully educated by her father, becomes a model of feminine propriety, but for West's Marianne, unlike Austen's, the consequences of sensibility are irremediable. Indulged and protected by her grandmother, she matures into a sentimentalist: "the portrait of an amiable and ingenuous mind, solicitous to excel, and desirous to be happy, but destitute of natural vigour or acquired stability; forming to itself a romantick standard, to which nothing human ever attained; perplexed by imaginary difficulties; shaking under fancied evils."[2] Predictably, poetic justice is served in the conclusion by Louisa's happy marriage and Marianne's failed one.

More interesting for the purposes of this discussion than either of her two preceding works is West's third novel, *A Tale of the Times* (1799). Optimistically, Prudentia Homespun predicts in the opening pages of this work that her defiance of English sympathizers with the Revolution will earn her notoriety and increase her sales. The plot is a not altogether successful combination of courtship and seduction stories, with education a contributing cause in both. Once again, West divides our interest between two women, Geraldine Monteith, who loses her husband's affection and her reputation through her relationship with the Deist Fitzosborne, and Lucy Evans, whose long-suffering love for Edward is rewarded by their marriage at the end of the novel.

The story begins with Geraldine Powercourt's marriage to James, Earl of Monteith. Daughter to a benevolent father and a foolish, selfish mother, Geraldine has been informally adopted by Mrs. Evans, who has done what she could to strengthen her character. Geraldine owes "every female grace and suitable accomplishment" to "an experienced governess and celebrated masters," but it is to "the instructions of Mrs. Evans, and to the tender friendship of her daughter Lucy" that her mind is "indebted for its richest treasures."[3] Lucy, while lacking her friend's "expensive accomplishments," is yet "very pretty, very sensible, very amiable, and as well educated as the daughter of a country clergyman need wish to be." Interestingly, Prudentia/West describes her as intellectually superior to her expensively schooled friend, for "she had read much, she had thought more; her leisure for study and reflection was greater than her friend's, and her mind imperceptibly acquired superior energy" (1:104-5). West's point is not so much that the woman of inferior class is naturally a better person as that her life is less taken up by frivolous social activities. To her usual theme—that a carefully managed education prepares a woman to face life's misfortunes and hazards—the author adds the issue of education as a means of spiritual growth (a theme implicit in Wollstonecraft and developed even more fully in Mary Brunton's *Discipline*).

Geraldine's story, like that of Wollstonecraft's Mary, is prefaced by negative exempla of women who have been weakened by miseducation. The young woman's mother, who by twenty-five has lost her beauty and health, does not have the mental resources to bear a sick chamber because "her education taught her rather to conceal than to subdue the irritability of her disposition; and, being solely confined to the acquirement of a few external accomplishments, no mental treasures were laid up in store against the bitter day of adversity" (1:73-74). Another interpolated story illustrating the same lesson centers on Geraldine's sister-in-law. This young woman's preparation for life involves avoiding "whatever was bad for the eyes, bad for the shape, and bad for the complexion" and acquiring "whatever was perfectly elegant and suitable for a young lady of the first fashion" (1:256-57).

At first, Geraldine's married life seems to epitomize the benefits of female education, and Monteith Castle resembles a Bower of Bliss governed by "Una instead of an Acrasia": "She had acquired a knowledge of all fashionable works, and here again instruction and materials only waited to be required. Her library, her conservatory, and her hot-house attracted general attention, and transfused general pleasure, because their respective treasures were not kept merely to gratify the ostentation of the possessor, but were permitted to impart their mental riches and odiferous sweets to any who wished to read a book or cultivate an off-set" (2:29-30).

But as every Eden must have its spoiler, so Geraldine's is pillaged by a young man who systematically penetrates her orthodox defenses against what Deism and Natural Law seem to sanction. Artful in his seduction, Fitzosborne's persuasive reasoning against social forms prepares for Geraldine's ruin, which he (like Lovelace) insures with drugs. Geraldine's fatal error is that (like Milton's Eve) she pridefully entertains her free-thinking friend's arguments without inferring from them that his principles are dangerously libertine. And, in a way, her ruin bespeaks the conservative myth in regard to female education— that knowledge is directly associated with a fall from moral and sexual innocence. But Jane West is not content with a simplistic conservatism, for she presents in Lucy Evans a conflicting case of a woman whom knowledge informs and strengthens. Geraldine's "ruin" is accomplished in reputation only, but it is enough; for once society's prejudice has been aroused, she is proscribed from ever reentering her domestic paradise.

For all its interest as a period piece, *A Tale of the Times*, like all of West's novels, has several troubling flaws. One of the most forceful scenes in the novel is one in which the two plots converge, when Lucy Evans and her accepted suitor penetrate Fitzosborne's machinations and futilely attempt to persuade Geraldine that she is in danger. Yet the predominance of slow-paced scenes between Geraldine and Fitzosborne and the attendant neglect of the secondary plot involving Lucy Evans and Edward often make the novel tedious. A second flaw in this novel is that, as had been her practice in the two earlier works, West interlards her chapters with poetry, ignoring (she admits in a footnote) the complaints of her critics. The wittiest sallies of Prudentia Homespun cannot redeem the dull implausibility of characters who wax poetic for pages at a time. But even if West does not always meet our expectations as readers, it is important to remember that this self-educated novelist was extremely popular with her contemporaries, who decoded with full understanding the piquancy of an old-maid authoress quizzing the intellectual ability of her own sex and doubting the felicities of marriage.

TWELVE

Mary Brunton

THE DISCIPLINED HEROINE

MARY BRUNTON was more attentive to character than Mary Wollstonecraft, more conscious of detail than Jane West. Her witty use of native Scots personality had affinities with Maria Edgeworth and Sir Walter Scott, both of whom she admired. Known today primarily for her influence on Jane Austen, Brunton deserves consideration in her own right as one of the better novelists of the early nineteenth century.

The *Memoir* of her life and writings that her husband published after her death provides us unusual insight into Mary Brunton's opinion of her role as novelist. Looking forward to a time when the novel would no longer be a "nickname for a book," she defended the genre as having classical potential: "I protest, I think a fiction containing a just representation of human beings and of their actions—a connected, interesting, and probable story, conducting to a useful and impressive moral lesson—might be one of the greatest efforts of human genius. Let the admirable construction of fable in Tom Jones be employed to unfold characters like Miss Edgeworth's—let it lead to a moral like Richardson's—let it be told with the eloquence of Rousseau, and with the simplicity of Goldsmith—let it be all this, and Milton need not have been ashamed of the work!"[1]

Brunton mentioned only one among the female authors who preceded her, and she was frankly timid about being recognized as a woman novelist. While she championed the genre's potential, she did not aspire to literary fame, she explained to her mother, because "to be pointed at—to be noticed and commented upon—to be suspected of literary airs—to be shunned as literary women are, by the more unpretending of my own sex; and abhorred, as literary women are, by the pretending of the other!—My dear, I would sooner exhibit as a rope-dancer."[2] Brunton's reservations about writing remind us that the sexual/textual trope continued to inhibit women's free textual expression.

Brunton's demur, her recognition and avoidance of the social consequences for "exhibiting" women, also suggests the author's willingness to use whatever sleight of hand was necessary to continue functioning as a literary woman without being recognized as one. To her advantage, Brunton had the complete cooperation of an appreciative husband. He listened to each day's effort in the evening, and when a final draft of the first novel was prepared, made notes for her consideration. She writes of finishing her second novel at three o'clock in the morning and waking Mr. B. "out of his first sleep" to hear of Ellen's wedding. Even with a supportive husband, though, female authorship was problematic, and Brunton found when she was forced to acknowledge authorship of *Self-Control* (1811) that "all the excellencies of the book are attributed to Mr. B., while I am left to answer for all its defects" (23).

Well received, *Self-Control* quickly went into a second edition. Among its enthusiasts was Jane Austen, who, appreciating Brunton's wit, read the novel twice. In the description of the minor character July Dawkins, one finds a technique that would have appealed to the author of *Northanger Abbey* (1818). July, the landlady's sentimentally educated daughter, both recalls Charlotte Lennox's "female quixote" and anticipates Austen's Catherine Morland:

After reading Evelina, she sat with her mouth extended in a perpetual smile, and was so very timid, that she would not for the world have looked at a stranger. When Camilla was the model for the day, she became insufferably rattling, infantine, and thoughtless. After perusing the Gossip's Story, she, in imitation of the rational Louisa, suddenly waxed very wise—spoke in sentences—despised romance—sewed shifts—and read sermons. But, in the midst of this fit, she, in an evil hour, opened a volume of the Nouvelle Eloise, which had before disturbed many wiser heads. The shifts were left unfinished, the sermons thrown aside, and Miss Julia returned with renewed *impetus* to the sentimental.[3]

In such ironic appraisals, which reveal, coincidentally, the author's resistance to the usual literary patterns supplied for identificatory readers, Brunton stands with the best courtship novelists—Lennox, Burney, Edgeworth, and Austen.

As Brunton herself recognized when it was published, though, *Self-Control* is flawed. The novel begins well enough with Laura's disillusionment when, instead of proposing marriage as she expects, her suitor tries to seduce her. Laura imposes a two-year trial for the repentant Hargrave, while she and her father leave for London to improve their disintegrating finances. London is the scene of interesting adventures in the first volume, but the reader's attention flags in the next, when Laura (left unprotected at her father's death) goes to live with Lady Pelham. This guardian's relentless urging on Hargrave's behalf—even after he is discovered to have been involved in an adulterous affair—is both tedious and implausible. Moreover, as Jane Austen noted, the plot leaves "Nature" and "Probability" behind when, toward the conclusion, Laura is shipped off to America, where she first hopes for the help of sympathetic Indians and finally manages her own escape in a canoe.[4]

By the time *Discipline* (1814) was published, Mary Wollstonecraft's insights about women's education, about its psychologically and economically oppressive effects, had been in print for well over a decade. Yet in few works of fiction had this aspect of woman's position been probed so thoroughly as it was in Brunton's second novel. Extraordinary in this novel is a first-person narrator/heroine through whom Brunton explores differences in subject positions between a woman who at first is thoroughly invested in fashionable education and later is brought to reject self-objectification and to consider herself as preparing for eternal life. In a series of almost emblematic scenes, Brunton depicts, first, the framing of female consciousness within a society that is male-centered and patently bourgeois, and then, her heroine's gradual and difficult growth beyond that circumscribed understanding to a position that modern readers would term feminist and Brunton probably would identify as Christian.

Anticipating the Victorians and following the trend established by such courtship novelists as Wollstonecraft, Burney, and Austen, Brunton dwells on childhood as a crucial period of formation for her heroine's psyche.[5] From her earliest years, Ellen's self-concept is formed by hearing her merchant father regret the waste of her talents: "It is a confounded pity she is a girl. If she had been of the right sort, she might have got into Parliament, and made a figure with the best of them. But now what use is her sense of?" The lesson she internalizes is not only that women are inferior, not "of the right sort," but also that they have no duty in life, nothing more to do, in Mr. Percy's words, than to amuse themselves until they are married. Correspondingly, in boarding school Ellen learns only to read a little French and Italian, to draw landscapes, to recite her catechism, and to dress fashionably. Her sole proficiency is in music, on which she squanders seven hours a day. Yet, trivial as her education is, it compares favorably with the experience of a friend, whose brother has enrolled her at school merely with the goal of settling her in marriage:

Let no simple reader, trained by an antiquated grandmother in the country, imagine my meaning to be that Miss Arnold was practised in the domestic, the economical, the submissive virtues; that she was skilled in excusing frailty,

enlivening solitude, or scattering sunshine upon the passing clouds of life!—
I only mean that Miss Arnold was taught accomplishments which were
deemed likely to attract notice and admiration; that she knew what to withdraw from the view, and what to prepare for exhibition; that she was properly
instructed in the value of settlements; and duly convinced of the degradation
and misery of failure in the grand purpose of a lady's existence. [16]

Here Brunton addresses the identificatory reader directly ("let no
simple reader"), explaining the demeaning effect of educating solely
for marriage. Such a young woman cooperates in her own objectification, experiencing herself as commodity, always conscious of the
eligible men whose approval she must gain. Clearly, the reader is to
receive Miss Arnold as the negative exemplum, yet the heroine herself
enjoys little more in the way of intellectual preparation. In fact, at the
beginning of the novel, Ellen may be understood as occupying a better
position only insofar as she is an heiress and thus assured of having
suitors, while her fortuneless friend must hope to attract them by
other means.

Most tellingly, Brunton stresses the resemblance between Miss
Arnold's education and a mercantile apprenticeship—"she knew
what to withdraw from the view, and what to prepare for exhibition."
This focus, an extension of bourgeois language, an incipient capitalism
that menaces female agency, is characteristic of the novel as a whole.
Brunton brings this tension to bear by repeatedly associating woman
with artifice—the reflection of a mirror, the glitter of jewels, the allure
of an inlaid dressing box. In several memorable scenes, the narcissistic
and self-objectifying tendencies brought on by commodification
achieve thematic significance. The author is particularly adept at using
the scopic to associate human motives with the marketplace—with
competition, terms of exchange, the consumer's desirous gaze. In one
instance, Ellen's anticipation of her first season is heightened by hearing that an old boarding-school rival, Lady Mary de Burgh, has already won a certain fame: "When this intelligence was conveyed to
me, I was standing opposite to a large mirror. I glanced towards it,
recalled with some contempt the miniature charms of my fairy com-
petitor, and sprung away to entreat my father would immediately
remove to town" (30-31). To his daughter's ambition, Mr. Percy contributes his own, providing her the wherewithal (her mother's jewels)
to make a splendid appearance and later enjoying an ancillary power
over her suitors. But Brunton's critique is not directed at one class
only, for while she dwells on the evils of consumerism and commodification, she does so at the expense not only of the bourgeoisie
but of their betters as well.

Ellen triumphs at her first ball because she has secured the attentions of her rival's brother, Lord Frederick de Burgh, whose suggestive "eye-glass set with brilliants" (35) focuses on her. Other suitors follow, their ocular tributes recorded in the *Morning Chronicle,* much to her father's entertainment: "He delighted to read, in the Morning Chronicle, that at Lady G——'s ball, the brilliancy of Miss Percy's jewels had never been surpassed, save by the eyes of the lovely wearer. . . . Indeed he took great pleasure in bringing my suitors, especially those of noble birth, to the point of explicit proposal, and then overwhelming them with a tremendous preponderance of settlement" (38). Her father's power plays leave no doubt of Ellen's investment in the system of patriarchal exchange that affords little quarter for the individuated woman. Ellen perceives her suitors in the same terms through which she reads herself, explaining Lord Frederick's ascendancy among them as an effect of her competition with his sister and describing him in objectifying, scopic language: "He was handsome, showy, extravagant, and even more the fashion than myself. He danced well, drove four-in-hand, and was a very Oedipus in expounding anagrams and conundrums" (38). But this application of spectacle to a male character is uncommon; most often Brunton uses the scopic to underline woman's objectification in a system whose motives—greed, materialism—are unrelentingly aligned with a market economy managed by men.[6]

When Ellen attends an estate auction, held "in consequence of an execution in the house of a lady of high fashion," for instance, the author is concerned not only to demonstrate the corrupt motives of those women "who wished to be relieved of their time, their money, or their curiosity" (74), but also to explore the implications of the scene for the heroine herself, who becomes another kind of artifact. From the beginning of this plot incident, Brunton calls to the reader's attention the significance of how a woman is viewed. This typical conduct-book theme is introduced when Ellen, describing Lady St. Edmunds as "my dear enchantress," persists in attending the auction with her despite Miss Mortimer's warning, "Well may you give her that name . . . for she is drawing you into a circle where nothing good or holy must tread; and if you will follow her to the tempter's own ground, you must bid farewell to better spirits" (74). At the sale, perhaps in unconscious denial that she can be corrupted, Ellen assumes the role of spectator, sketching "a group, in which a spare dame, whose face combined no common contrast of projection and concavity, was darting from her sea-green eyes sidelong flames upon a china jar, which was surveyed with complacent smiles by its round and rosy purchaser" (75).

From "amused spectator," though, Ellen is converted to "a keen actor," snatched into the scene of exchange when the auctioneer offers "a tortoise-shell dressing-box, magnificently inlaid with gold." Brunton dwells on the resemblance between box and bidders. "It was every way calculated to arrest the regards of fine ladies; for, like them, it was useless and expensive in proportion to its finery." Desire for the dressing-box quickly levels Ellen with the subject of her caricature, as she with difficulty outbids another, who "proceeded, with smiles not quite of courtesy; till, in exchange for my discretion, my temper, and a hundred and fifteen pounds, I had gained the tortoise-shell dressing-box" (75).

In her haste, Ellen forgets that she does not have the ready money to pay for her purchase. Applying first to Lady St. Edmunds and then to another young woman of fortune, Ellen is doubtful about the propriety of accepting the guineas offered by Lord Frederick until Lady St. Edmunds rallies her, asking "in a very audible whisper, what sort of interest I expected Lord Frederick to exact, which made me so afraid of becoming his debtor" (76). When Ellen accepts his assistance and jokingly asks what security he will require, Lord Frederick takes advantage of his position and, "drawing from my finger a ring of small value, said, with more seriousness than I expected, 'This shall be my pledge; but you must not imagine that I shall restore it for a few paltry guineas' " (77). The implicit contract is important. Mr. Percy has already refused Lord Frederick's offer for his daughter's hand, yet Ellen unwittingly finds herself involved with the rejected suitor in a way that she does not wish to be—she owes him guineas and interest. More than that, Lord Frederick's actions, his claiming her ring as pledge, advert to the exchange he really seeks, that of marriage. Ellen, initially a spectator at the auction, has become bidder, center of attention, and ultimately, commodity. In effect, Lord Frederick has purchased an option for her hand.

Hence the scene is a precocious examination of the cooperation that develops between capitalism and affective individualism. As its staging suggests, it is women who are primarily responsible for consuming the new commodities produced by bourgeois capitalism. But in eighteenth-century England, while women are the consumers, men are the producers, both of goods and of capital, and, like Ellen, a woman can only obtain the wherewithal to purchase by making herself available in the marriage market.

A third scene through which Brunton exposes the effects of female socialization begins with Ellen's desire to attend what for the period had become a catchword for the scopic, namely a masked ball. As precedents for this masquerade, readers of Brunton's novel would have recalled, among others, Harriet Byron's and Cecilia's unpleasant experiences (Harriet's attempted abduction by Hargrave and Cecilia's harassment by the disguised Monckton). But in Brunton's treatment, carnival or masquerade becomes as much an individual temptation for the heroine as it is an external occasion for license. The novel brings the conventional conduct-book emphasis to the question of Ellen's attending the masked ball, and Miss Mortimer, as she had earlier, stands as an agent of conscience, a voice for prudence, against Ellen's accepting the invitation.[7] Reluctantly, Ellen promises to return the tickets, but when the time for the masquerade draws near, her friend Miss Arnold persuades her to change her mind, to break her promise. Describing Ellen's anxiety about her costume, Brunton again underscores the fevered emotion associated with the scene of display: "Never did lover, waiting the hour of meeting, suffer more doubts and tremours than I did, lest Mrs. Beetham should disappoint me of my evening's paraphernalia." Ellen locks herself into her dressing room "because I could not, without constraint, allow even Miss Arnold to witness those rehearsals of vanity, which I was not ashamed to exhibit before Him who remembers that we are but dust" (83).

Ironically, Ellen's narcissistic posturing is interrupted by a rehearsal of another kind: "I was practising before a looking-glass the attitudes most favourable to the display of my dress and figure, when my attention was drawn by the sound of bustle in the staircase. I opened my door to discover the cause of the noise, and perceived some of the servants bearing Miss Mortimer, to all appearances lifeless" (83-84). While Ellen has been practicing attitudes before her mirror, her friend, in consultation with her doctor, has learned that she must undergo a dangerous operation for a life-threatening disease (apparently cancer). Later, Ellen finds Miss Mortimer in an attitude of prayer, "upon her knees, her hands clasped in supplication; the flush of hope glowing through the tears which yet trembled on her cheek; her eyes raised with meek confidence, as the asking infant looks up in his mother's face." With Miss Mortimer's natural virtue, the heroine contrasts its false image, asserting, "I was not unacquainted with the attitude of devotion. *That* I might have studied even at our theatres, where a mockery of prayer often insults both taste and decency" (84). Brunton enforces the conjunction between artifact (Ellen's costume) and display (her posturing before the mirror, the theatrical representation of prayer), and their opposition to nature (to the corporeal realities of "dust," disease, and the "asking infant").

Despite Miss Mortimer's tears over the broken promise, Ellen accompanies Miss Arnold to the masquerade, where, though she has vowed to be discreet, she makes nothing less than a spectacle of herself. Her first opportunity for display presents itself when Lady St. Edmunds encourages the two "Turks" (Lord Frederick and Ellen) to dance, as a group of "Spaniards" has done. Recollecting an earlier disgust with "a description of this Mohammetan exhibition, so well suited to those whose prospective sensuality extends even beyond the grave," Ellen refuses, claiming ignorance. Not to be denied, Lady St. Edmunds persuades her to imitate the tamer Turkish dances often represented on stage. Before describing her performance with Lord Frederick, the heroine/narrator inserts a commentary on what might be called the sexual politics of dancing:

Blessed be the providential arrangements which make the majority of woman-kind bow to the restraints of public opinion! Hardened depravity may despise them, piety may sacrifice them to a sense of duty: but, in the intermediate classes, they hold the place of wisdom and of virtue. They direct many a judgment which ought not to rely on itself; they aid faltering rectitude with the strength of numbers; for, degenerate as we are, numbers are still upon the side of feminine decorum. Had I been unmasked, no earthly inducement would have made me consent to this blamable act of levity; but, in the in-toxication of spirits which was caused by the adulation of my companions, the consciousness that I was unknown to all but my tempters induced me to yield. [92]

The phrase "restraints of public opinion" is the apparent antecedent of Brunton's pronouns; these "restraints," she affirms, "hold the place of wisdom and virtue" in the intermediate classes. The paragraph demonstrates a precocious insight roughly equivalent to the modern observation that one cannot escape ideology; at the same time it takes a highly reflexive stance on the side of prudence. Clearly, the author, while supporting the idea of Christian virtue, recognizes that it is achieved at some expense, the "restraints of public opinion" often being repressive to women.

Ellen's next mistake that evening merely compounds her previous one. Fatigued and heated by dancing, she has just been served a large glass of champagne when for the second time a black domino cautions her in a low voice. But, "with a careless smile," she drinks the liquor (93), and then allows Lord Frederick to lead her into an unoccupied apartment, where the danger of the "poisoned cup" becomes real. At first they are accompanied by Miss Arnold and a companion, who walk about examining the drawings hung in the room. But after they leave, Ellen, unmasked and seated on a sofa, foolishly submits to remaining with Lord Frederick, who is "proposing an expedition to Scotland": "He was even in the act of attempting to snatch a kiss,—

for a lord in the inspiration of champagne is not many degrees more gentle or respectful than a clown,—when the door flew open, and admitted Lady Maria de Burgh, Mrs. Sarah Winterfield, and my black domino." Once again, the narrator emphasizes the emblematic visual effect, observing that, "our indiscretions never flash more strongly upon our view than when reflected from the eye of an enemy" (94).

The retreat into the sumptuous apartment, and its consequences, recall Miss Mortimer's warning that Ellen is being led into a charmed circle where the good will not follow, a prophecy further borne out in a later scene in which Lord Frederick presses his suit. By this time, Ellen, a habitual visitor at Lady St. Edmunds's house, is among the few intimates received in an opulently decorated boudoir, a secret room of sensual delight: "Nothing which taste could approve was wanting to its decoration,—nothing which sense desires could be added to its luxury. The walls glowed with the sultry scenes of Claude, and the luxuriant designs of Titian. The daylight stole mellowed on the eye through a bower of flowering orange trees and myrtles; or alabaster lamps imitated the softness of moonshine. Airy Grecian couches lent grace to the forms which rested on them; and rose-coloured draperies shed on the cheek a becoming bloom" (144-45). The appeal is to all the senses, but it is the visual that most distinguishes the "temple of effeminacy" (145). Brunton's strategy is complex, for while the phrase "temple of effeminacy" echoes the contemporary misogynist association between inordinate sensuality and the female, it also returns to Brunton's earlier equation (in the auction scene) of material excess, moral degeneracy, the scopic, and the fine lady.

The turning point of the plot is Ellen's disillusionment with the fashionable life she has been leading, followed by a reform that is at once a spiritual conversion and, more to the point here, a feminist awakening. Brunton details Ellen's progress from imprudence to discipline—from unquestioning acceptance to resistance and finally to rejection of the patriarchally defined role of fine lady. As the patterns of spiritual and feminist awakening are inextricably interwoven with the courtship story, it will be useful here to consider the three together by following the plot movement toward Ellen's marriage.

From the beginning, even while Ellen is carrying on a flirtation with the rhetorically glib Lord Frederick, she acknowledges the force of Miss Mortimer's arguments: "You have told me that you mean one day to change your plan of life—to put away childish things,—to begin your education for eternity. Is Lord Frederick well fitted to be your companion,—your assistant in this mighty work?" (47). Ellen has already met the kind of grave man Miss Mortimer seems to describe, but, with her marketplace values, she does not begin to appreciate her father's friend, Mr. Maitland, until he becomes famous (hence desirable) for his Parliamentary speeches against slavery: "The newspapers panegyrised him; and fashion, rank, and beauty crowded round the happy few who could give information concerning the age, manners, and appearance of Mr. Maitland. Not all his wisdom, nor all his worth, could ever have moved my vain mind so much as did these tributes of applause" (117-18). Ellen responds to Maitland's obvious infatuation with her by playfully testing her power, claiming "love is out of the question with me. The creatures that dangle after me want either a toy upon which to throw away their money, or money to throw away upon their toys. A heart would be quite lost upon any of them" (137). But later her mediated desire for him, for the flattery of his courtship, is thwarted by his perception that she is unsuited to domestic life: "At four-and-thirty a man begins to foresee, that, after the raptures of the lover are past, the husband has a long life before him; in which he must either share his joys and his sorrows with a friend, or exact the submission of an inferior" (140). Maitland's terms are reminiscent of the kind of moral constancy and domestic tranquility that Edmund Leites describes as characterizing Puritan theories regarding marriage.

Interestingly, Ellen's shift in subject position, her conversion to Maitland's/Miss Mortimer's understanding of marriage and life gradually permeates her language, beginning with her embarrassed explanation to Lady St. Edmunds that she rejects Lord Frederick because she has begun to think she would like to respect her husband. But it is only when, through her father's bankruptcy and suicide, and her consequent loss of all her fair-weather friends, including the fortune-hunting Lord Frederick, that her re-education may begin in earnest. Removed from the corruptive influence of fashionable life, Ellen spends her time with Miss Mortimer learning, in the spiritual sense, to know herself: "From the first month of my residence with Miss Mortimer I may date a new era of my existence. My mind had received a new impulse, and new views had opened to me of my actions, my situation, and my prospects. An important step had been made towards a change in my character. But still it was only a step. The tendencies of nature, strengthened by the habits of seventeen years, remained to be overcome, and this was not the work of a month, or a year" (183-84). The discipline to which Brunton's title refers is not only contemplation, scriptural study, and good works, however; with Miss Mortimer's encouragement, Ellen devotes "many . . . leisure hours to books of instruction and harmless entertainment"; her evenings were "commonly enlivened by reading history, travels, or criticism" (190).

To this regimen the author makes a signal addition in the person of Sidney, Miss Mortimer's physician and Ellen's would-be suitor, who "was a man of sense; and therefore, by a very few efforts I convinced him that he could be nothing more" (198-99). It is after she has rejected him as her suitor, curiously, that Ellen begins to study chemistry under Sidney's guidance, using his library and apparatus: "By means of these, and a degree of patience not to be expected from any man but a lover, he contrived to initiate me into the first rudiments of a science, which has no detriment except its unbounded power of enticing those who pursue it" (199). It is precisely the fact that he is not a lover that makes this brief vignette so interesting, for such instances of male-female friendship are highly unusual in novels of this period.

Brunton apparently sets out to make at least two points here. First, by eschewing the usual feminine behavior, by overcoming the vanity of conquest, Ellen makes spiritual progress, as well as gaining a friend. The second point is about the nature of education: "In the course of my experiments, I made a discovery infinitely more important to me than that of latent heat or galvanism; namely, that the prospect of exhibition is not necessary to the interest of study" (199). Miss Mortimer's lingering death concludes this stage of Ellen's reform, and with the force of hagiography, exemplifies the author's enlarged notion of education: "At last, the great work was finished. Her [Miss Mortimer's] education for eternity was completed; and, from the severe lessons of this land of discipline, she was called to the boundless improvement, the intuitive knowledge, the glorious employments of her Father's house" (207). The concept that Brunton attributes to Ellen and points for her readers is that education (in this broader spiritual sense) properly continues to the end of life and beyond.

Orphaned a second time by her friend's death, Ellen foresees that she will face difficulties common to her sex: "What chance had the customs of society left open to the industry of women? The only one which seemed within my reach was the tuition of youth. . . . When, indeed, I considered how small a part of the education of a rational and accountable being I was after all fitted to undertake, I shrunk from the awful responsibility of the charge" (211). When she does find a position as governess, it is in the household of one of society's female products, a worst-case scenario of what social custom encourages in women. At their first meeting, Ellen finds Mrs. Boswell "bedizening herself and a pretty little fair-haired girl with every possible variety of bauble" (254). The woman is so poorly educated that she is "utterly incapable of anything that deserves the name of conversation." Nor does she read—"six pages a week of a novel, or of the Lady's Magazine, were the utmost extent" (260). Her character is low, suspicious, and conniving; and she resorts to manipulation and deceit to manage her husband and her child. As if all this were not enough to convince the reader of her point, the author, in a Gothic flight, has Mrs. Boswell commit Ellen to an asylum because she suspects that her husband is growing fond of the governess. On the whole, the interpolated story has little probability to recommend it, but the unrelieved caricature of Mrs. Boswell does demonstrate the strength of Brunton's opinion that women have greater duties than to amuse themselves and that intellectual improvement is required so that they may fulfill them.

Finally released from the asylum, Ellen is struggling to earn her living selling small decorative items she has made when she recognizes a woman carrying a baby as her old friend Juliet Arnold, "altered by sickness, want and sorrow" (305). Juliet's story is one more in the series of little histories through which the novelist seeks to adjust her reader's view of woman's role. Concurrently, and in opposition to Juliet's tale, Brunton brings into the plot Cecil Graham, a courageous young Scotswoman, left penniless in London because of her soldier husband's absence. While they are quite different in character, both women have suffered distinctly female misfortunes at the hands of men. Tubercular Juliet Arnold, it turns out, was deceived by Lord Glendower (Lady Maria de Burgh's suitor), who, having persuaded her into "a Scottish expedition," then refused to marry her. Cecil Graham's hardship was of quite another kind, for in obedience to her father she gave up the young man she loved and married one of his choosing. Again, Brunton's view—this time of patriarchally arranged marriage—is multidimensional, presented through several subject positions.

Although Juliet Arnold has been duped in a way no respectable woman was likely to be taken in, and though for her there is not even a deathbed repentance, Brunton does draw our attention to elements in her story that represent a kind of feminist triumph. Uniquely, this fallen woman claims to have provided for her child's legitimacy: "What I did cannot be blamed. I had heard something of the Scotch laws in regard to marriage; and refused to see Glendower, unless he would at least persuade the people of the lodging-house that I was his wife. Afterwards, I contrived to make him send me a note, addressed to Lady Glendower. The note itself was of no consequence, but it answered the purpose, and I have preserved it. I took care, too, to ascertain that the people about us observed him address me as his wife; and in Scotland this is as good as a thousand ceremonies" (308).

If Ellen cannot approve of the means Juliet has taken, and if Brunton withholds her approval, doubtful of Juliet's spiritual state at her death, there nonetheless remains an unusual poetic justice in the conclusion of her episode. The wealthy aristocratic rake is made to acknowledge the rights of a woman he has reduced from middle-class dependence to destitution: "Juliet's marriage was sanctioned; and though her death left Lord Glendower at liberty to repair, in some sort, the injury which he had done to Lady Maria, the rights of his first-born son could not be transferred to the children of his more regular marriage" (334).

Similarly uncommon is the exemplum of Cecil, for even while Brunton is describing what seems to be a typical father-daughter conflict over the choice of marriage partner, she uses the story not, as one might expect, to endorse a liberalization of marriage practice but rather to condemn filial disobedience: "And you dutifully submitted to your father," Ellen says, her heart swelling as she "contrasted the filial conduct of this untutored being with my own" (264). And yet, even while Brunton depicts Cecil's sacrifice as leading to a satisfactory marriage, she also draws in full the extremity of the young woman's pain, as Cecil compares her wedding dance to a wake and describes her former lover gone mad with grief.

The ideal woman in the novel is not the self-sacrificing Cecil Graham, however, but her cousin, Charlotte. This character appears just in time to take Ellen to Scotland, where ostensibly her brother Henry (who turns out to be Maitland) will return part of Mr. Percy's fortune, which he has recovered for Ellen. Charlotte is eminently strong, a woman of sensibility whose sudden presence in Juliet Arnold's sickroom is obviously staged for contrast:

Her stature was majestic; her figure of exquisite proportion. Her complexion, though brunette, was admirably transparent; and her colour, though perhaps too florid for a sentimental eye, glowed with the finest tints of health. Her black eyebrows, straight but flexible, approached close to a pair of eyes so dark and sparkling, that their colour was undistinguishable. No simile in oriental poetry could exaggerate the regularity and whiteness of her teeth; nor painter's dream of Euphrosyne exceed the arch vivacity of her smile. Perhaps a critic might have said that her figure was too large, and too angular for feminine beauty; that it was finely, but not delicately formed. Even I could have wished the cheek-bones depressed, the contour somewhat rounded, and the lines made more soft and flowing. But Charlotte Graham had none of that ostentation of beauty which provokes the gazer to criticize. [328]

Brunton's description implies that this woman exceeds objectification or reduction; she eludes representation ("no simile . . . nor painter's dream") because, as the last line explains, she does not perceive herself that way. Charlotte Graham has "none of that ostentation of beauty"; in other words, she does not practice self-objectification. In common with her cousin Cecil, Charlotte has in her eyes "a keen sagacity, which seemed accustomed to look beyond the words of the speaker to his motive." But she is more than just a woman of sensibility; she is, the author's words suggest, the woman unsubjugated: "Her manners had sufficient freedom to banish restraint, and sufficient polish to make that freedom graceful; yet for me they possessed an interesting originality. They were polite, but not fashionable; they were courtly, but not artificial. They were perfectly affable, and as free from arrogance as those of a doubting lover; yet in her mien, in her gait, in every motion, in every word, Miss Graham showed the unsubdued majesty of one who had never felt the presence of a superior; of one much accustomed to grant, but not to solicit indulgence" (329).

Uncircumscribed by demeaning constructions of the female role, Charlotte is, moreover, a fitting counterpart to her brother Henry: "His extensive information, his acquaintance with scenes and manners which were new to us all, did indeed render his conversation a source of instruction, as well as of amusement; but no man was ever more free from that tendency towards dogma and harangue, which is so apt to infect those who chiefly converse with inferiors. He joined his family circle, neither determined to be wise nor to be witty, but to give and receive pleasure. His was the true fire of conversation; the kindly warmth was essential to its nature, the brilliance was an accident" (371). Brunton's description of Henry implies in the Scottish household a kind of haven where individuated women share equitably in the family circle, where the relationship between man and woman is companionate rather than hierarchical, one conducive to moral constancy.

If Henry is necessarily a kind of authority figure in relation to his clan, he is not so in regard to his sister and to Ellen. Hence, while Brunton acknowledges a place for patriarchy, she relegates it altogether to the exterior world, a move that coincidentally parallels John Locke's separation of the domestic from the political scene. By so doing, she obviates an inherent problem for any woman writer, that of finding a denouement for her feminist tale, of allowing both for socially constituted male authority and for a resistant female subject position.

More than the founding of a domestic utopia, the marriage between Maitland and Ellen is also an appropriate conclusion to Ellen's somewhat truncated spiritual biography. In her words, she has become "a humbled creature, thankful to find, in his sound mind and steady principle, a support for her acknowledged weakness;—a traveller to a better country, pleased to meet a fellow-pilgrim, who animating her diligence and checking her wanderings, might soothe the toils of her journey, and rejoice with her forever in its blessed termination" (374-75).

PART V

The Denouement:
Courtship and Marriage

THIRTEEN

Courtship

"WHEN NATURE PRONOUNCES
HER MARRIAGEABLE"

WHEN JOHN BENNET dated a woman's trials and sorrows from the time "when Nature pronounces Her Marriageable," he did not caution his boarding-school audience that they were likely to experience conflict with the older generation over their affective rights, over prerogatives of love and choice.[1] Yet throughout the latter half of the eighteenth century and well into the nineteenth, one finds textual evidence of persistent generational conflict concerning marriage choice: whose decision was it? and what was the basis for deciding?

In effect, the eighteenth-century shift in the balance of power between children and parents was a moment of flux in patriarchy, with companionate marriage ideology justifying the daughter's break from family control.[2] Companionate marriage necessarily altered power relations within the family. Citing evidence of this shift in the balance of power in Jane Austen's novels, Igor Webb observes that "what happens to the children is a sign of the author's judgment of his or her society, and often this judgment is overtly aimed at a novel's main responsible . . . adult, figure. . . . The older generation exemplifies the society." Despite their immaturity, then, the children are "possessed of a knowledge the adults do not have."[3] On the whole, Webb is correct in suggesting that Austen is concerned with generational conflict over marriage. But his argument that in her novels "residual and emergent elements have almost equal force" implies that Austen inhabits a mid-point in a simple developmental continuum toward the social acceptance of married love. In other words, the psychodynamic shift that the eighteenth and early nineteenth centuries experienced in its original intricacies and inconsistencies is too easily foreshortened and silhouetted by our distant historical perspective. As the following two instances from the year 1772 (and the discussion later in this chapter of Susannah Minifie Gunning's *Barford Abbey*) suggest, the balance of opinion about reasons for marrying shifted very slowly and by no means consistently; well before the turn of the century there were writers who lent strong support to the feminist cause of self-determination in marriage, and well after the turn of the century there were writers who continued to depict generational conflict as a natural part of courtship stories.

The first example, a pamphlet entitled *Considerations on the Cause of the Present Stagnation of Matrimony* (1772), explains the decline in marriage as resulting in part from the interference of parents and guardians whose motives are financial rather than filial:

Since the Smithfield bargain is so much insisted on by parents, (and the term itself is borrowed from the market that bears that name) it might not be amiss if proper pens were provided in Smithfield, and certain days fixed, whereon they might bring their daughters to market; that if a man, after having viewed them, should be inclined to bid money for any one, he might have nothing more to do, than to ask the proprietor his price. . . . one cannot but think, that it would contribute very much to the pleasure of travelling . . . to see the several fathers driving up their daughters to market, like so many flocks of geese or turkies.[4]

The author's use of marketplace language—"Smithfield bargain," market "days," "proper pens," "proprietor," and "price"—underscores the criticism of such parents. Notably absent are the subject positions of daughters, yet that very absence constitutes a protest when the author offers his opinion—"one cannot but think" that traveling would be more pleasurable if one could see "several fathers driving up their daughters to market"—and concludes the description with the satiric force of simile—"like so many flocks of geese or turkies." In other words, the paragraph arraigns fathers, suitors, trade, and society, leaving the reader with the daughters as the sole point for satiric identification.

Published the same year, Sarah Robinson Scott's novel *The Test of Filial Duty* (1772) bears similar witness both to the emotional and ideological tensions of the paradigm shift from arranged to companionate marriage, and to the change in power relations between parents and daughters. An extraordinary scene in this epistolary novel describes another kind of bringing to market, the introduction of two young people whose parents "intend" them for each other:

My mother, who saw my confusion, and pitied me, took my hand, and would have placed me on the sopha by her, but Sir Edward prevented my immediately sitting down by introducing his son, with a hint of his business, which he thought very arch . . . he signified it by a laugh; and thus putting the finishing stroke to my confusion, a seat was really become absolutely necessary. But still, I knew not what to do with my eyes: if I looked at my father, he gave me a significant smile; if at Sir Edward, I received a nod of importance, implying that he had done me a notable favor in bringing me so fine a lover; my mother's countenance shewed she sympathized so tenderly with my uneasiness, as increased my distress; and, as for Mr. Edmondbury, I durst not glance toward him. All were silent, and I perceived their eyes were on me. In this dilemma I found no resource but in fixing mine on one point, as steadily, and with a person as prim, as if I were sitting for my picture. Sir Edward was entirely absorbed in the expectation of my being instantly charmed with his son; my father and mother were watching to see if their daughter did not make the same impression on him; and how long the foolish dumb scene would have continued I know not, had we not been summoned to dinner, which was ordered earlier than usual in complaisance to Sir Edward.[5]

The scene, epitomizing the distressed situation of the woman commodified within an exchange system, clearly invites the sympathy of identificatory readers. Depicting herself as the center of an invasive scopic attention, the heroine fixes her own eyes as though "sitting for my picture." Her complete physical stasis emphasizes Charlotte's objectification; she is there on approval—prim, passive, silent, still. While physically she has been altogether quiescent, her language works to opposite ends. Writing the above account for a friend, Charlotte displaces with situational and verbal irony the possibility that two young people can fall in love on command. Sir Edward has come upon the "business" of introducing his son, "so fine a lover." Nonetheless, the scene is not unrelieved satire but a more telling exploration of conflicting human feelings; Charlotte's parents, while participating in the patriarchal ethic, are clearly benevolent, concerned with making her happy. She is to some degree grateful for their concern. And it is plain from Charlotte's perception of "their eyes . . . on me" that her acquiescence is not a foregone conclusion, that she must in some measure be sued for and won.

In fact, the ambivalence of this early scene turns out to be prophetic of the author's inability or reluctance to resolve the conflict between affective individualism and patriarchal exchange. In this novel, so tendentiously titled *The Test of Filial Duty*, Scott hesitates between the two contending forces. Hence, with as much reason as Charlotte has to mistrust Mr. Edmondbury's suit, ultimately she does fall in love with him. In this way, Scott accommodates the traditional parental prerogative ("filial duty") while legitimizing the young woman's right to suit herself in marriage. That is, Scott effectually compromises between the generations or between the two subject positions (dutiful daughter and affective individual) her heroine so clearly inhabits, while at the same time illustrating the strains women suffered on the subject of marriage.[6]

What one observes in both of these texts from the year 1772, but particularly in this latter one by Scott, is a hesitation on the author's part about which side to choose in the generational conflict.

Yet in the course of the century there had been substantive changes in the ways marriages were made. After Lord Hardwicke's Act of 1753 eliminated the opportunity for most clandestine marriages, and after socially exclusive gatherings were institutionalized, parents had much less to fear from allowing a measure of social freedom to their adolescent children, and women had more opportunity to exert their newfound affective rights.[7] Local matchmaking was fostered by the building of assembly rooms in town after town during the period. In country towns there were balls, card parties, and assemblies, "particularly at the four assizes or at the major annual fairs or horse-racing events." At the national level "the institution of the London season, lasting from early in the New Year to June, and the subsequent season at a major watering place like Bath, provided the necessary facilities for the development of acquaintances across county boundaries."[8] By the beginning of the nineteenth century, the complex British marriage market was serving the interests of both the landed elite and the wealthy bourgeoisie.

Against the social backdrop of increased opportunity for companionate marriage, women who allowed themselves to be settled by their parents were regarded as being just as culpable as women who selected their partners solely because their time was running out. In the real world, the role of old maid was among the least desirable for women, and yet the number of upper-class women who never married was rising in the eighteenth century, growing to as much as 20 or 25 percent.[9] While novels posited ideal behavior for women who faced the very real danger of becoming the universal targets of jokes, then, they also cautioned women against marrying solely to avoid remaining old maids. As one of Fanny Burney's characters explains in *Camilla* (published in 1796, three years after the forty-one-year-old author married the French emigré d'Arblay), women often married for the wrong reasons: "their friends urged them . . . they had no other establishment in view . . . nothing is so uncertain as the repetition of matrimonial powers in women . . . those who cannot solicit what they wish, must accommodate themselves to what offers."[10] Courtship novels were replete with minor characters like Elizabeth Bennet's friend Charlotte, who, rather than living out their lives as old maids, chose matches that were at best indifferent.

Other women, confused by the choices before them and not

knowing how to select the true lover over the false, could make irrevocable mistakes. There was evidence, even in the magazines, that
women appreciated sketches detailing the kinds of choices they had
to make. As editor of the *Female Spectator*, Eliza Haywood featured a
letter from one "Bellamonte" who sought advice about three suitors
she described. Haywood judged that one suitor was sincere, one a
sentimentalist, and the third a "modern Narcissus."[11] A decade later
Frances Brooke's *Old Maid* took up similar questions, with "Mary
Singleton, Spinster" confiding to her readers, "Our sex, in the affair
of love, the most important of female life, and on which our whole
happiness in a great measure depends, is by no means upon an equal
footing with the other."[12] The question of choice was still current
enough in 1799 that the *Lady's Monthly Museum* satirically canvassed
women's motives for marrying:

Some few grovelling spirits among the ladies may, indeed, form a systematic
plan of advancing their interests, or gratifying their ambition, by a matrimonial connection. Some, even, who pass current in the muster-roll of virtuous women, may yet be base enough to dispose of their persons, by a
species of legal prostitution, to the highest bidder. But are there not many
amiable females, who surrender themselves into the arms of the enraptured
objects of their fondest regards, from the tenderest, from the most exalted
principles of esteem and affection? Others, again, mistake the transient glow
of passion, or the fond delirium of imagination, for the fervours of a rational
attachment, and rush presumptuously into the marriage state without reflection: while some placid souls, . . . bestow themselves on the first man
with whom it may be convenient to unite, merely as casualties of the moment
may favour them, or as their friends may advise, without being directed by
any motives of love or interest.[13]

From the charged diction with which the writer describes women's
sundry undesirable motives, it is clear that marrying from "the most
exalted principles of esteem and affection" was still an ideal by no
means generally achieved.

What then were the attributes a woman should look for in a de-
clared lover? According to the principles by which marriages had been
arranged, all requirements could be summed up in the word *equality*.
Within the earlier practice, equality referred to the grounds on which
the nobility and its middle-class imitators settled their daughters—
equal status and fortune. But as I have suggested in discussing the
heroine's blazon, from at least the middle of the eighteenth century
the term *equality* was complicated by a semantic shift coincident with
the change in marriage patterns. Equality of fortune and family status,
once prioritized in marriage arrangements, now became somewhat

less important. Along these lines, Alan Macfarlane observes that while most women who married peers before 1720 brought fortunes in money (£25,000 on the average), after that it was "very likely that whether they loved each other was increasingly important."[14]

Within the ideology of companionate marriage, inequality became a matter not so much of familial or dynastic concern as of individual psychological concern. As Frances Brooke explained in her periodical, "Marriage, where the disproportion of rank and fortune is very great, especially if the disadvantage is on the woman's side, seldom turns out happy." So much delicacy and circumspection are required that "it is next to impossible that their lives, can be passed agreeably. Equality is necessary to friendship; and without friendship marriage must be at best insipid, but oftener a state of perfect misery." The wealthier partner could not be sure that he was not loved solely for his money. Moreover, he might subsequently regret his choice and, feeling cheated of an equal fortune, make both lives miserable.[15]

Having already expressed herself quite plainly in her magazine, Brooke wrote another discussion of equality into her novel *Emily Montague* (discussed in chapter 6). Self-congratulatory, Brooke's groom urges parents to insure similar happiness for their children by considering that there must be parity of age, education, understanding, sentiment, and fortune to make a marriage.[16] Even more directly, Mary Ann Hanway's *Ellinor* (1798) advocates equal marriages by first describing an unequal union between a destitute man of "blood" and a wealthy tradesman's daughter, and then admonishing authorially, "We wish to impress on the minds of our young readers, for whose amusement, and, we hope, *instruction* , these sheets were penned, that the only chance for substantial pleasure in the marriage state is, where the ages, situation of life, and intellectual acquirements, are nearly on an *equality*."[17]

While some allowances were made for the exigencies of love, then, marriages between equals—in fortune and in family prestige—were considered safest. For those whose love prompted them to forget equality, public censure was a problem, at least where class boundaries were concerned. Richardson's *Pamela* (1740), though distinguished from the general pattern of courtship novel by its preoccupation with sexual pursuit, does offer some insight into contemporary wisdom about equality in marriage. Mr. B. warns Pamela about the criticism that will follow their marriage: "Here is Mr. B., with such and such an estate, has married his mother's waiting maid." He predicts that those who disapprove of his marriage will do so from principle: "The world sees not your perfections and excellencies."[18] As

Mr. B. suggests, the choice between social prudence and individual privilege was usually a difficult one.

The accommodation between the traditional understanding of equality (of fortune and class/status) and the new requirements of affective individualism is especially well articulated in Susannah Minifie Gunning's *Barford Abbey* (1768). Gunning's epistolary novel opens with a letter in which Lady Mary Sutton offers a home to Fanny Warley, whose guardian has just died. The orphaned Fanny will join her new guardian in Europe when means can be arranged, and in the interim she is invited to visit Barford Abbey. Though she is surrounded by new friends, Fanny, of unknown parentage, lives self-consciously on the margin of the exchange system. She hesitates to accept the invitation to Barford Abbey, for instance, because she remembers her deceased guardian's caution about the steward's son. "She well knew my poor expectations were ill suited to his large ones."[19] And when Fanny meets Sir James and Lady Powis, owners of the estate on which the abbey is located, their friendship, welcome as it is, only reinforces her consciousness that her mysterious birth places her outside the exchange system.

The reader's initial impression of this aristocratic couple, who insist on terming their steward Jenkings "friend" rather than "servant" and who invite a strange young woman to their house, is that they are benevolently egalitarian. But Jenkings and his wife understand that, when a fortuneless young woman visits a noble family with an eligible ward, she must be reminded of her place: "Mrs. Jenkings informed me, his Lordship [Lord Darcey] was a ward of Sir James's just of age;—his estate genteel, not large;—his education liberal,—his person fine,—his temper remarkably good.—Sir James, said she, is for ever preaching lessons to him, that he must marry *prudently*;—which is, that he must never marry without an immense fortune" (1:21-22). Sir James, it seems, is overly concerned about patrilineal matters, a fault that years earlier had caused his estrangement from their only son, who made an imprudent love match.

Yet even while the author gives full expression to the cautions against making an unequal match, she conveys through Sir James's troubled rhetoric the sense that ultimately his position is untenable. Thus Fanny's host includes in his description of the surrounding estates a description of the eligible bachelors who live on them. In effect, Sir James acknowledges his sympathy with her situation: the locale has "more smart young men, *Miss Warley*, than are to be met with in *every* county" (1:31). On the one hand, Sir James seems willing to assume that Fanny may find a husband in one of the elegant houses surrounding Barford Abbey, and to that end he takes a benevolent interest in defining her prospects. On the other, his speech serves to divert attention from Lord Darcey, the eligible bachelor who walks by his side. Ironically, though Sir James disapproves of a neighbor whose fortune will allow him to "purchase a *coronet* for his daughter" (1:32), it is just such an advantageous but emotionally impoverished match that he implies for Lord Darcey when he cautions, "Was Miss Warley a girl of fortune, I should think her born for you, Darcey.— As that is not the case,—take care of your heart, my Lord" (1:43).

The fact is that Sir James's initial disapproval of Darcey's growing affection for Fanny is an isolated authoritarian stance not only against his own heart but against his wife, Mr. and Mrs. Jenkings, Darcey and his friend Molesworth, and, in a reduplicative way, his estranged son, Mr. Powis. Gunning's epistolary novel allows her both to position Fanny squarely in the middle of two contending systems of nuptial practice and to encourage reader identification with her heroine's conflicting subject positions. From patriarchal ideology Fanny has nothing to hope, but from within the newer affective ideology she may legitimately challenge Darcey when it seems that he has been insincere in his attentions and does not intend to marry her. Meanwhile, the reader knows that Darcey hesitates to declare his love only because he promised his dying father to take Sir James's advice in regard to marriage.

The valuation of love over avarice, of benevolent and feminist sympathies over patriarchal ones is reaffirmed in Gunning's emotionally heightened conclusion. Finally giving in to his fondness for Fanny, Sir James approves Darcey's choice, but unfortunately not until Fanny has already left to join her guardian in France. Coincidentally, Sir James's prodigal son and his wife return, revealing that Fanny is their daughter. Thus, despite the almost radical egalitarianism that Gunning incorporates in her descriptions of the Powises, she renders hazily if at all an answer to the question of whether equality of family status and fortune still obtains as a requirement for marriage. Even if Sir James has been won over to the side of companionate marriage, the discovery that Fanny is his granddaughter effectually renders questions of social or financial prudence moot by the end of the novel.

In a last excess of complication, news arrives that Fanny has been lost in a shipwreck. Eventually discovered to have remained on shore because of a case of smallpox, Fanny returns to the Powises', where she is ecstatically welcomed to the familial relationships she had lacked. The concluding marriage represents the rule of heart over head, sanctioning the affective rights of the young in general, and of women in particular. Gunning enforces the point of her story through a wedding guest who writes to her mother, "Can you believe, after beholding Lord and Lady Darcey, I will ever be content with a moderate share of happiness?—No; I will die first—To see them at this instant would be an antidote for indifference" (2:182). For Gunning's identificatory female reader, the message must have been clear: *choice* and *love* were the terms of felicity belonging to woman's emergent role as affective individual.

FOURTEEN

Maria Edgeworth

BELINDA AND A
HEALTHY SCEPTICISM

INTRODUCED to London society as one of Mrs. Stanhope's nieces, the heroine of *Belinda* (1801) must brave the stigma of being associated with a matchmaker who prides herself "upon having established half a dozen nieces most happily, that is to say, upon having married them to men of fortunes superior to their own."[1] Probing the issues of love and choice through secondary characters as well as through the conflicting subject positions of her heroine, Maria Edgeworth articulated a broad range of ideological positions with regard to marriage and to women's roles.

Edgeworth's matchmaking aunt, anticipating Jane Austen's Mrs. Bennet, consistently employs a mercantile logic to persuade Belinda "that a young lady's chief business is to please in society, that all her charms and accomplishments should be invariably subservient to one grand object—the establishing herself in the world" (1). Young women of fortune can afford to enjoy themselves, to hesitate before choosing among their suitors, but Mrs. Stanhope warns that nothing is "more miserable than the situation of a poor girl, who, after spending not only the interest, but the solid capital of her small fortune in dress, and frivolous extravagance, fails in her matrimonial expectations (as many do merely from not beginning to speculate in time)" (3). Thus Belinda is urged to experience herself as a perishable commodity or failing stock and to take her profit while she can get it.

Having just arrived, Edgeworth's heroine overhears the gossip already circulating in London about herself and Mrs. Stanhope. She learns that, from the perspective of the young men surrounding the masked muse of tragedy, she, Belinda Portman, is but the latest commodity for a hawkster relation: "I take it she hangs upon hand; for last winter, when I was at Bath, she was hawked about every where, and the aunt was puffing her with might and main. You heard of nothing, wherever you went, but of Belinda Portman, and Belinda

Portman's accomplishments: Belinda Portman, and her accomplishments, I'll swear, were as well advertised as Packwood's razor strops" (19). Indeed, her aunt encourages Belinda to be opportunistic, variously urging her to be on the lookout for a good settlement, to take pains with her appearance when she meets Clarence Hervey, to accept the wealthy but foolish Sir Philip Baddely, to look pragmatically at the possibility (which reaches the aunt as gossip) that she may be Lord Delacour's next choice when his wife dies from the illness she apparently suffers. Innocent of design herself and mortified at being associated with fortune hunting, Belinda gleans from one of the young men a line that could serve as a moral for other scheming guardians and parents: "Girls brought to the hammer this way don't go off well" (19).

   Indeed, Mrs. Stanhope inadvertently furnishes Belinda with testimony against the kind of marriage she specializes in when she writes to complain of Belinda's "sister and cousins, who had married with mercenary views, had made themselves miserable, and had shown their aunt neither gratitude nor respect" (208). By this point, having been some time in London, Belinda has witnessed only disappointment in domestic arrangements. Against the immediate background of Mrs. Stanhope's letter detailing the misalliances of her female relatives and her own observation of the Delacour establishment, when she visits the Percival household she appreciates it as a kind of domestic utopia:

She found herself in the midst of a large and cheerful family, with whose domestic happiness she could not forebear to sympathize. There was an affectionate confidence, an unconstrained gaiety in this house, which forcibly struck her, from its contrast with what she had seen of Lady Delacour's. She perceived that between Mr. Percival and Lady Anne there was a union of interests, occupations, taste, and affection. . . .
   Lady Anne Percival had, without any pedantry or ostentation, much accurate knowledge, and a taste for literature, which made her the chosen companion of her husband's understanding, as well as of his heart. He was not obliged to reserve his conversation for friends of his own sex, nor was he forced to seclude himself in the pursuit of any branch of knowledge; the partner of his warmest affections was also the partner of his most serious occupations; her sympathy and approbation, and the daily sense of her success in the education of their children, inspired him with a degree of happy social energy, unknown to the selfish solitary votaries of avarice and ambition. [208-9]

   Beyond providing Belinda a model of domestic life founded on companionate marriage, the Percival household affords her lessons on how to select the right suitor. Choosing, as the disillusioned Lady Delacour has explained, is no easy process: "But let her judge by what she feels when a dexterous mercer or linen-draper produces pretty thing after pretty thing—and this is so becoming, and this will wear for ever, as he swears; but then that's so fashionable;—the novice stands in a charming perplexity, and after examining, and doubting, and tossing over half the goods in the shop, it's ten to one, when it begins to get late, the young lady, in a hurry, pitches upon the very ugliest and worst thing that she has seen" (30). Significantly, Lady Delacour's warning that a young woman's choice among suitors can be as difficult as selecting a new gown echoes Richardson, returning to the "mercer's shop" image first introduced over forty years earlier in *Sir Charles Grandison* (1753). The lesson is that courtship choices, like those made in shopping, can be confusing—an appropriate warning from one whose life has been dominated by the consumerism of the fashionable world.

In fact, the issue of courtship choices occupies no small part of Edgeworth's attention. Among the obstacles to the kind of companionate marriage she herself enjoys, Lady Anne explains, one must first contend with the ephemeral and irrational nature of love: "Our affections . . . arise from circumstances totally independent of our will. . . . They are excited by the agreeable or useful qualities that we discover in things or in persons . . . or by those which our fancies discover" (232). The subtext of their conversation is Belinda's confusion over Clarence Hervey; having heard of his rumored affair with a young woman named Virginia, she wonders how "without Ithuriel's spear," women are to know good from evil. Choice is rendered still more difficult, agrees Lady Anne, by the usual practice of courtship: "In the slight and frivolous intercourse, which fashionable belles usually have with those fashionable beaux who call themselves their lovers, it is surprising that they can discover any thing of each other's real character. Indeed they seldom do; and this probably is the cause why there are so many unsuitable and unhappy marriages. A woman who has an opportunity of seeing her lover in private society, in domestic life, has infinite advantages; for if she has any sense, and he has any sincerity, the real character of both may perhaps be developed" (232). In its usual practice, courtship is so constrained by unrealistic social expectations that two people may marry with little knowledge of each other's character.

Gaining sufficient knowledge of a lover's character takes time and entails the risk that "after the world suspects that the two people are engaged to each other, it is scarcely possible for the woman to recede." But even if "the drawn sword of tyrant custom [is] suspended over her head by a single hair," Mr. Percival and Lady Anne's judgment is that beyond a certain point, a woman's "respect for the opinion of the world . . . is weakness" (239). Thus, with apparent respect for the drawn sword of custom, for hegemonic ideology, Edgeworth nonetheless issues what may be read as a feminist challenge to contemporary courtship practice.

Ironically, it is from this feminist subject position that Belinda discourages Lady Anne's suit for her ward, Mr. Vincent. With much the same sentiment as Richardson's Harriet Byron rejects Sir Hargrave Pollexfen, she explains: "He is very handsome, he is well bred, and his manners are unaffected . . . but—do not accuse me of caprice—altogether he does not suit my taste; and I cannot think it sufficient not to feel disgust for a husband—though I believe this is the fashionable doctrine." When her friend counters that by living in the same household, she may grow accustomed to Mr. Vincent, Belinda pleasantly retorts, "I do not doubt but one might grow *accustomed* to Caliban" (234). Neither respect nor simple familiarity will suffice for marriage, according to Edgeworth's heroine.

As well as challenging their courtship roles, Edgeworth is concerned to examine other roles women are socialized to reject or accept, and this she often accomplishes through intertextual reference. Refracting woman's position, the author brings to bear a series of representational misconstructions, usually set apart, rhetorically or visually framed for the reader's attention.[2] The new woman is to be neither an Amazon nor an Eve; neither a fashionable woman, nor a Sophie, nor a Griselda.

In one negative exemplum, Harriot Freke, the most extreme of Edgeworth's offenders against "femininity," is visually framed for our attention, depicted standing on a cliff practicing manual exercise with a firearm. By this point we already know her as outrageously masculine in pranks and dress, for it was she who promoted the female duel in which Lady Delacour was wounded by a powder flash (the wound that makes Lady Delacour fear for her life). Later, when Harriot Freke forces her way into the Percival household, intending to lure Belinda to cabal against Lady Delacour, her speech ominously echoes Satan's seduction of Eve in *Paradise Lost*. Belinda, though, is no Eve, injudiciously proud of her own strength, and she reminds Freke that it is not Milton "but Satan, who says, 'Fallen spirit, to be weak is to be miserable' " (219). This passage—Belinda's assertion of her own weakness even as she demonstrates her strength—suggests a female ideal. Rather than enslaving women, delicacy, in Lady Anne's words, "conduces to their happiness" (222).

Most unusual among the several little histories in the novel is the

subplot involving Clarence Hervey's misguided Rousseauism, his attempted education of a second Sophie, whom he plans to marry when
she reaches adulthood.[3] Once more, Edgeworth uses internal framing
to demonstrate the insufficiency of the implied female role. As the
young woman he has chosen matures, Hervey begins to recognize
that while she is beautiful when represented on canvas as St. Pierre's
Virginia, she is, in comparison with Lady Delacour and Belinda, an
insipid and potentially embarrassing companion for a man of the
world. On Virginia's side, too, the experiment fails, for rather than
falling in love with Hervey, she becomes obsessed by a spectral sailor
whose original she saw in a picture (or perhaps briefly in person?).
Beyond demonstrating the futility of trying to raise a woman outside
of and consequently unshaped by society, the scene reminds us that
love is irrational and no more determinable by the means Hervey uses
than by the usual manipulations of patriarchy. Having read romances,
Virginia has already been substantially brought to understand herself
in relation to a world, if only an attenuated one of heroes and heroines.
Thus she laments having seen the "fatal picture," which supplants
in her dreams her dutiful affection for Hervey: "When I read of heroes
in the day, that figure rises to my view, instead of yours, in my dreams;
it speaks to me, it kneels to me. . . . I saw you weltering in your blood;
I tried to save you, but could not. I heard you say, 'Perfidious, un-
grateful Virginia! you are the cause of my death!' Oh, it was the most
dreadful night I ever passed! Still this figure, this picture, was before
me; and he was the knight of the white plumes; and it was he who
stabbed you; but when I wished him to be victorious, I did not know
that he was fighting against you" (453).

Virginia's experience resembles Mr. Percival's explanation of first
love: "From poetry or romance, young people usually form their earlier ideas of love, before they have actually felt the passion; and the
image which they have in their own minds of the *beau ideal* is cast
upon the first objects they afterward behold" (247). Implicitly,
through her precocious dramatization of animus possession, Edgeworth displaces duty, reason, and gratitude—conventional terms for
marriage—with irrationality, fancy, and love.

Of the instructive voices in the novel, Lady Ann Percival's is most
attractive, probably representing Edgeworth's own opinions, both on
courtship and on roles for women. Yet while Edgeworth clearly presents Lady Anne as a model "domestic" woman, she is not, as Dr.
X—— warns Hervey, "an old-fashioned spiritless, patient Griselda"
(90). No doubt suggesting a pattern for the ideal woman Mary Brunton
depicted in her novel *Discipline* (1814), published thirteen years later,
Edgeworth records Clarence Hervey's realization that no represen-

tation can do Lady Anne justice: "Clarence Hervey was so much struck with the expression of happiness in Lady Anne's countenance, that he absolutely forgot to compare her beauty with Lady Delacour's. Whether her eyes were large or small, blue or hazel, he could not tell; nay, he might have been puzzled if he had been asked the colour of her hair. Whether she were handsome by the rules of art, he knew not; but he felt that she had the essential charm of beauty, the power of prepossessing the heart immediately in her favour" (91). Fittingly, when Belinda herself sketches Lady Percival and her children, she copies a portrait, registering once more the novelist's recognition that, as inadequate as conventional techniques or terms are, they are the only ones available to the artist or writer.

Significantly, it is their common desire to relocate the world-weary Lady Delacour in the kind of domestic life the Percivals enjoy that ultimately unites Clarence Hervey and Belinda in the final pages of the novel. Similarly, when she herself has been reconciled to husband and daughter, Lady Delacour self-consciously choreographs the other characters, physically placing them in a highly symbolic tableau, an assemblage of domestic portraits:

What signifies being happy, unless we appear so?—Captain Sunderland— kneeling with Virginia, if you please, sir, at her father's feet: you in the act of giving them your blessing, Mr. Hartley. . . . Clarence, you have a right to Belinda's hand, and may kiss it too: nay, Miss Portman, it is the rule of the stage. Now, where's my Lord Delacour? he should be embracing me, to show that we are reconciled. Ha! here he comes—Enter Lord Delacour, with little Helena in his hand—very well! . . . Now, Lady Delacour, to show that she is reformed, comes forward to address the audience with a moral—a moral! Yes,
    "Our *tale* contains a *moral*; and, no doubt,
    You all have wit enough to find it out." [463]

In this highly self-reflexive scene, Edgeworth affirms what her text has repeatedly suggested through framed representations and re- fractions of negative exempla—that the most desirable role for woman is a domestic one, a partnership within companionate marriage. Yet, at the same time, the fact that Edgeworth chooses to have Lady De- lacour arrange the scene serves as her acknowledgement that even in fiction the domestic tableau ("being happy") is achieved with diffi- culty.

Published some eight years later, Edgeworth's *Manoeuvring* (1809) displays a similar concern with marital happiness, and so complete was the paradigm change in favor of companionate marriage by this

time that the title referred uncompromisingly to parental "maneuvering," to the unfortunate machinations of a mother concerned to
"settle" her children in good marriages. Mrs. Beaumont wishes to
marry her daughter to Sir John Hunter, "heir presumptive to a great
estate" because there was in his family a certain reversionary title.[4]
By Mrs. Beaumont's calculations, Miss Hunter, Sir John's younger
sister, will be an ideal match for her son; she not only possesses an
independent fortune of two hundred thousand pounds but is also so
"childish and silly" that her mother-in-law might depend on man-
aging her. With one exception, all the maneuverer's plots fail. Ironically, in the case of her own marriage alone is Mrs. Beaumont's
plotting successful, but the young man she snares turns out to be a
maneuverer in his own right, a disappointed heir become fortune
hunter who is quite venal enough to marry a rich widow.

Edgeworth's apparent point, in this novel, as in *Belinda*, is to
illustrate the kind of courtship that leads to domestic happiness, yet
she admits that from her audience's perspective her lovers may be
dull. As she had in *Belinda*, she breaks through the conventional descriptions, this time of the concluding wedding, with a commentary
on the difficulty of representing love: "Happy love, though the most
delightful in reality, is the most uninteresting in description; and
lovers are proverbially bad company, except for one another: therefore
we shall not intrude on Captain Walsingham and Amelia, nor shall
we give a journal of the days of courtship; those days which, by
Rousseau, and many people, have been pronounced to be the hap-
piest; by others, the only happy days of existence; and which, by
some privileged or prudent few, have been found to be but the prelude
to the increasing pleasures of domestic union" (135).

Here, as elsewhere, Edgeworth signals her reluctance to depend
on the conventionally depicted ideal—in this case, love in marriage—
as a matter of course or convention. Through her metatextual commentary, Edgeworth reminds her readers not to take their happiness
for granted; she adverts to love's individual pleasures, pleasures
which, though the "most delightful in reality," defy representation.

FIFTEEN

Jane Austen

THE BLAZON OVERTURNED

JANE AUSTEN's novels, along with those by Maria Edgeworth, Mary Brunton, and Susan Ferrier, were the last grand flourish of the courtship novel, sounded at the beginning of a century that was to modulate domestic themes with public ones, bridging into the Victorian. Like her literary forbears who wrote women's courtship novels, Austen interrogated the terms and the practices of the marriage market— the commodification of women by society—and like them she suggested alternatives to the subject positions society made available to women in her period.

Not surprisingly, the blazon in one shape or another was Austen's standard beginning, and parallel connivances at the marriage market shaded many of her parents and guardians, legitimizing their daughters' resistance.[1] One of the social proscriptions that Austen took apparent pleasure in examining was that against unequal matches, especially advice against marriages involving class or status inequities. *Mansfield Park* (1814), for instance, begins by recording the community's ironic admiration at how well Lady Bertram has married, how far her brilliant match exceeded the expectations raised by her blazon: "About thirty years ago, Miss Maria Ward of Huntingdon, with only seven thousand pounds, had the good luck to captivate Sir Thomas Bertram, of Mansfield Park, in the country of Northampton, and to be thereby raised to the rank of a baronet's lady, with all the comforts and consequences of an handsome house and large income. All Huntingdon exclaimed on the greatness of the match, and her uncle, the lawyer himself, allowed her to be at least three thousand pounds short of any equitable claim to it."[2]

Austen's language refers the question of marriage to the marketplace, where Maria Ward's marriage may be judged a fortunate one in terms of economic and class interests. The blazon (here limited to family and fortune) is merely one means among several used to portray a foolish character, the ironic point being that Lady Bertram and all Huntingdon take seriously this reductive reading of her "good luck." Whether one judges equality in marriage on the basis of money, family status, virtue, or affect, Sir Thomas has decidedly not met his equal in vapid Lady Bertram.

In *Pride and Prejudice* (1813), especially, the blazon becomes a recurrent trope whose attendant issues—unequal matches, conniving parents, and resistant daughters—shape the entire novel. Particularly significant are Mrs. Bennet and Lady Catherine de Bourgh, two "maneuverers" (to borrow Edgeworth's word), whose encroaching voices menace those around them. Much as the reader understands the Bennets by their complicities and resistances to Mrs. Bennet, so the reader understands Lady Catherine de Bourgh's circle in relation to her. Both women represent versions of patriarchy, a pervasively influential but otherwise absent authority in the novel. Significantly, these maneuvering women body forth patriarchy against their sex, for in the absence of strong male characters it is their business to manage the traffic in women; it is they who adjudicate blazons.

A maneuverer in the extreme, Mrs. Bennet influences Austen's narrative voice, fixing the point of view from which the reader approaches the Bennet household. Hers is the ethic of the famous first lines: "It is a truth universally acknowledged, that a single man in possession of a good fortune, must be in want of a wife. . . . this truth is so well fixed in the minds of the surrounding families, that he is considered as the rightful property of some one or other of their daughters."[3] Hers is the depreciation of affective relationships from which the reader repeatedly recoils: "A single man of large fortune; four or five thousand a year. What a fine thing for our girls" (2). Mrs. Bennet assumes the attitude of a customer in an ill-stocked market, enlisting her husband in the competition by encouraging him to visit the eligible Mr. Bingley before their neighbors' daughters engross all the young bachelor's attention. From the subject position of a maneuvering mother, we understand the initial description of Darcy at the assembly: "Mr. Darcy soon drew the attention of the room by his fine, tall person, handsome features, noble mien; and the report which was in general circulation within five minutes after his entrance, of his having ten thousand a year" (7). Darcy's blazon is devalued, and his attraction diminishes immediately, however, when the Bennets and their neighbors realize that his aristocratic pride will prevent his entering into any "exchange" with them. Thereafter, Mrs. Bennet's dislike of Darcy is settled until his taking Elizabeth off her hands surprises her into apology. In proportion to his fortune and possessions, Mr. Darcy becomes "charming" and Lizzy is "sweetest"; Mrs. Bennet reduces their marriage, as she has all the others, to material terms—"pin-money," "jewels," "carriages," and "a house in town."

On Darcy's side, no less than on Lizzy's, there is a maneuvering woman, Lady Catherine. Our prepossession against her begins with Mr. Collins's visit. His constant reference to her as an absent authority on everything from chimneypieces to his own marriage comprises the first step in Austen's dismantling of this patriarchal and aristocratic figurehead. Collins's courtship visit to the Bennet household is one of many parodic shadows that surround the true courtships between Jane and Bingley and between Elizabeth and Darcy. But it also prepares for the later garden scene between Lady Catherine and Elizabeth. For Mr. Collins, the object is to find a wife, as Lady Catherine has advised. With little embarrassment, then, he transfers his suit from Jane to Elizabeth and finally to Charlotte Lucas. His formal rhetoric is of a piece with his studied compliments for Lady Catherine and, the reader suspects, is as interchangeable as the object of his intentions.[4] Mr. Collins, fearing that he will be "run away with" by his feelings for Elizabeth, launches into his reasons for marrying as though he were arguing a case in court. It is clear from his subsequent speech that his third motive, Lady Catherine's "particular advice and recommendation," is most pressing and that his marriage is merely another studied compliment for his patron. He concludes his proposal with an ironic coupling of affection and fortune: "And now nothing remains for me but to assure you in the most animated language of the violence of my affection. To fortune I am perfectly indifferent, and shall make no demand of that nature on your father, since I am well aware that it could not be complied with; and that one thousand pounds in the 4 per cents. which will not be yours till after your mother's decease, is all that you may ever be entitled to" (96). Collins's inflated diction reveals the paucity of his affection and the fullness of his disappointment with Elizabeth's fortune.

In his inability to credit her refusal, Collins resorts more directly to the market patois, which has all along been his measure of the match. In effect, he calls out the blazon which should remind Elizabeth that he offers wares she cannot afford to refuse: "It does not appear to me that my hand is unworthy your acceptance, or that the establishment I can offer would be any other than highly desirable. My situation in life, my connections with the family of De Bourgh, and my relationship to your own, are circumstances highly in my favour; and you should take it into farther consideration that in spite of your manifold attractions, it is by no means certain that another offer of marriage may ever be made you. Your portion is unhappily so small that it will in all likelihood undo the effects of your loveliness and amiable qualifications" (97-98). Collins's reminder of Elizabeth's inadequate bargaining position does not affect her decision, which, unlike his proposal, is individual and sincere: "Do not consider me now as an elegant female intending to plague you, but as a rational creature speaking the truth from her heart" (98).

Ironically, the next proposal Elizabeth receives also borrows its terms from Lady Catherine. Just as Collins's proposal betrayed its inadequacy by its conflicted rhetoric, so Darcy's first declaration reveals its insufficiency by a double-voicedness. Darcy's love for Elizabeth is sincere, but the language of family and class pride suffuses his proposal: "He spoke well, but there were feelings besides those of the heart to be detailed, and he was not more eloquent on the subject of tenderness than of pride. His sense of her inferiority—of its being a degradation—of the family obstacles which judgment had always opposed to inclinations, were dwelt on with a warmth which seemed due to the consequence he was wounding, but was very unlikely to recommend his suit" (168). Darcy's ardent love is undercut by the patriarchal considerations that invade his language; his aunt's voice obtrudes, as it were, on his own sincere passion. His suit is a reminder that the language of trade is not reserved to one class. Like Collins's, Darcy's first proposal depends to no small degree on marriage market calculations, on the blazon by which he refers to Lizzy's connections as "inferior," and on that basis he anticipates (as he later admits) her acceptance of the offer.

Lizzy's reply, as in the earlier scene with Collins, simultaneously alludes to and rejects the commonly received wisdom and its formulaic language: "In such cases as this, it is, I believe, the established mode to express a sense of obligation for the sentiments avowed" (169). Experiencing no gratitude, however, Lizzy expresses none. As the exchange becomes more heated, she diverges even further from the normative language of patriarchally ordered courtship, tracing her "disapprobation" to his "arrogance . . . conceit, and . . . selfish disdain of the feelings of others." Her dislike she characterizes as "immovable": "I had not known you a month before I felt that you were the last man in the world whom I could ever be prevailed on to marry" (172). By the standards of her maneuvering mother or of Darcy's proud aunt, Elizabeth's answer, like Harriet Byron's to Sir Hargrave Pollexfen ("You do not . . . hit . . . my fancy"), is inexplicable.

Implicitly, in her divergence from marriage-market calculations and decorums, Austen's heroine recommends to the identificatory reader the new ethic for female behavior, the new subject position from which to consider societal wisdom about equal marriages. Before the author can bring Elizabeth and Darcy to the point of seeing beyond "pride and prejudice," however, she must elaborate on the extent to which an individual woman may withstand the demands of patriarchy. This she does through the scene in which Lady Catherine confronts Lizzy with the rumor of her engagement to Darcy. Austen heightens the effect by the setting she chooses, the same copse to which Mr. Bennet, Jane, and Lizzy variously retreat when they are emotionally troubled. It is the copse in which Lizzy has just read her aunt's letter explaining Darcy's generous interventions in arranging the runaway Lydia's marriage.

Lady Catherine speaks with the vested authority of her family and class as she explains the prior engagement that exists between Darcy and her daughter: "From their infancy, they have been intended for each other. It was the favourite wish of *his* mother, as well as of her's. While in their cradles, we planned the union" (315). The agents for this exchange may be female, but its nature remains "patriarchal"—concerned not for individual good but for familial well-being, the transmission of property and status. But Lizzy denies the validity of this claim, despite the brandished weapons of patriarchy against her own marriage to Darcy—"honour, decorum, prudence, nay, interest, forbid it" (315). In frustration, Lady Catherine resorts, as had Collins and Darcy, to the calculated taxonomy of the blazon: "My daughter and my nephew are formed for each other. They are descended on the maternal side, from the same noble line; and, on the father's, from respectable, honourable, and ancient, though untitled families. Their fortune on both sides is splendid. They are destined for each other by the voice of every member of their respective houses; and what is to divide them? The upstart pretensions of a young woman without family, connections, or fortune" (316).

The argument, forceful as it appears, is the predictable, the inflexible, authoritative word of patriarchy. To it, Lizzy returns several radical arguments. First, rejecting Lady Catherine's arguments for class endogamy ("descended . . . from the same noble line"), she insists that, as a gentleman's daughter, she is Darcy's equal.[5] Lizzy questions Lady Catherine's premise that Darcy may be brought to marry Miss de Bourgh at all. Finally, Lizzy asserts that she will not be intimidated and that Lady Catherine has no right to interfere in her affairs: "Neither duty, nor honour, nor gratitude . . . have any possible claim on me, in the present instance. No principle of either, would be violated by my marriage with Mr. Darcy. And with regard to the resentment of his family, or the indignation of the world, if the former *were* excited by his marrying me, it would not give me one moment's concern—and the world in general would have too much sense to join in the scorn" (318). Lizzy's charged rhetoric and the stand she takes against patriarchal exchange mark her as a resistant figure worthy of emulation by young women readers of Austen's period.

Moreover, Lady Catherine's intended disruption of Lizzy's and Darcy's engagement is the very encouragement needed to bring the engagement on, for his aunt's account of the meeting proves to Darcy that he need not give up hope. Lizzy, he believes, would have acknowledged an irrevocable decision against him "frankly and openly." It is to her earlier candid refusal that he attributes his reform, explaining that he was spoiled from childhood, "allowed, encouraged, almost taught . . . to be selfish and overbearing, to care for none beyond my own family circle, to think meanly of all the rest of the world, to *wish* at least to think meanly of their sense and worth compared with my own" (328). He is grateful for the humbling experience of his first proposal: "I came to you without a doubt of my reception. You shewed me how insufficient were all my pretensions to please a woman worthy of being pleased" (328). Darcy humbled is the patriarchy humbled, as his words make clear; Lizzy has taught him that the measure for marriage is no longer his blazon—his fortune and class prestige—but his "pleasing," which can only be assessed from her subjective point of view. Within the newer system of companionate marriage, the terms of the blazon are emptied of value.

Granted, as Nancy Armstrong's *Desire and Domestic Fiction* so convincingly demonstrates, the sexual dynamics of Austen's novel—of all the courtship stories I have discussed—may be read as masking underlying class dynamics.[6] But to read them solely in this way is both to undervalue the dynamic relationship between female writers and readers and to impose an anachronistic mistrust of the domestic on one's reading of eighteenth-century texts. After all, Austen and her predecessors in the courtship novel wrote long before women made up any appreciable part of the labor force, long before they had any political rights. To value their heroines according to their contexts, then, we must begin by understanding that in the eighteenth century, affective individualism—narrowly defined as the right of choosing a partner within heterosexual marriage—was a feminist cause.

If we love Lizzy best among Austen's heroines, though, it is not solely for the feminist subject position she delineates but also for her redemptive role in relation to Darcy, whom she leads out of the confines of pride into the new territory of rhetorical freedom. The change is especially marked in two scenes at the conclusion of the novel. In the first, when Lizzy calls for Darcy's explanation of his love, he attributes it to the "liveliness of her mind." As she rephrases it, he was "disgusted with the women who were always speaking and looking, and thinking for *your* approbation alone" (338). The passage marks Lizzy's difference, her individuality, as compared with the designing women Darcy has known. When they decide to announce their engagement to Lady Catherine, Lizzy teases, "And if I had not a letter to write myself, I might sit by you, and admire the evenness of your writing, as another young lady once did. But I have an aunt, too, who must not be longer neglected" (339-40). Lizzy distances herself from self-objectification, and by remembering that she too has a letter to write, she substitutes an active purposiveness for Miss Bingley's earlier passivity.

That Lizzy's verbal freedom makes a substantial change in Darcy's life, and that his conversion to more feminist and more egalitarian principles is to be lasting, is further evident in Austen's brief treatment of their life at Pemberley after marriage. From Georgiana's viewpoint, the change in her brother is startling: "At first she often listened with an astonishment bordering on alarm, at her [Elizabeth's] lively, sportive, manner of talking to her brother. He, who had always inspired in herself a respect which almost overcame her affection, she now saw the object of open pleasantry. Her mind received knowledge which had never before fallen in her way. By Elizabeth's instructions she began to comprehend that a woman may take liberties with her husband, which a brother will not always allow in a sister more than ten years younger than himself" (345). This we may understand as the real object lesson for Austen's readers; like Lizzy, they are to take liberties with the facade of patriarchy, to domesticate the Darceys of the world. Elizabeth does not "pollute" the shades of Pemberley, as Lady Catherine feared, but rather brings the utopian promise of the estate to fulfillment.

CONCLUSION

GIVEN OUR late-twentieth-century horizons of expectation about marriage, it goes against current modes of critical thought to suggest that such a genre as the courtship novel could advance feminist positions. We distrust the sacrifices of autonomy and individual achievement that "domestic bliss" has entailed for women, and we understand that the heterosexually rendered model of affective relationships—"husband-wife"—excludes substantial numbers of the population. There is no question but that eighteenth- and early nineteenth-century courtship novels, read against today's social conditions, yield little that modern readers of even the most conservative women's magazine would label "feminist."

Yet the sole act of writing was enough to distinguish Eliza Haywood, Charlotte Lennox, Mary Brunton, and other courtship novelists as women of unusual courage. By braving the sexual/textual trope, they set themselves apart from their sisters even as they selectively appealed to women through the kinds of stories they chose to tell, the kinds of lessons they tried to point. Writing at a time when the decorums of marriage were shifting, with emphasis increasingly falling on the affective relationship of wife and husband, courtship novelists quietly championed women's rights to choose marriage partners for personal, relational reasons rather than for familial, economic ones. Hence, while uninitiated twentieth-century readers may see courtship novels as no more than quiet renderings of domestic stories, eighteenth- and nineteenth-century women readers were much more likely to feel personally interested in what they perceived as a progressive, feminist attention to their subject positions.

Specifically appealing to young women readers, courtship novelists focused attention on courtship issues, on the brief and limited opportunity for autonomy that women enjoyed before they married; their common agenda was to disturb established ideas about how dutiful daughters and prudent young women should comport themselves during their courtships. Insofar as novelists problematized the subject positions through which contemporary women viewed themselves, they may be seen as the Enlightenment equivalent of suffragettes and ERA activists. To read this subgenre bound by the works of Samuel Richardson and Jane Austen, then, is to appreciate the fact that numbers of British writers in the period 1740–1820 were protesting at least part of the socially encoded disadvantages suffered by women: as students, as writers and speakers, and as daughters and wives.

CHRONOLOGY OF COURTSHIP NOVELS

1740   Samuel Richardson, *Pamela*
1741   Samuel Richardson, *Pamela*, part two
1744   Mary Collyer, *Felicia to Charlotte*, vol. 1
       Eliza Haywood, *The Fortunate Foundlings*
1749   Mary Collyer, *Felicia to Charlotte*, vol. 2
1752   Charlotte Lennox, *The Female Quixote*
1753   Haywood, *The History of Jemmy and Jenny Jessamy*
1753-54   Samuel Richardson, *Sir Charles Grandison*
1758   Charlotte Lennox, *Henrietta*
1762   Charlotte Lennox, *Sophia*
1768   Susannah Minifie Gunning, *Barford Abbey*
1769   Frances Moore Brooke, *The History of Emily Montague*
1772   Sarah Robinson Scott, *A Test of Filial Duty*
1777   Henry Mackenzie, *Julia de Roubigné*
1778   Fanny Burney, *Evelina*
1782   Fanny Burney, *Cecilia*
1788   Mary Wollstonecraft, *Mary, a Fiction*
       Charlotte Smith, *Emmeline*
1789   Charlotte Smith, *Ethelinde*
1790   Helen Maria Williams, *Julia*
1791   Elizabeth Inchbald, *A Simple Story*
1792   Thomas Holcroft, *Anna St. Ives*
1793   Jane West, *The Advantages of Education*
       Susannah Minifie Gunning, *The Memoirs of Mary*
       Mary Wollstonecraft (attributed to Gilbert Imlay), *The Emigrants*
1794   Mary Hays, *Memoirs of Emma Courtney*
1796   Fanny Burney, *Camilla*
1797   Jane West, *A Gossip's Story*
1798   Mary Ann Hanway, *Ellinor*
       Mary Wollstonecraft, *Maria; or, The Wrongs of Woman*
1799   Jane West, *A Tale of the Times*
1801   Maria Edgeworth, *Belinda* Maria Edgeworth, *Angelina*
1804   Amelia Opie, *Adeline Mowbray*
1808   Hannah More, *Coelebs in Search of a Wife*
1809   Maria Edgeworth, *Manoeuvring*
1811   Jane Austen, *Sense and Sensibility* Mary Brunton, *Self-Control*
1812   Amelia Opie, *False or True*
1813   Jane Austen, *Pride and Prejudice*
       Eaton Stannard Barrett, *The Heroine*

1814   Jane Austen, *Mansfield Park*
       Mary Brunton, *Discipline*
       Maria Edgeworth, *Patronage*
1816   Jane Austen, *Emma*
1818   Jane Austen, *Northanger Abbey*
       Jane Austen, *Persuasion*
       Susan Ferrier, *Marriage*
1824   Susan Ferrier, *Inheritance*

NOTES

Introduction

1. Tony Tanner, *Adultery in the Novel: Contract and Transgression* (Baltimore: Johns Hopkins Univ. Press, 1979), 16.

2. See C.B. Macpherson, *The Political Theory of Possessive Individualism: Hobbes to Locke* (Oxford: Clarendon Press, 1962); Alan Macfarlane, *The Origins of English Individualism* (New York: Cambridge Univ. Press, 1978); and J.G.A. Pocock, *Virtue, Commerce, and History: Essays on Political Thought and History, Chiefly in the Eighteenth Century* (Cambridge: Cambridge Univ. Press, 1985).

3. Despite the considerable criticism it has received for obscuring distinctions of class and gender, Lawrence Stone's *The Family, Sex and Marriage in England, 1500-1800* (New York: Harper and Row, 1977) remains valuable for the wealth of literary and documentary evidence it assembles in relation to changing conceptions of marriage among the English gentry and nobility. Randolph Trumbach's *The Rise of the Egalitarian Family* (New York: Academic Press, 1978), focusing on the practice of aristocratic families, enforces the point that companionate marriage became the social ideal; even for younger sons of the nobility, "it had become distasteful . . . to use marriage for financial gain" (71). John R. Gillis comments in *For Better, For Worse: British Marriages, 1600 to the Present* (New York: Oxford Univ. Press, 1985) that by 1850 middling and upper-class marriage practices converged toward their common interests, companionate marriage and capital accumulation: "While young people were told they must marry for love and were given a certain latitude in the choice of mates, the courtship process was carefully constructed to prevent misalliance" (135). For their surveys of the scholarship on the question, see Rita Goldberg, *Sex and Enlightenment: Women in Richardson and Diderot* (Cambridge: Cambridge Univ. Press, 1984), 51-55; Janet Todd, *Sensibility: An Introduction* (New York: Methuen, 15-16; and Roy Roussel, *The Conversation of the Sexes: Seduction and Equality in Selected Seventeenth- and Eighteenth-Century Texts* (New York: Oxford Univ. Press, 1986), 86-87.

4. Courtship, much simpler when women are perceived as interchangeable, is complicated when women are permitted individual choice. Alan Macfarlane observes, in *Marriage and Love in England: Modes of Reproduction, 1300-1840* (New York: Basil Blackwell, 1986), that "the elaborate and widespread courtship system is hence both an expression and a contributory cause of the individualistic social system which had developed early in England" (308-9).

5. Ibid., 291-94.

6. See Edmund Leites, *The Puritan Conscience and Modern Sexuality* (New

Haven: Yale Univ. Press, 1986) for a discussion of Puritan interest in moral autonomy.

7. Samuel Richardson's novels initiate, or at least coincide with, the beginning of a preoccupation with ingenue heroines and their courtships that extends through some two dozen authors and culminates in the early nineteenth-century novels of Jane Austen. See the appendix for a chronological list of authors and works.

Recently Nancy Armstrong has argued compellingly, in *Desire and Domestic Fiction* (New York: Oxford Univ. Press, 1987), that "stories of courtship and marriage offered their readers a way of indulging, with a kind of impunity, in fantasies of political power that were the more acceptable because they were played out within a domestic framework where legitimate monogamy—and thus the subordination of female to male—would ultimately be affirmed" (29). While acknowledging the conscriptive hegemonic forces to which minority texts are always subject, my study of the feminized novel differs from Armstrong's in focusing on the female tradition and on women's issues.

8. Nancy Miller in "Rereading as a Woman: The Body in Practice," in *The Female Body in Western Culture*, ed. Susan Suleiman (Cambridge: Harvard Univ. Press, 1986) proposes that to reread as a woman is "to imagine while reading the place of a woman's body; to read reminded that her identity is also re-membered in stories of the body" (355-56).

9. Sandra M. Gilbert and Susan Gubar, *The Madwoman in the Attic* (New Haven: Yale Univ. Press, 1979), 154-55. Gilbert and Gubar return to this question in *The War of the Words*, vol. 1 of *No Man's Land: The Place of the Woman Writer in the Twentieth Century* (New Haven: Yale Univ. Press, 1988), 227-71.

10. Jane Spencer, *The Rise of the Woman Novelist* (Oxford: Basil Blackwell, 1986), 25ff, 78-79.

11. For a thorough summary of this debate, see the first chapter of Margaret Homans, *Bearing the Word: Language and Female Experience in Nineteenth-Century Woman's Writing* (Chicago: Univ. of Chicago Press, 1986).

12. Gilbert and Gubar, *Madwoman in the Attic*, 7.

13. For a discussion of *l'écriture féminine*, see Toril Moi, *Sexual/Textual Politics: Feminist Literary Theory* (London: Methuen, 1985), 108-26.

14. Nancy Chodorow, *The Reproduction of Mothering* (Berkely: Univ. of California Press, 1978).

15. Homans, *Bearing the Word*, chapter 1.

16. Some recent examples are Terry Eagleton, *The Rape of Clarissa* (Minneapolis: Univ. of Minnesota Press, 1982); Jon Stratton, *The Virgin Text: Fiction, Sexuality, and Ideology* (Sussex: Harvester Press, 1987); and Armstrong, *Desire and Domestic Fiction*.

17. Armstrong, *Desire and Domestic Fiction*, 51.

18. Jane Austen, *Pride and Prejudice*, ed. Frank W. Bradbrook (London: Oxford Univ. Press, 1970), 345.

19. M.M. Bakhtin, *The Dialogic Imagination*, trans. Michael Holquist and Caryl Emerson, ed. Michael Holquist (Austin: Univ. of Texas Press, 1981), 342.

20. Paul Smith, *Discerning the Subject*, vol. 55 of *Theory and History of Literature* (Minneapolis: Univ. of Minnesota Press, 1989), xxix.

21. According to Smith (ibid., chapter 1), Marxism has not yet come to terms with the ways individual experience may empower resistance.

22. Smith, *Discerning the Subject*, 5.

23. Ibid., 137.

24. Arguing along somewhat similar lines, Linda S. Kauffman, *Discourses of Desire: Gender, Genre, and Epistolary Fictions* (Ithaca: Cornell Univ. Press, 1986) demonstrates the interrelatedness of amorous epistolary discourse, which is eventually assimilated into such novels as *Clarissa*. Originating in the milieu to which Ovid's *Heroides* are a response, certain motifs also appear in the novel: rebellion against fathers and lovers, against their control of women and speech, against their representations of women (122).

One. *The Courtship Novel*

1. John Bennet, *Letters to a Young Lady, on a Variety of Useful and Interesting Subjects; Calculated to Improve the Heart, Form the Manners, and Enlighten the Understanding* (Newburyport: John Mycall, 1792), 2:101.

2. Ann Rosalind Jones, "Surprising Fame: Renaissance Gender Ideologies and Women's Lyric," in *The Poetics of Gender*, ed. Nancy K. Miller (New York: Columbia Univ. Press, 1986), 76.

3. Kauffman, in *Discourses of Desire*, traces the influence of amorous epistolary discourse from the earliest extant textual example, Ovid's *Heroides*, through the modern novel. Kauffman argues that a heroine's simultaneously incorporating and responding to her passionate lover's letter, her prose record of frustrated desire, becomes part of the novel's dialogicity. Text implies, becomes, an alternative sign for body.

4. Margery Kempe, *The Book of Margery Kempe*, in *The Norton Anthology of English Literature*, ed. M.H. Abrams et al. (New York: Norton, 1986), 1:375.

5. Ibid., 1:377.

6. Eliza Haywood, *The Rash Resolve* (1724; reprint, New York: Garland, 1973), viii-ix.

7. Alexander Pope, *The Dunciad*, in *The Poems of Alexander Pope*, ed. John Butt (New Haven: Yale Univ. Press, 1963), bk. 2, lines 149-51.

8. The term *feminization* is variously used to describe literature of this period by Stone, *Family, Sex and Marriage*; Eagleton, *Rape of Clarissa*; Goldberg, *Sex and Enlightenment*; and Armstrong, *Desire and Domestic Fiction*.

9. Mary Poovey develops the theory that the idealization of female behavior influenced women writers, in *The Proper Lady and the Woman Writer* (Chicago: Univ. of Chicago Press, 1984), 3-47.

10. Stone, *Family, Sex and Marriage*, 225-28.

11. See note 3 to the Introduction, above.

12. Armstrong, *Desire and Domestic Fiction*, 15.

13. Jean Hagstrum, *Sex and Sensibility: Ideal and Erotic Love from Milton to Mozart* (Chicago: Univ. of Chicago Press, 1980), 160.

14. For discussions of the spiritualization of the domestic scene, see Gilbert and Gubar, *Madwoman in the Attic*, 17-27; Poovey, *Proper Lady*, 26-30; and Hagstrum, *Sex and Sensibility*, 152-53.

15. See, for example, Zillah R. Eisenstein, *The Radical Future of Liberal Feminism* (New York: Longman, 1981), and Linda J. Nicholson, *Gender and History: The Limits of Social Theory in the Age of the Family* (New York: Columbia Univ. Press, 1986).

16. Leites, *Puritan Conscience*, 48.

17. Ibid., 134, 139.

18. Armstrong, *Desire and Domestic Fiction*, 14, 112.

19. Hagstrum, *Sex and Sensibility*, 2.

20. Smith, *Discerning the Subject*, chapter 1.

21. Paula Backscheider makes this association between courtship novels and other contemporary texts in "I Died for Love," in *Fettr'd or Free? British Women Novelists, 1670-1815*, ed. Mary Anne Schofield and Cecilia Macheski (Athens: Ohio Univ. Press, 1986), 153.

22. Joyce Hemlow, "Fanny Burney and the Courtesy Books," *PMLA* 65 (1960): 755. See Goldberg, *Sex and Enlightenment*, 24-65, for a discussion of the relationships between conduct books and the novel.

23. John E. Mason, *Gentlefolk in the Making* (1935; reprint, New York: Octagon Press, 1971), develops the idea that a work of conduct literature defines a discrete group (4).

24. On the relationship between Richardson's novels and conduct books, see Margaret Anne Doody, *A Natural Passion: A Study of the Novels of Samuel Richardson* (Oxford: Clarendon Press, 1974), 32-77; Goldberg, *Sex and Enlightenment*, 24-65; and Sylvia Kasey Marks, *Sir Charles Grandison: The Compleat Conduct Book* (Lewisburg: Bucknell Univ. Press, 1986).

25. See Chauncey Brewster Tinker, *The Salon and English Letters: Chapters on the Interrelations of Literature and Society* (New York: Macmillan, 1915), and Joyce M. Horner, *The English Women Novelists and Their Connections with the Feminist Movement (1688-1797)*, Smith College Studies in Modern Languages, no. 11 (Northampton, Mass., 1929-30).

26. Irene Tayler and Gina Luria, "Gender and Genre: Women in British Romantic Literature," in *What Manner of Woman*, ed. Marlene Springer (New York: New York Univ. Press, 1977), treat the literature of the "Feminist Controversy" as precursor to that of the Romantic period, making the connection between Jane Austen and the turbulence of the 1790s.

27. Among conduct writers who must have felt Wollstonecraft's presence were John Bennet, Mrs. Bonhote, John Burton, Hester Chapone, Erasmus Darwin, Maria and Edward Edgeworth, James Fordyce, William Duff, Mary Hays, Catherine Macaulay, and J. Hamilton Moore. And then there were the courtship novelists of the eighties and nineties: Fanny Burney, Susannah Minifie Gunning, Mary Ann Hanway, Mary Hays, Elizabeth Inchbald, Thomas Holcroft, Charlotte Smith, Jane West, and Helen Maria Williams.

28. For more on this topic, see Michael G. Ketcham, *Transparent Designs: Reading, Performance, and Form in the "Spectator" Papers* (Athens: Univ. of Georgia Press, 1985).

29. Quoted in Cynthia L. White, *Women's Magazines, 1769-1968* (London: Michael Joseph, 1970), 28.

30. The *Ladies Magazine*, Dec. 30, 1749–Jan. 13, 1750.

31. Ibid.

Two. *Eliza Haywood*

1. For further discussion of this point, see Mary Anne Schofield,*Eliza Haywood* (Boston: Twayne, 1985), 8.

2. Bakhtin, *Dialogic Imagination*, 342. See my discussion of this term in the Introduction, above.

3. In *Novels of the 1740s* (Athens: Univ. of Georgia Press, 1982), Jerry Beasley notes that, as *Tom Jones* was to do, Haywood's *Fortunate Foundlings* "capitalizes on the extraordinary popular interest in Captain Corum's royally chartered foundling hospital" (176).

4. Eliza Haywood, *The Fortunate Foundlings* (1744; reprint, New York: Garland, 1974), 19.

5. Eliza Haywood, *The History of Jemmy and Jenny Jessamy* (1753; reprint, New York: Garland, 1974), 1:47.

Three. *Mary Collyer*

1. For further information on Collyer's works, see Catherine S. Green, "Mary Collyer," in *British Women Writers*, ed. Paul and June Schlueter (New York: Garland, 1988).

2. Mary Collyer, *The Virtuous Orphan*, ed. Ronald Paulson (1735; reprint, New York: Johnson Reprint, 1979).

3. *Monthly Review* 2 (Jan. 1750).

4. Beasley, *Novels of the 1740s*, 169.

5. Mary Collyer, *Felicia to Charlotte* (1744, 1749; reprint, New York: Garland, 1974), 1:2.

6. See my discussion of Edmund Leites's theory in chapter 1.

Four. *Early Feminist Reception Theory*

1. Jane Barker, Preface to *Exilius: or, The Banished Roman* (1715; reprint, New York: Garland, 1973).

2. For her discussion of "proper" women writers, see Poovey, *Proper Lady*.

3. Jane Barker, Preface to *A Patch-Work Screen for the Ladies* (1723; reprint, New York: Garland, 1973).

4. Penelope Aubin, *The Life and Adventures of the Lady Lucy* (1726; reprint, New York: Garland, 1973), x-xi.

5. Mary Davys, Preface to *The Reform'd Coquet* (1724; reprint, New York: Garland, 1973), ix-x.

6. Samuel Richardson, Preface to *Clarissa: or The History of a Young Lady*, ed. John Butt (New York: Dutton, 1967).

7. Eagleton, *Rape of Clarissa*, 4, 15.

8. Barbara Johnson, *A World of Difference* (Baltimore: Johns Hopkins Univ. Press, 1987), 79.

9. Eagleton, *Rape of Clarissa*, 73.

10. Smith, *Discerning the Subject*, 56-69.

11. Miller, "Rereading as a Woman," 355.

12. As Judith Newton explains in the Introduction to *Feminist Criticism and Social Change* (New York: Methuen, 1985), ideology is "a complex and contradictory system of representations (discourse, images, myths) through which we experience ourselves in relation to each other and to the social structures in which we live" (xix).

13. Born in frontier America, where her father was an army officer in charge of a company of foot (not governor or lieutenant governor of New York, as she later pretended), Lennox left at fifteen to finish her education in England. There she found her guardian aunt irretrievably insane, and shortly after arriving received news of her father's death. Despite the patronage of two noblewomen, Lennox's case was as unfortunate as any heroine's, and she took the usual escape route, marrying Alexander Lennox in 1748. The best that can be said of her bargain was that it was through her husband's employment by William Strahan (printer of the *Dictionary*) that Charlotte Lennox became Samuel Johnson's protegée, and that her husband's improvidence made her writing career a necessity.

By the time she was twenty and had been married a year, Lennox had tried the stage, published her *Poems on Several Occasions* (1747), and started her first novel. *Harriot Stuart* (1750) was an implausible story with typed characters who expounded stilted romantic sentiments, yet Johnson hosted an all-night fete in honor of "Mrs. Lenox's first literary child" at Devil Tavern—ceremonies including a crowning with laurel and a specially ordered apple pie. Once begun, his literary sponsorship continued, and over the next eleven years he contributed six dedications and at least that many reviews and proposals to Lennox's cause. In 1751, she produced the first of several translations (*The Memoirs of the Duke of Sully*) and wrote most of her second novel, *The Female Quixote*. She had been advised by Johnson and Richardson, and when the novel went to press she received a good review from yet another of London's literati, Henry Fielding.

See Duncan Isles's appendix, "Johnson, Richardson, and *The Female Quixote*," in Charlotte Lennox, *The Female Quixote*, ed. Margaret Dalziel (London: Oxford Univ. Press, 1970).

14. Lennox, *Female Quixote*, 7-8.

15. See Patricia Meyer Spacks, *The Adolescent Idea: Myths of Youth and the Adult Imagination* (New York: Basic Books, 1981), 129-36, and Spencer, *Rise of the Woman Novelist*, 187-92, for their discussions of *The Female Quixote*. Both

Spacks and Spencer interpret the novel as a myth of female adolescent power, yet they recognize Arabella's passivity. Neither, however, gives full attention to the cooptive effect of masculinist representations of women.

16. Judith Fetterley, *The Resisting Reader* (Bloomington: Indiana Univ. Press, 1977), xxii, 7.

17. Rachel Brownstein, *Becoming a Heroine* (New York: Viking, 1982), 292-96; Gilbert and Gubar, *Madwoman in the Attic*, 17-27; and Poovey, *Proper Lady*, 3-47, among others, have discussed the insidious effects of being heroinized.

18. On a writerly level, parodic fetishism is a "literalization," a female strategy similar to those Homans links with woman's preoedipal experience in *Bearing the Word*, 1-39.

19. Erasmus Darwin, Appendix to *A Plan for the Conduct of Female Education* (1797; reprint, New York: Garland, 1973), 33.

20. Ibid., Introduction.

21. Kristina Straub traces the way "pessimistic cultural perspectives on femininity create the ideological prospect of eighteenth-century women's lives" in *Divided Fictions: Fanny Burney and Feminine Strategy* (Lexington: Univ. Press of Kentucky, 1987), 10-22.

22. Katharine Rogers, Appendix to *Feminism in Eighteenth-Century England* (Urbana: Univ. of Illinois Press, 1982).

23. See Judith Lowder Newton, *Women, Power, and Subversion: Social Strategies in British Fiction, 1778-1860* (Athens: Univ. of Georgia Press, 1981). Newton supposes that women writers used their novels to work through painful personal encounters "with culturally imposed patterns of male power and female powerlessness." In the case of Fanny Burney's *Evelina*, the impulse may have been the author's shock at being "reduced to merchandise in the marriage market" (10).

Five. *Charlotte Lennox*

1. Charlotte Lennox, *Henrietta* (1758; reprint, New York: Garland, 1974), 1:3.

Six. *Frances Moore Brooke*

1. Samuel Johnson, James Boswell, and Hannah More were among her well-wishers the evening before her departure for Canada. Young Fanny Burney writes approvingly of Frances Brooke in *The Early Diary of Fanny Burney*, ed. A.R. Ellis (1889; reprint, Freeport: Books for Libraries Press, 1971): "Mrs. Brooke is very short and fat, and squints; but has the art of showing agreeable ugliness. She is very well bred, and expresses herself with much modesty upon all subjects; which in an authoress, a woman of known understanding, is extremely pleasing" (1:283).

2. Frances Brooke, *The History of Emily Montague* (1769; reprint, New York: Garland, 1974), 1:9.

Seven. *The Blazon and the Marriage Act*

1. Christopher Lasch observes in "The Suppression of Clandestine Marriage in England: The Marriage Act of 1753," *Salmagundi* 26 (Spring 1974): 99-104, that by the Puritan Interregnum, clandestine marriage was understood as a celebration of vows without witnesses; later, it was redefined as a union without parental consent.

2. Gillis, *For Better, For Worse*, remarks that middling and upper-class marriage practices converged. Their common interests were companionate marriage and capital accumulation: "While young people were told they must marry for love and were given a certain latitude in the choice of mates, the courtship process was carefully constructed to prevent misalliances" (135). Trumbach, in *Rise of the Egalitarian Family*, focusing on the practices of aristocratic families, enforces the point that companionate marriage became the social ideal, observing, for instance, that even for younger sons of the nobility, "it had become distasteful . . . to use marriage for financial gain" (71).

3. Cited in H.J. Habakkuk, "Marriage Settlements in the Eighteenth Century," *Transactions of the Royal Historical Society* 32 (1949): 25.

4. Erica Harth, "The Virtue of Love: Lord Hardwicke's Marriage Act," *Cultural Critique* 19 (Spring 1988): 123-54, quoted from 143, 154. For a similar study of ideological change, see Neil McKendrick et al., *The Birth of a Consumer Society* (Bloomington: Indiana Univ. Press, 1982).

5. *A Serious Proposal for Promoting Lawful and Honourable Marriage Adress'd to the Unmarried, of both Sexes* (London, 1750), 27.

6. Ibid., 39, 43. That this egalitarianism did not extend to class structure is implicit in the terms of social distinction ("Gentleman independent," "Profession," "Trade," and "Calling"), which refer to the developing middle class. Read along the lines proposed by Michael McKeon's *The Origins of the English Novel, 1600-1740* (Baltimore: Johns Hopkins Univ. Press, 1987), the *Serious Proposal* does not evince any obvious program for reforming "status inconsistency," McKeon's term for the recognition of "a disparity between present experience and the expectations created by reference-group identification" (172-73). The only status inconsistencies the pamphlet seeks to redress are those of generation (presumably, the ladies' and gentlemen's offices will empower the younger generation to marry without the interference of avaricious parents and guardians) and those of gender (significantly, the pamphleteer selects a woman for the case study). Gender, incidentally, is largely absent as a site of status inconsistency in McKeon's otherwise exhaustive systematization of the social, economic, and political forces behind the novel.

7. Michel Foucault, *The Order of Things*, ed. R.D. Laing, World of Man Series (New York: Pantheon, 1970).

8. As Michel Foucault explains in *The History of Sexuality*, trans. Robert Hurley (London: Allen Lane, 1978), the rule of tactical polyvalence means

that discourse is never one-dimensional: "Discourse can be both an instrument and an effect of power, but also a hindrance, a stumbling-block, a point of resistance and a starting point for an opposing strategy" (1:101).

9. As Trumbach explains, in *Rise of the Egalitarian Family*, "Patriarchy presumed that there was property not only in things but in persons and that ownership lay with the heads of households" (119). It was this tendency to commodify that contemporary literature adverted to. With the expediency of *Village Voice* personals, one pamphleteer assembled advertisements from the lovelorn of both sexes, "Chiefly Comic. Directed from Vauxhall, Ranelagh, Marybon, Cuper's," titling them *Love at First Sight; or, the Gay in a Flutter* (London, 1750).

10. Samuel Richardson, *Sir Charles Grandison*, ed. Jocelyn Harris (London: Oxford Univ. Press, 1972), 1:9.

11. Richardson's novel clearly implies a female reader, for we experience Greville's letter over Harriet's shoulder, as it were, rereading the words he writes for Lady Frampton but has sent to Harriet via her cousin Lucy. Hence, it is quite appropriate to "imagine . . . the place of a woman's body," as Miller proposes in "Rereading as a Woman" (355-56).

12. Greville's taxonomic description seeks both to appropriate, to commodify Harriet, and to obscure her nature as an autonomous female subject. On both counts, the rhetorical strategy is reductive: if Harriet is merely the sum of her parts, she is less than human and thus consumable. And by dwelling on the qualities of her parts, Greville displaces his fear of Harriet as Other. As fetish, Greville's taxonomy is remarkable on two counts: first, the fetish is usually attributed to a later period, the nineteenth century and, second, female difference is usually displaced to one metonymic part (breast, foot, etc.) rather than several.

13. While Harth, in "Virtue of Love," suggests a difference in the language used by the houses of Parliament to argue the Hardwicke Act, it is clear that the language of commerce was shared by them. Thus, in novels and pamphlets, either class may employ it to blame the other for consumerist attitudes.

14. Nancy Vickers notes in "This Heraldry in Lucrece' Face" (in Suleiman, *Female Body*) that from the sixteenth century, *blazon* meant "to describe in proper heraldric language, to paint or depict in colors, to inscribe with arms . . . in some ornamental way, to describe fitly, to publish vauntingly or boastfully, to proclaim" (quoted from the *OED*). In French, *blason* could be either "a heraldric description of a shield" or a poetic description of "an object praised or blamed by a rhetorician-poet" (213). Vickers observes that the legacy of description is "shaped predominantly by the male imagination"; it is a product of "men talking to men about women" (209). Vickers, like Julia Kristeva (*Desire in Language: A Semiotic Approach to Literature and Art*, ed. Leon S. Roudiez, trans. Thomas Gora et al. [New York: Columbia Univ. Press, 1980]), emphasizes the tendentiousness of the blazon, which foreshadows a later reversal or discovery (in Lucrece's case, Collatine's laudatory description foreshadows the tragedy of her rape).

15. Kristeva, *Desire in Language*, 53.

16. Fanny Burney, *Evelina, or The History of a Young Lady's Entrance into the World*, ed. Edward A. Bloom (1778; New York: Oxford Univ. Press, 1968), 18.

17. Maria Edgeworth, *Manoeuvring* (1809), vol. 5 of *Tales and Novels* (1857; reprint, New York: AMS Press, 1967).

18. Maria Edgeworth, *Belinda* (1801), vol. 3 of *Tales and Novels* (1857; reprint, New York: AMS Press, 1967), 1.

19. Eaton Stannard Barrett, *The Heroine, or Adventures of Cherubina* (1813; reprint, New York: Frederick A. Stokes, 1928), 1.

20. Jane Austen, *Northanger Abbey*, in *Northanger Abbey, The Watsons, and Sanditon*, ed. John Davie (New York: Oxford Univ. Press, 1971), 1-5.

21. Jane Austen, *Sense and Sensibility*, ed. Claire Lamont (London: Oxford Univ. Press, 1968).

22. Edward Said, *Beginnings: Intention & Method* (1975; reprint, New York: Columbia Univ. Press, 1985), 90. One could argue as well with Pocock, *Virtue, Commerce, and History*, that a revival of the Greek ideal of republicanism shaped social and political relations of the period. "Because so many of the components of the good life can be had for money, we are under a constant temptation to mistake money for the *summum bonum*, and an individual drawn wholly into the life of monetarised exchange relationships would be living in a commodified parody of the natural and divine order" (104). If the conception of virtue was seen as threatened by exchange relations, presumably this was so as well for women as for men.

Eight. *Fanny Burney*

1. Darwin, Appendix to *A Plan for the Conduct of Female Education*, 33.

2. Fanny Burney, *Cecilia*, intro. Judy Simons (London: Virago Press, 1986), 1-2.

3. Julia Epstein, *The Iron Pen: Frances Burney and the Politics of Women's Writing* (Madison: Univ. of Wisconsin Press, 1989), 159.

4. See Straub, *Divided Fictions*, 109-51, for a discussion of Cecilia's troubled attempts at working.

5. Mary Ann Caws, in *Reading Frames in Modern Fiction* (Princeton: Princeton Univ. Press, 1985), points out that "to frame is to privilege what is contained within the boarders of the picture" (21).

6. Eve Kosofsky Sedgwick, *Between Men: English Literature and Male Homosocial Desire* (New York: Columbia Univ. Press, 1985), discusses the relationship between patriarchal exchange and male bonding. "Homosocial" is a particularly apt description of the attitudes of Cecilia's guardians, whose views of her marriage are uniformly concerned with what her male partner will gain or lose by the bargain.

7. Spencer discusses another of Burney's heroines in *Rise of the Woman Novelist*, commenting that Camilla "has never really been free at all and she certainly will not be in the future. . . . Our last glimpse of her shows her smothered in the care of parents and husband together" (167). In a similar

way, Straub (*Divided Fictions*) observes that in *Cecilia*, "Male protectors are consistently portrayed, from the novel's beginning, as outside the realm of secure domesticity or as somehow antithetical to it" (113).

8. Terry Castle, *Masquerade and Civilization* (Stanford: Stanford Univ. Press, 1986), 263, 270.

9. Straub suggests that all of Burney's novels "portray the heroine's key act of power—the turning point in the plot by which she gains social definition in the novel—as both an act of self-alienation, a splitting-off of the act of control from the personal, desiring self that authorizes it, and as a successful strategy of social manipulation" (153).

10. Straub, *Divided Fictions*, 119.

11. Margaret Anne Doody, *Frances Burney: The Life in the Works* (New Brunswick: Rutgers Univ. Press, 1988), 118.

12. Smith, *Discerning the Subject*, 137, 5.

13. Straub, *Divided Fictions*, 176.

Nine. *Richardson and Wollstonecraft*

1. James Fordyce, *Sermons to Young Women* (Boston: Thomas Hall, 1796), 127.

2. A.R. Humphreys, "The Rights of Women in the Age of Reason," *Modern Language Review* 41 (1946): 156-69, outlines the classical debate about women's education and its influence on the eighteenth century. W. Lyon Blease, *The Emancipation of English Women* (1910; reprint, New York: Arno Press, 1977) includes information about women's education. Dorothy Gardiner's *English Girlhood at School* (London: Oxford Univ. Press, 1929) is a thorough history of women's education, several chapters of which treat the period in question. Phyllis Stock's *Better Than Rubies: A History of Women's Education* (New York: Putnam, 1978) is less detailed but offers a more recent perspective. Shirley Nelson Kersey's *Classics in the Education of Girls and Women* (Metuchen: Scarecrow Press, 1981) is a documentary history of women's education, collecting representative selections from Plato through Heloise Edwin Hersey. Barbara Schnorrenberg's "The Eighteenth-Century Englishwoman," in *The Women of England*, ed. Barbara Kanner (Hamden, Conn.: Archon Books, 1979), is a valuable bibliographic essay that lists primary and secondary materials on education. Also treating women's education is Rogers's *Feminism in Eighteenth-Century England*.

3. Stone, *Family, Sex and Marriage*, 348.

4. Phyllis Stock, *Better Than Rubies*, 99.

5. Jean-Jacques Rousseau, *Émile; or On Education*, trans. Allan Bloom (New York: Basic Books, 1979), 136.

6. Susan Moller Okin, *Women in Western Political Thought* (Princeton: Princeton Univ. Press, 1979), 99.

7. John Gregory, *A Father's Legacy to His Daughters* (1774; reprint, New York: Garland, 1974), 32.

8. In addition to the sources cited in note 2 above, see Horner, *English Women Novelists*, 47-81 and Tinker, *Salon and English Letters*, 123-253.

9. Richardson, *Sir Charles Grandison*, 1:51.

10. Armstrong quotes Walter Ong to this effect, in *Desire and Domestic Fiction*, 28.

11. Ibid., 132.

12. Robert Hare argues persuasively in his Introduction to Mary Wollstonecraft, *The Emigrants* (1794; reprint, Gainesville: Scholars' Facsimiles and Reprints, 1964) that there is no reliable evidence that Gilbert Imlay wrote anything at all. The descriptions and topography of the novel and of the other work attributed to him, *A Topographical Description of the Western Territory of North America*, are drawn from identifiable reference books. There is, moreover, no evidence in Wollstonecraft's letters to him that Imlay had either literary interests or feminist sympathies.

13. Nancy K. Miller describes two forms (euphoric and dysphoric) of women's story in *The Heroine's Text: Readings in the French and English Novel, 1722-1782* (New York: Columbia Univ. Press, 1980). In "dysphoric" texts, such as Wollstonecraft's, the heroine is not reconciled to society at the conclusion.

14. Mary Wollstonecraft, Advertisement to Mary, in *"Mary, a Fiction" and "The Wrongs of Woman"*, ed. Gary Kelly (London: Oxford Univ. Press, 1976).

15. Mary Poovey, "Mary Wollstonecraft: The Gender of Genres in Late Eighteenth-Century England," *Novel* 15 (Winter 1982): 113.

16. For an interesting discussion of the relative places of sensibility and reason in Wollstonecraft's literary reviews, see Mitzi Meyers, "Sensibility and the 'Walk of Reason': Mary Wollstonecraft's Literary Reviews as Cultural Critique," in *Sensibility in Transformation: Creative Resistance to Sentiment from the Augustans to the Romantics*, ed. Syndy M. Conger (Rutherford: Fairleigh Dickinson Univ. Press, 1990).

17. Poovey, "Mary Wollstonecraft," 112.

18. Mary Wollstonecraft, *A Vindication of the Rights of Woman*, in *The Works of Mary Wollstonecraft*, ed. Janet Todd and Marilyn Butler (London: William Pickering, 1989), 5:65.

19. Jacques Lacan, *Écrits: A Selection*, trans. Alan Sheridan (New York: Norton, 1977), 1.

Ten. *Bluestockings and Amazons*

1. Harrison Steeves discusses "little histories" in *Before Jane Austen* (New York: Holt, Rinehart, and Winston, 1965).

2. Poovey, *Proper Lady*, 43.

3. Pierre Maranda, "The Dialectic of Metaphor: An Anthropological Essay in Hermeneutics," in *The Reader in the Text*, ed. Susan Suleiman and Inge Crossman (Princeton: Princeton Univ. Press), 190.

4. Michel Foucault, *An Introduction*, vol. 1 of *The History of Sexuality*, trans. Robert Hurley (New York: Pantheon Books, 1978), 100.

5. Richardson, *Clarissa*, 4:496.

6. Fanny Burney, *Camilla, or A Picture of Youth*, ed. Edward A. Bloom and Lillian D. Bloom (New York: Oxford Univ. Press, 1972), 50-51.

7. Susannah Minifie Gunning, *Memoirs of Mary, A Novel* (London, 1793), 3:223.

8. See Felicity Nussbaum, *The Brink of All We Hate* (Lexington: Univ. Press of Kentucky, 1984) for a literary history of Amazons.

9. Burney, *Evelina*, 361.

10. Mary Ann Hanway, *Ellinor* (1798; reprint, New York: Garland, 1974), 2:302.

11. Amelia Opie, *Adeline Mowbray* (1805; reprint, New York: Garland, 1974), 1:37-38.

12. For further discussion of the negative connotations of *sentimentalist*, see Hagstrum, *Sex and Sensibility*, 6-7, and Todd, *Sensibility*, 6-7.

13. Letter from Mrs. Bradshaigh, in *The Correspondence of Samuel Richardson* (1804; reprint, New York: AMS Press, 1966), 4:240.

14. Maria Edgeworth, *Angelina*, vol. 1 of *Tales and Novels* (1801; reprint, New York: AMS Press, 1967), 227.

15. Mary Brunton, *Self-Control* (1811; reprint, New York: Garland, 1974).

16. Charlotte Smith, *Desmond* (1792; reprint, New York: Garland 1974), 2:165-66.

17. Stone, *Family, Sex and Marriage*, 352.

18. Maria and Richard Lovell Edgeworth, *Practical Education* (1798; reprint, New York: Garland, 1974), 2:522.

19. Hannah More, *Coelebs in Search of a Wife* (1799), in *The Works of Hannah More* (New York: Harper and Brothers, 1848), 2:308.

Eleven. *Jane West*

1. Jane West, *The Advantages of Education: or, the History of Maria Williams* (1793; reprint, New York: Garland, 1974), 1:3-4.

2. Jane West, *A Gossip's Story* (1797; reprint, New York: Garland, 1974), 1:47.

3. Jane West, *A Tale of the Times* (1799; reprint, New York: Garland, 1974), 1:101.

Twelve. *Mary Brunton*

1. Alex Brunton, "A Memoir of the Life and Writings of the Author, Including Extracts from Her Correspondence," in Mary Brunton's *Discipline: A Novel* (London: Richard Bentley, 1849), 37. In the Introduction to the Pandora reprint of *Discipline* (1814; reprint, New York: Pandora Press, 1986), Fay Weldon incorrectly attributes the *Memoir* to Brunton's brother. Text citations are to the Pandora edition.

2. Here I disagree with Katrin R. Burlin, " 'At the Crossroads': Sister

Authors and the Sister Arts," in *Fettr'd or Free?* ed. Schofield and Macheski. Burlin cites Brunton's reluctance to be known as a woman writer as an instance of "real aesthetic and critical weakness" (68). Having just completed her second novel, Brunton writes to a friend (Mrs. Izet), and the passage is more representative of her natural elation and her recognition in her own novel of the unfulfilled promise of the genre than of a recipe for future work.

3. Mary Brunton, *Self-Control* (1811; reprint, New York: Garland, 1974), 1:121-22.

4. Jane Austen, *Jane Austen's Letters*, 2d ed., ed. R.W. Chapman (London: Oxford Univ. Press, 1952), letter 86, p. 344.

5. Aside from Burney's *Camilla*, there is little precedent in feminocentric novels for the two chapters Brunton devotes to Ellen's formative years.

6. See Sarah W.R. Smith, "Men, Women, and Money: The Case of Mary Brunton," in *Fettr'd or Free*, ed. Schofield and Macheski.

7. For further discussion of masquerade, see Castle's *Masquerade and Civilization*. Castle does not, however, discuss Brunton's novel.

Thirteen. *Courtship*

1. Bennet, *Letters to a Young Lady*, 2:101.

2. Macfarlane, *Marriage and Love in England*, 122.

3. Igor Webb, *From Custom to Capital: The English Novel and the Industrial Revolution* (Ithaca: Cornell Univ. Press, 1981), 46-47.

4. *Considerations on the Cause of the Present Stagnation of Matrimony*, 17.

5. Sarah Robinson Scott, *The Test of Filial Duty. In a Series of Letters Between Miss Emilia Leonard, and Miss Charlotte Arlington* (London, 1772), 1:66.

6. Stone cites a prolonged argument over the rights of parents and children and over interest and love in *Family, Sex and Marriage*, 280-84. See also Goldberg, *Sex and Enlightenment*, 53-55.

7. Gillis, *For Better, For Worse*, 136.

8. Stone, *Family, Sex and Marriage*, 316.

9. Ibid., 380.

10. Burney, *Camilla*, 643-44.

11. Eliza Haywood, *The Female Spectator: Being Selections from Mrs. Eliza Haywood's Periodical* (1744-46), ed. Mary Priestley (London: John Lane, 1929), 84-100.

12. Frances Brooke, *Old Maid* (London, 1756), no. 7, 42.

13. As cited in Stone, *Family, Sex and Marriage*, 273, from *Lady's Monthly Museum*, 2 (1799): 288.

14. Macfarlane, *Marriage and Love in England*, 296-97.

15. Brooke, *Old Maid*, no. 7, 42.

16. Brooke, *History of Emily Montague*, 4:125.

17. Hanway, *Ellinor*, 1:314.

18. Samuel Richardson, *Pamela*, in *The Novels of Samuel Richardson*, intro. William Lyon Phelps (1902; reprint, New York: AMS Press, 1970), 2:9.

19. Susannah Minifie Gunning, *Barford Abbey* (1768; reprint, New York: Garland, 1974), 1:8-9.

Fourteen. *Maria Edgeworth*

1. Edgeworth, *Belinda*, 18.

2. These are instances of what Caws, in *Reading Frames in Modern Fiction*, terms architectural design (22).

3. According to Marilyn Butler, *Maria Edgeworth: A Literary Biography* (Oxford: Clarendon Press, 1972), Edgeworth borrowed the attempt to educate a wife from Thomas Day's similar experiment with Sabrina Sidney (243).

4. Edgeworth, *Manoeuvring*, 6.

Fifteen. *Jane Austen*

1. For a different reading of Austen's consciousness of market practice, see Webb, *From Custom to Capital*.

2. Jane Austen, *Mansfield Park*, ed. John Lucas (1814; reprint, London: Oxford Univ. Press, 1970), 1.

3. Austen, *Pride and Prejudice*, 1.

4. Janis P. Stout argues convincingly, in "Jane Austen's Proposal Scenes and the Limitations of Language," *Studies in the Novel* 14 (1982): 316-26, that the author's reticence in "true" love scenes reveals her distrust of language to convey sincere feeling. Hence the verbosity of Collins's proposal, Lady Catherine de Bourgh's disuasive speech, and Darcy's initial proposal all reveal a lack of integrity in the speakers.

5. Lillian S. Robinson observes, in *Sex, Class & Culture* (1978; reprint, New York: Methuen, 1986), that Lizzy denies the prerogatives of class and wealth (185).

6. See my Introduction for more discussion of Armstrong's *Desire and Domestic Fiction*.

INDEX

accomplishments, feminine, 112-13, 146-47

affective individualism, 1-2, 14-18, 27, 29, 34, 38-39, 52, 65, 89, 143; and relationships, 154, 161

Amazon, 104-5, 108-10

angelisme, 16

aphonia, 27, 84, 86

Armstrong, Nancy, 4-5, 15-16, 18, 94, 158, 166 n 7

arranged marriage, 46, 65, 69-74, 124, 131, 141, 150, 154-59

Aubin, Penelope, 25, 43-44

Austen, Jane, 153-59; and Barrett, 77-78; and blazon, 72, 78-79, 153-59; and Brunton, 120-21; and Edgeworth, 146; and female pedant, 47; and feminism, 45; and generational conflict, 137; and marriage, 54; and novel, 80

—Mansfield Park: blazon in, 153-54; status inequity in, 153-54

—Northanger Abbey: female pedants in, 47; influenced by Barrett, 78; novel in, 80

—Pride and Prejudice: blazon in, 154-59; Marxist reading of, 4-5; pedant in, 108; title of, 89

—Sense and Sensibility: blazon in, 79; influenced by West, 116

authority and language, 144, 157

Bakhtin, Mikhail, 5-6, 26

Barbauld, Anna Laetitia, 21

Barker, Jane, 25, 43

Barrett, Eaton Stannard, 47, 77-78

Behn, Aphra, 3, 12

Bennet, John, 11, 137

Blake, William, 22

blazon, 72, 77-80, 114, 141, 153-59, 173 n 14

bluestockings, 21, 33, 104-8

body/text association, 43, 120

Brooke, Frances Moore, 62-66, 171 n 1; and affective individualism, 65; and arranged marriage, 65; and companionate marriage, 65; comparative study of women, 63; female subject positions, 64; 66; and Richardson, 63; and sensibility, 64, 66

Brownstein, Rachel, 48

Brunton, Mary, 153, 161; and arranged marriage, 131; and Austen, 120-21; and childhood, 122; and commodification, 123-25; and conduct books, 124; and female socialization, 125; and identificatory reader, 123; and male-female friendship, 130; and masquerade, 125-28; and Memoir by her husband, 120; and objectification, 124; and patriarchy, 124, 133; and representation, 133; and resistance, 133; and sensibility, 132-33; and sexual/textual trope, 120; and scopic, 123-28; and women's education, 111, 122-34; and writing, 120-21; Discipline, 122-34, 150; Emily Montague, 62-66, 142; Old Maid, 62, 141-42; Self-Control, 111, 121

Burke, Edmund, 21

Burney, Fanny: and bluestockings, 21; and courtesy novel, 19; and female pedants, 106; and feminism, 45; and marriage, 54, 140; 111; Camilla, 106, 111, 140; Evelina, 80, 109

—Cecilia, 80-90; affective individualism in, 89; aphonia in, 84, 86; authoritative discourse in, 85, 90; blazon in, 76, 80; clandestine marriage in, 87; commodification in, 81; companionate marriage in, 89; consumerism in, 82; and female authority in, 87; female autonomy in, 81; framed scene in, 81-82; Hardwicke Act in, 87; heiress in, 81; ideology in, 84-85; individual versus society in, 80-85; mercantile rhetoric in, 90; paralysis in, 86; patriarchy in, 81, 83, 87, 90; resistance in 82, 86; self-alienation in, 88-89; sensibility in, 80; sentimentalism in, 80

Castle, Terry, 82-84, 87, 89-90

Cixous, Hélène, 4

clandestine marriage; 87; definition of, 172 n 1; and Hardwicke's Marriage Act, 87, 140; and West's *Advantages of Education*, 115

class endogamy, 69-70, 157

class or status inequity, 33, 141-43, 153-54

Collyer, Mary: life of, 32; and Marivaux translation, 32-33; and sensibility, 33

—*Felicia to Charlotte*: affective individualism in, 34, 38-39; bluestocking readers of, 33; class or status inequity in, 33; companionate marriage in, 39; emergent feminism in, 37-38; female epistolary friendship in, 34; fetishism in, 36; male rhetoric in, 35-37; metatextual commentary in, 37; misogyny in, 36; moral constancy in, 35; power inequity in, 37; Richardson influenced by, 33-39; sensibility in, 34-35, 38; sexual politics in, 37; somatic relationship in, 39

—*Virtuous Orphan, The*: Richardson influenced by, 32; sensibility in, 33

commodification: and Austen, 153-59; and Brunton's *Discipline*, 123-25; and Burney's *Cecilia*, 81; and *Considerations on the Cause of the Present Stagnation of Matrimony*, 138; and courtship novel, 69-79; and Edgeworth's *Belinda*, 146-48; and marriage, 138-40; and patriarchy, 173 n 9; and representation of women, 71-79, 173 n 12; and Scott's *Test of Filial Duty*, 138-39

companionate marriage: and blazon, 158; and Burney's *Cecilia*, 89; and choice, 65; and class and status in-

equity, 141-43; and Edgeworth's *Belinda*, 147-52; and generational conflict, 137-38, 140; and history, 165 n 3, 172 n 2; and ideology, 1, 14, 137-38

conduct books: and female pedants, 108; and masquerades, 126; and periodicals, 14, 19; and Wollstonecraft, 168 n 27; and women's novels, 22, 110; and view of women, 124

conflict, generational, 2, 65, 137-38, 140, 178 n 6

Considerations on the Cause of the Present Stagnation of Marriage, 138

counterideology: possibility of, 5, 45; and West's Prudentia Homespun, 114

courtship: and Edgeworth's *Belinda*, 146-52; and heroine's coming out, 2; and roles for women, 149-50; and system, 165 n 4

courtship novel: and conduct books and periodicals, 14, 19; and epistolary form, 63; and feminist issues, 161, 166 n 7; and gendered rhetoric, 3; and male and female spheres of action, 3; and Marxist criticism, 44-46; and passion, 16; and reception, 19; and sensibility, 14-15, 107; and sexual politics, 3; and women's roles, 62; and women writers, 18

courtship novelists: and marriage, 53-54

Darwin, Erasmus, 80

Davys, Mary, 25, 43, 44

domestic fiction, 18, 158

Doody, Margaret, 84, 86-87

Eagleton, Terry, 44-46

Edgeworth, Maria: and Austen, 146; and female pedants, 47; and feminism, 45; and marriage, 54, 147-52; *Angelina*, 111; *Manoeuvring*, 151-52; *Practical Education*, 112

—*Belinda*: accomplishments in, 146-47; blazon in, 77; Brunton influenced by, 150; commodification in, 146-48; companionate marriage in, 147-52; courtship choices in, 148;

ficatory readers in, 30; moral constancy in, 31; negative exempla in, 30; separate plots in, 30
hegemony: and feminism, 37, 45, 149, 116 n 7; male, 6-7, 72; and rhetoric, 12, 31, 35-37
heiress: in Burney's *Cecilia*, 88
Hemlow, Joyce, 19
Homans, Margaret, 4, 49
humanism, liberal, 16

ideology: and companionate marriage, 1-2, 14, 30, 137-38; and counterideology, 5, 49; and experience, 19, 84-85, 170 n 12; and patriarchy, 20
Imlay, Gilbert: and Wollstonecraft, 96, 100-101, 102, 176 n 12
individuation, 5
Irigaray, Luce, 4

Johnson, Barbara, 45
Johnson, Samuel, 21, 47, 109
Jones, Ann Rosalind, 11

Kempe, Margery, 12
Kristeva, Julia, 74

Ladies Magazine, 39
Lady's Monthly Museum, 141
language: acquisition of, 3-4; and authority, 144, 157; and sensibility, 112, 179 n 4
Leites, Edmund, 15-18, 31, 129
Lennox, Charlotte: and Brunton, 121; and Darwin, 51; and life, 170 n 13; and marriage, 53; and Richardson, 20, 45; and sentimentalism, 110; and sexual/textual trope, 161
—*Female Quixote*: antiromance in, 47, 50; companionate marriage in, 51; feminist reception theory in, 50-51; fetish in, 49; gender and genre in, 47; heroinization in, 47-50; male hegemony in, 51-52; resistance in, 48, 170 n 15
love, 15, 152; conjugal, 17

Macfarlane, Alan 70, 142
Malthus, Thomas, 26

maneuvering, 76-77, 151-52, 154-56
Manley, Delariviere, 12
Maranda, Pierre, 104-5
marketplace rhetoric: and marriage, 138-39, 146-48
marriage: and capital, 165 n 3; and choice, 11, 65, 71, 145, 148, 152, 165 nn 3, 4; and class, status, or economic equity, 2, 141; and generational conflict, 2; and heterosexual roles, 1; and marketplace, 112, 138-40, 153, 156, 171 n 23; and mercantile language, 146-48; and novelists, 53-54; and patriarchal exchange, 70-74, 76. *See also* arranged marriage; companionate marriage
masquerade, 87, 90, 125-28
Miller, Nancy, 46, 96
misalliance, 116, 147
moral constancy, 17, 35
More, Hannah, 21; *Coelebs in Search of a Wife*, 21, 113

novel, feminized, 13-14. *See also* courtship novel; English novel
Nussbaum, Felicity, 108

objectification, 124, 139, 159
Okin, Susan Moller, 94
Opie, Amelia, 110

patriarchy: and arranged marriage, 81, 87, 90, 124, 133, 150, 154-59; and companionate marriage, 137; and exchange, 11, 71-72, 74-75, 77, 124, 131, 174 n 6; and Hardwicke Marriage Act, 70; and ideology, 112, 144, 158; and representation, 72, 173 n 9; and women's conduct literature, 11, 133
pedant, female, 47, 105-8
Philips, Katherine, 3
Poovey, Mary, 5, 16, 19, 48, 96, 98-99, 104
Puritans: and affective individualism, 2, 15-17, 166 n 6

reader: female, 173 n 11; identificatory, 47-48, 53, 114, 123, 156, 166 n 8